DOOLEY
A FAMILY MEMOIR

WITH KEVIN O'BRIEN

HEROBOOKS

PUBLISHED BY HERO BOOKS
1 WOODVILLE GREEN
LUCAN
CO. DUBLIN
IRELAND

Hero Books is an imprint of Umbrella Publishing
First Published 2022
Copyright © Joe, Johnny and Billy Dooley & Kevin O'Brien

ISBN 9781910827598

Cover design and formatting: jessica@viitaladesign.com
Photographs: Inpho and the Dooley family collection

DEDICATION

To the memory of our late father Sean and our mother Betty
for all their guidance and support

CONTENTS

PROLOGUE

PHOTO SECTION 1: A Family's Journey to Croke Park Glory 19

PART 1.. 25

PART 2.. 39

PART 3.. 57

PART 4.. 81

PART 5.. 99

PART 6.. 111

PART 7.. 125

PART 8.. 139

PART 9.. 147

PART 10 161

PART 11 177

PART 12.. 205

PART 13.. 217

PART 14.. 231

PART 15.. 247

PHOTO SECTION 2: The Dooley Brothers in the famous Green, White and Gold 267

EPILOGUE

ACKNOWLEDGEMENTS

WE WERE ALL very lucky to be born into a family where we had a very happy upbringing and were thought great lessons that have stood to us in life and sport. You would never be let ahead of yourself in our house.

A very special thanks to our parents Sean and Betty for all they did for us; it was not easy to rear nine children and keep them all on track.

Thanks to our siblings Seamus, Mary, Kieran, Sandra, Patricia and Eilish, and their partners, for all their support over the years.

We remember the family people that went before us, and wore the Offaly jersey with pride and distinction... our grandfather Jim Carroll, and grand-uncles Joe Carroll and Tom Dooley.

There are some many people who contributed directly to our success on the field. Thanks to our teachers, Damien White in Clareen National School, who threw in the ball and got us going, and Brother Denis and all the Presentation Brothers and teachers in Birr Community School who fostered the game brilliantly.

Thanks to all the people in Clareen and Seir Kieran GAA club for their support and encouragement over the years, and all our fellow players and friends in the club... there are too many to mention. We created our own history and had great times and memories doing it which we will cherish forever. Thanks also to the managers and underage coaches who looked after us over the years, including Gerry Kirwan and Michael 'Chip' Connolly who managed us to senior success. We were lucky to have great club officers down through the years and past players who kept the game strong in the parish in both good and lean times.

With the county, we were lucky to play with a great bunch of men at all levels in the 1980s and 90s. To this day, many of them are still close friends, and we can meet every single one of them and have a good chat about past and current days.

We were lucky to win a few All-Irelands, see parts of the world we might never have seen only for the great game but, most of all, we made friendships and memories that will last a lifetime. Thanks to all the excellent management teams and selectors and backroom people who looked after us over the years, especially those who managed us to national success… Diarmuid Healy, Éamonn Cregan and Derry O'Donovan, Michael Bond, Padraic Horan and Pat Joe Whelehan.

Thanks to our own clubman Tony Murphy for all his hard work as team secretary over a long number of years. We also especially remember one of our selectors Pat McLoughney, who has passed to his eternal reward. Thanks to all the officers and volunteers of Offaly County Board who supported us always.

Thanks to Liam Hayes of Hero Books for approaching us to write a family memoir. It was often mentioned to us individually but would never have happened only for Liam. He has been very professional to deal with and his editing of the book has been brilliant.

A big thank you to a local Tullamore journalist Kevin O'Brien for his patience and all his hard work in building this book. He has put huge time and effort into this project and left no stone unturned, interviewing all our family members. We think he has done a brilliant job.

Finally, we wish to thank our own families for all their patience and support over the years… Joe's wife Marie, and Shane, Aidin and Niamh; Billy's wife Fiona, and Sean, Conor and Gearoid; and Johnny's wife Sinéad, and Jack, Emma and Hannah.

There was a lot of minding of children, washing of gear… keeping out of the way before big games when we were a bit edgy, and dealing with disappointments and success. You all made huge sacrifices and that is very much appreciated. We are also very proud of the way all of our own families have carried themselves in life.

We made a conscious effort to tell our story as honestly and straightforward as we could. We hope you enjoy the read. All proceeds from the book will be donated 'Dóchas Offaly Cancer Support Centre' who provide a brilliant service for anyone effected by cancer.

Joe, Billy and Johnny Dooley
August 2022

★★★

AS I WAS nearing the end of writing this book, the Offaly minor hurlers reached the All-Ireland final for the first time in 33 years.

The world revisited on these pages recalls a glorious time when the Faithful County regularly competed for All-Ireland titles.

In 1985, Joe Dooley won his first All-Ireland senior medal. A year later, Billy Dooley was part of the Offaly squad that took home the county's maiden All-Ireland minor hurling title. In 1987, Billy and Johnny Dooley both featured on the victorious minor side against Tipperary.

In 1989, Johnny played for the last Faithful team to take home the Irish Press Cup.

Those wins paved the way for the glory days of the 1990s, when the Offaly hurlers lifted the Liam MacCarthy Cup twice during one of the most extraordinary periods in the history of the game.

Few families have contributed more to sport in the county, or indeed nationally, than the Dooleys. It's been a privilege to work on this project with Joe, Billy and Johnny over the last year. I am thankful to them for trusting me to tell their stories, plus the patience and good humour they showed in reliving their memories. Thanks also to their wives Marie, Fiona and Sinéad for their generous hospitality when welcoming me into their homes.

The wider Dooley family made hugely valuable contributions. It was a great pleasure to hear stories from Betty, Seamus, Mary, Kieran, Sandra, Patricia and Eilish. Without you, this book would not have been possible.

My thanks to Liam Hayes of Hero Books for giving me this opportunity. From first suggesting the idea, to your expert advice during the process, it's been a pleasure.

Adrian Russell and Niall Kelly gave it their blessing from the outset. To my talented colleagues at *The42*, it's a great honour to work alongside you every day.

I received my first break in journalism over 15 years ago. I owe a huge debt of gratitude to Kevin Corrigan and the *Tullamore Tribune* for providing me with the chance to pursue this career.

Since I was young, Tullamore GAA club has been a constant presence in my life. For fostering my love of the game, to the lifelong friends I've made and the great days we've enjoyed on the field, I'm always proud to say I'm a Blue.

A special thanks to my many close friends for your interest in this project and the words of encouragement along the way.

Finally, to my family and especially my parents Benny and Caroline, I'm eternally grateful for your support over the years.

Kevin O'Brien
September 2022

PROLOGUE

Pattaya, Thailand
December, 2000

JOHNNY

THERE WERE TWO types of cells in the police station… a big inner chamber, and smaller cells near the front.

We were placed in a cell by the reception, which wasn't too bad. At least we were somewhat visible to the outside world. Visitors could talk to us through the bars. It wasn't brilliant, but it wasn't terrible either. After a while, the Thai police led us down a hallway that had more cells on either side.

We entered this open plan area… maybe 30 by 30 feet in size. There wasn't any natural lighting, apart from a skylight way above on the ceiling that allowed a sliver of light in.

There were about 30 of us in that cell. Concrete walls, concrete floors… no beds. Everyone was lying on the ground.

The first thing that struck me was the amount of prisoners missing limbs. There were lads without arms and legs everywhere. Space was confined. Everyone was lying across one another. Some, we learned afterwards, were illegal immigrants in Thailand, without travel papers or whatever.

There was one toilet over in the corner, up on a big high pedestal. Basically a hole in the ground for everyone to share.

The condition of the chamber was disgusting. Everywhere you looked there were these little flies and maggots running up and down... hundreds and thousands of these insects crawling all around the walls and floor. At certain times this bell would go off. All the prisoners would all rush to the front bars to queue up for this tiny little bag of rice. Needless to say, we weren't queueing up. Our appetite had long since deserted us.

There was another cell across the way that had a big, huge guy in there all on his own. I was thinking to myself, *What's this lad's story?* It looked like he was the King Kong of the jail.

All sorts of things flashed through my mind. Every hour felt like a week. I tried to get some sleep. I shut my eyes for a few minutes to see if I could forget about where I was. It wasn't easy. You hear stories about people getting locked up abroad... the conditions in cells and all these things. But you couldn't even imagine how grim this was.

When we were escorted into the cell, I glanced across at a few of my Offaly teammates. They didn't say a word... but the look in their eyes told its own story.

How have we managed to get ourselves into this mess?

★★★

BILLY

TEAM HOLIDAYS ARE a great way for a squad to tighten bonds and friendships away from the field. Nowadays, county teams go on more in-season training camps than we ever did, but the trips away at the end of a season, particularly after winning an All-Ireland, were the real icing on the cake.

Hard training sessions and winning trophies bring a group closer together, yet there's nothing quite like the stories and slagging that emerge from a team holiday.

The trips away with your own crew open a different window into the soul of your squad. You see the other side of fellas. Hurling talk tends to be kept to a minimum. The hours spent sitting sipping cold ones and dining out together are where you really get to know their character. Chatting about stuff that would never come up when you're beside a lad togging out in a dressing-room or on a bus to a game.

Of course, lads cut loose. They find themselves in hairy situations. The unplanned, unscripted stuff... that's the real gold. It's funny. In the depths of January, we could be standing on the end line in Birr about to begin one of Derry O'Donovan's infamous 20-minute runs, when Johnny Pilkington might remind everyone of an incident involving one of the lads from a trip away. His comedic timing was second to none.

We'd be in stitches laughing, briefly forgetting about the physical torture ahead of us. That's the kind of stuff that can get you through a winter of slogging on mucky pitches... when Croke Park on a summer's evening seems like light years away.

★★★

JOE

WE WERE FORTUNATE with Offaly during the 1990s that we got a few trips away on the back of our success. We had some great holidays over the years. Our first one as a group came after the 1994 All-Ireland. Having fallen at the first hurdle in Leinster the previous two years, we sort of came out of nowhere to win it.

Our reward was a two-week holiday to Florida after Christmas. We had to raise some money for the trip and I was the player representative on the fundraising committee. It was chaired by Kieran Keenaghan, a great Offaly hurling man, who was well supported by some good GAA men from around the county... Sean Maunsell, Liam Claffey, Peadar Kavanagh and Tony Murphy among them.

Everyone arrived in Dublin Airport to get the flight wearing the official team gear. We felt important, like we were the best hurlers in Ireland.

It was great to be going away and especially with wives and girlfriends and a nice bit of spending money in our pockets as well.

We were all young. It was the first time everybody really got to know each other well. I was closest to Michael Duignan on the team and we generally socialised together. Edel, Michael's girlfriend at the time, and my wife Marie became great friends. They were very close right up to the time of Edel's sad passing in 2009. She was a lady and great fun on a night out. We've a lot of great memories from our time together.

One night the team ended up singing karaoke in the hotel bar in Clearwater. Some lads could sing and others didn't have a note in their head. I'd put Billy and Martin Hanamy in the latter category. They did a duet of *I Shot the Sheriff* and almost cleared out the hotel. That performance is remembered to this day…for all the wrong reasons. They haven't sang since. They weren't asked to either.

★★★

BILLY

WE WEREN'T LONG back from that holiday when we played Galway in the league in Ballinasloe.

They beat us out the gate, 1-28 to 1-1. At half-time, we still hadn't scored and Galway had 20 points on the board. For a team that had been in the All-Ireland four months earlier, it was shocking stuff. We were never a league team, but that was embarrassing. They walked all over us.

Éamonn Cregan went berserk in the dressing-room. I never saw him as angry, before or after. I'd say he wasn't far from walking away before the second-half threw in. He knew there was going to have to be a lot of cobwebs blown out… and quickly.

★★★

JOE

IN 1998 WE flew to South Africa via London. It was a long flight but we took full advantage of the complimentary food and drink on board. It was a brilliant trip, with plenty of tourist attractions in and around Cape Town… wonderful sights and scenery. We visited the Cape of Good Hope, Table Mountain and Robben Island. We spent another enjoyable afternoon in the Stellenbosch wine region visiting wineries.

Some great friends and supporters of the team came with us. Simon Lyons from Banagher video recorded most of the holiday. Tom and Eileen Mangan, owners of Doheny and Nesbitt, and Seamus and Mary Coakley from Clareen travelled as well.

If we'd won the 2000 All-Ireland we were to go to Australia, but Kilkenny beat us... and that put an end to that. We had to settle for Thailand. We started off in Bangkok for a few days. We were staying in a fabulous hotel but at the entrance there was a small shebeen. It was a fairly rough and ready kind of place. And we all took a shine to it.

That became our meeting up point every evening after our day's sightseeing. The owner of that shebeen almost became a millionaire over our few days there... she was heading to the supermarket every hour to try and restock the fridges with refreshments. Our next stop was Pattaya, a seaside resort on the eastern coast of Thailand.

During the week about 12 of us, some players and their partners, went on an activity day and took a boat out to an island. We did some jet-skiing and paragliding. Then we hired out these motorbikes. They were like Honda 50s. We did a tour of the island on dirt track roads. We arrived at a shooting range and got to test our accuracy with some Magnum P45s.

One of the younger members of our panel, Colm Cassidy, nearly killed himself on the motorbike. He lost control on a gravel road and managed to jump off before it careened off into a deep valley. Fortunately, Colm wasn't harmed... he got a lift back with one of the lads.

The motorbike wasn't recovered.

We arrived back at the base and returned the rest of the motorbikes. The lads in the rental shed looked them up and down every way they could, searching for any marks or damage. That was their gig. If any were damaged, they'd charge you for it. But they forgot to count them, and we forgot to tell them. We jumped on our boat and headed back to the mainland as quickly as we could... scot-free, we thought. When we arrived, there was a delegation there waiting for us.

'Where's the motorbike?'

We had to part with a few bob to try and calm things down. It wasn't a great start to the day... but things were about to get a lot worse. We went our separate ways, and a few of us went for dinner and had a few drinks. We were probably dehydrated from all our activities. One drink led to another and before long, a handful of us ended up in some dingy bar playing pool.

I brought a good camera with me on that trip and carried it around in a plastic bag that day. Two of the lads were playing pool and I went to move the bag… the camera was gone!

There were a good few locals in the bar at the same time. We were fairly certain one of them had taken it. We brought it up with them that a camera had gone missing. We had a bit of drink on board… and one word borrowed another. Things quickly heated up… it went from zero to 90 in a matter of seconds.

A small melee broke out and there were Thai lads coming at us from every direction.

There were plenty of punches thrown.

★★★

JOHNNY

WE ALL ENDED up out on the street, which was very busy. I looked up the street and saw Thai lads swinging out of some of the Offaly boys.

While things were starting to get a little out of hand, it was, by and large, handbags. There was some pushing and shoving with a few punches thrown in, but nothing out of the ordinary. There were a few punches aimed in my direction. I never threw a punch in my life and I wasn't about to start in Thailand.

Click… click.

As quick as a flash, I felt these two handcuffs latching onto my wrists. Before you could snap your fingers, the police had arrived on the scene and cuffed a few of us. We were led on up into the back of this paddy wagon and brought on down to the local cell.

In the big open plan cell, I got chatting to an English lad who had been in there for three months. There was some issue with his passport. He had no contact from the outside world since he was brought in… he reminded me of Tom Hanks in *Castaway* with his big beard.

When he told me about his plight, I started to get a bit nervous. *Are we ever going to get out of here?*

We weren't being told anything by the police. The language barrier didn't help… we didn't even know why we were in there. We couldn't understand what we were supposed to have done wrong. It all happened so fast. To me it felt like a bit of a stitch up of some description. *Why are we all in here?*

We only had to spend one night there. We were released the next day. We were probably only held for about 16 hours… but it felt a lot longer. By the following morning, word was starting to spread back to the rest of the team and the partners about what had happened.

I'd have paid whatever I had in my bank account, which wasn't too much at the time, just to get out of there.

★★★

JOE

THE POLICE WERE effectively looking for a bribe. We paid a 'fine' of around a couple of hundred euros each which is big money over there. That solved everything. But we didn't have enough on us, so we had to wait for our partners to arrive.

They had been on a bit of an evening out themselves. So they didn't arrive at the police station until sometime the next morning. They got wind that we were all in bother. It must have been some shock when they heard about us, but they went to an ATM and came up with the cash to bail us out.

★★★

JOHNNY

WE WERE EXPECTING there would be a bit of fuss with the team management and county board when we got back, but in fairness they never said a word. We didn't care anyway, we just wanted to get out of there.

I hopped straight into the shower and tried to wash away all the slime and dirt. Wash away the memory of it all… but, it's one of those things that you can't undo. Thankfully, we can look back and laugh at it now. It was all part of the experience of going to Thailand. Whenever my kids are going on holidays and I advise them to be careful, they're quick to remind me of my past! It's all in good humour.

It wasn't a laughing matter by any means at the time. We were all more than a bit sheepish going back to the hotel. The other guys did some sniggering and laughing at our expense after that.

★★★

JOE

WE'D OFTEN LAUGH about that story now. We didn't for a long time, but now we can look back on it and say it was a bit of craic. Something to tell your grandchildren about. Word got back fairly quickly and it probably spread around the county as well, but it was never spoken about publicly. Not to us anyway.

We were surprised it never became a story in the media back home as we were a fairly high profile team at the time. We'd played in four All-Ireland finals over the previous seven years.

And we were one of four county teams in Pattaya at the time… Kilkenny were out there as well, as were the Kildare and Armagh footballers.

It was just one of those things. We had a lot of drink on board but a camera was stolen and that's what started it. Nobody ever owned up to taking it.

And needless to say, I never got the camera back!

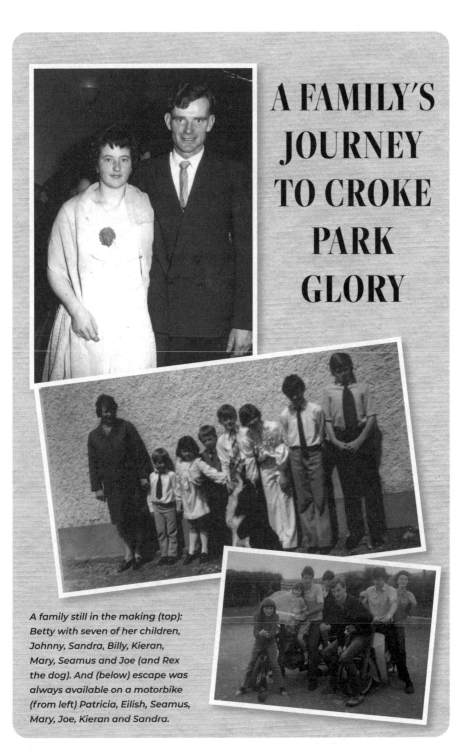

A FAMILY'S JOURNEY TO CROKE PARK GLORY

A family still in the making (top): Betty with seven of her children, Johnny, Sandra, Billy, Kieran, Mary, Seamus and Joe (and Rex the dog). And (below) escape was always available on a motorbike (from left) Patricia, Eilish, Seamus, Mary, Joe, Kieran and Sandra.

Betty pours tea for her sons in the days before the 1994 All-Ireland final (top), and all the Dooley sons with their mother.

Betty and Sean and their family (top) and happily surrounded by all their grandchildren in 2000.

Winning sons of Clareen and Seir Kieran, and their trophy haul of All Stars (from left) Billy, Eugene Coughlan, Joe, Kevin Kinahan and Johnny.

The Dooley family together in the sun for Aideen's wedding in 2015 (from left): Back – Sandra, Mary, Betty, Patricia and Eilish. Front – Kieran, Joe, Seamus, Billy and Johnny.

Joe and his family in Croke Park in 2021 after Offaly claimed the Christy Ring Cup (from left): Back – Shane's wife Anne Marie, Niamh, Marie, Aidin and Shane. Front – Joe and Aidin's husband Brendan.

Billy and Fiona, with their sons (from left) Gearóid, Conor and Seán.

Johnny and family... Emma, Sinéad, Hannah and Jack.

The Seir Kieran teams which claimed the Offaly Senior Hurling Championship crown in 1988 (top), 1995 (middle) and '96.

I

1995 All-Ireland final

Cregan

Where's Joe Dooley

Sid

Pilkington in the pub again!

Loughnane's scream

McIntyre

Wexford hopping

★★★

JOE

THERE'S 10 MINUTES to go in the 1995 All-Ireland final. We're leading Clare by three points and on course to retain our title. On the verge of becoming back-to-back All-Ireland hurling champions for the first time in Offaly's history.

Conditions on the pitch are heating up. It's a stifling atmosphere, but we're well used to it at this stage. Despite the 82,000 strong crowd, I can hear Ger Loughnane on the sideline... he's wired, urging Clare on.

Johnny Pilkington's goal left daylight between the teams. We missed a few chances to extend our lead and put them away. Now the Banner are driving at us. Ollie Baker powers into the game at midfield and gets a hook on me, when I have a point for the taking. Anthony Daly and Seanie McMahon are breaking forward from half-back. Jamesie O'Connor is zipping all over the attack hunting for an opening.

There's a break in play.

I look over to the sideline. My number is called. My race is run.

No 12 Joe Dooley is being replaced by No 17 Brendan Kelly. I never like being taken off. A switch to full-forward to curb the influence of Brian Lohan might have served me better, but the selectors probably had their minds made up about substitutions before the ball was thrown-in.

Still, I trot towards the bench thinking... *We're surely over the line here. We'll see this out.*

But as the minutes tick down, we're looking edgy. Little things start to go against us. Fergal Tuohy scores his fourth point of the day. Clare's fitness is starting to tell all over the pitch.

Is the pressure getting to us?

I glance at the clock. Five minutes to go.

Two points in it.

★★★

BILLY

WE'RE STILL CREATING chances. Plenty of them. We miss four straight shots… one after another. If we'd scored even two of them, we'd have closed it out.

Anthony Daly's point attempt from a long-range free hits David Hughes' crossbar and bounces back into play. It drops in front of Éamonn Taaffe. He sends the rebound into the net. The Clare crowd go into raptures.

Johnny equalises from a 50-metre free. Daly sends Clare back in front from a '65'. It's tit for tat now. Davy Fitzgerald is roaring at his backs… keeping them on their toes. Clare have a mean defence in front of him. They're very aggressive. I have Frank Lohan tracking me. He's only a young fella, but is a big strong lad… 6' 2" and very fast. It's a tough afternoon in his company.

Johnny Pilkington drops a shot off the post. I'm lurking in the area. It bounces just beyond my reach and Clare clear the danger. Small margins. Jamesie O'Connor sends over the insurance point from a free. And that is that.

Clare get their hands on the Liam MacCarthy Cup for the first time in 81 years. Our dreams of going back-to-back are in tatters.

★★★

JOHNNY

IN FAIRNESS TO Clare, they were a serious outfit. It wasn't fully appreciated at the time just how good they were. They proved their pedigree in 1997, when they won it again. They had the strongest defence and midfield in the country. From one to nine, nobody else came close. Up front they had a nice sprinkling of forwards that included Jamesie O'Connor and Sparrow O'Loughlin... but they were built from the back out to dominate teams.

All that being said, we were only beaten in the last five minutes. We hurled well that day and our backs were exceptional... Kevin Kinahan gave one of the greatest displays ever seen at full-back.

We led by 1-6 to 0-7 at half-time. There was very little between the teams. It did feel like the whole country was behind them and maybe even the referee, ever so slightly. There were a few 50-50 calls that we felt could have gone our way and didn't. But then again, Jamesie missed a few easy enough frees that he should have put over. Sometimes these things balance themselves out. You can make up all the excuses you like after you lose... but good teams make their own luck.

They were riding the crest of a wave that summer. We were the big story the year before, but in 1995 it was Clare. I'll never forget running out on the pitch before the game. When Clare came out... the whole stadium shook. We were usually well-supported but were definitely outnumbered two or three to one by Clare that day. They were electrifying and it was great for hurling.

We were hot favourites to win it. Perhaps we weren't managed as well as we could have been. Expectations should have been controlled better. If anything, the hype revved up between 1994 and '95... there were huge crowds going to our training sessions. Our supporters were on a high the same as we were.

★★★

JOE

LOSING A GAME that was within our grasp, it was a killer. To retain the Liam MacCarthy Cup would have been special. It would have put us in with an opportunity of going for three in-a-row in 1997.

Putting successive All-Ireland together is very difficult to do. The Kilkenny side of 1992 and '93 were the only ones who did it in the 90s. We were within two minutes of it in 1995... and just didn't get over the line. I always felt we were a better team in 1995 than in '94, when we beat Limerick with the famous comeback. Our pedigree was challenged after that win. When all the hysteria died down, there was a perception out there that we were lucky to win... that we stole an All-Ireland from Limerick.

It hurt us.

I think we peaked as a team in the Leinster final against Kilkenny in July of 1995. We went into the game as underdogs, despite being All-Ireland champions. Éamonn Cregan had us wound up. He felt we were disrespected. After beating them by nine points, we felt a great sense of achievement. From there on, we found it hard to stay as hungry as we should have been.

We had 11 points to spare against Down in the semi-final, but we were below par. It wasn't the best preparation for an All-Ireland final. Clare got a much sterner test against Galway.

We went somewhat off the boil. And that's no disrespect to Clare. We were expected to win... but the favourites tag never suited us.

After the 1994 All-Ireland a local band in Offaly called Stars on P45 brought out the Joe Dooley song. The first time I ever heard it was in Ferbane after we brought the Liam MacCarthy Cup down there.

It was seemingly well known in the area at the time. Ciaran 'Brownie' Guinan, who's a great singer and musician in Ferbane, and a few of his friends penned it. They brought it out on a cassette. It's a catchy tune... even to this day, people remember it.

Sang to the tune of *That's Amore* it goes:

When the ball's in the sky,
In Croke Park in July,
That's Joe Dooley

When the ball's in the air,
Who's that man in the square,
That's Joe Dooley

What a boy
Pride and joy of Uibh Fhaili,
He's in gold, white and green,
From the fields of Clareen,
That's Joe Dooley

It really caught fire during the championship in 1995.

After Clare beat us they were singing it down there all winter, with a slight twist at the end... *When the ball's in the sky, in Croke Park in July, where's Joe Dooley?*

To hear that was going on made it harder on me personally. I was in the limelight in the run into that All-Ireland. It was massively disappointing when it didn't work out. But the song made it back to number one in 1998 when we beat Clare. It still gets an odd airing to this day.

After Offaly games in Croke Park, my son Shane always seemed to be able to make his way past security and get into the dressing-rooms, whether we had won or lost. He was old enough to remember some of the great days in the 90s.

He managed to get in there after the game in 1995. He was nine-years-old and took the defeats hard, particularly that one. He couldn't believe we lost... he thought we couldn't be beaten.

We had enjoyed a great run through 1994 and '95. We hadn't been beaten in the championship in over two years. Sitting on my lap in the Hogan Stand dressing rooms, his eyes filled with tears, he was inconsolable.

He wasn't the only one.

★★★

JOHNNY

I FOUND THAT loss very tough to deal with. Because of the hype and the fact we were going for two in-a-row, which had never been done by an Offaly hurling team. We knew what it was like to win. And when you feel the pain of losing, it's multiplied by 50. Supporters were on a downer. All of a sudden... you go from hero to zero.

I'm not a good loser. I struggled with it for a few weeks. When you lose an All-Ireland, it's impossible to get it out of your head. You're playing it back over and over... all the little things you could have done that might have swung the game. *If I did that play slightly differently. Why did I make that pass? Why didn't I try something there?*

I could never bring myself to watch back a game like that... too painful. I've seen it since now on TG4 playbacks. It didn't pan out exactly how I'd remembered. We played far better than I thought on the day.

There's nothing you can really do to get over tough days like that. You just have to wait it out. I'm not saying it's easy. You stay tight with the team and let alcohol soothe the pain for a few days. That probably doesn't help the head either.

I'd put it down to a mild depression… what you feel after a disappointment like that.

I'm not making light of depression, but you do feel low for a week or two. You hardly want to leave the house. Like anything, it eventually dissipates. Going back training with the club helps, even though that's the toughest part of all.

Picking the hurl and gear bag back up and heading to that first training session is very difficult. The thought of hurling again can be the last thing you want to do. You might have a club championship match two weeks later. Get the dirty diesel out of the system… it's what you need to do.

Although I don't know if the pain of losing an All-Ireland final ever properly leaves you.

★★★

BILLY

AFTER THE MATCH, I told a reporter that it was the most disappointing day of my life. In a sporting sense, it still is. Without a doubt. It was tough going. I went into a lull for a period of time. You just have to go through it.

It took me a while to get the appetite back for the game. I lost plenty of county finals but to get over that All-Ireland was definitely the hardest thing I had to do. An All-Ireland is the pinnacle. It would have been great to put two back-to-back.

People think, *Ah sure they'll get over that and they'll be back again.*

You're training for 12 months… for nothing, really. And we trained extremely hard that year. But so be it, life is life. It wasn't to be.

I woke up on Wednesday morning feeling groggy after spending the day before on the beer with the team. I sat there staring out my bedroom window. I had nothing else in my head, only the game… I don't know how long I was there for, until I realised I needed to snap out of it.

I was getting married to Fiona in three days.

Our wedding was on the following Saturday. I had no choice but to change my tune fairly quickly. I couldn't be moping around the house for the week. I was lucky I had something to look forward to. It definitely helped.

Fiona and her mother Margaret put in a huge amount of work organising the wedding while I was preoccupied with the All-Ireland. So much time and effort went into getting everything in place for it... we got married in Kinnitty Church, and it was a brilliant day.

I felt it took us two years to get over the Clare defeat as a team.

We underwent some transition as well. We lost some good players from the panel after 1995. You can't lose talent like that and expect someone to come in and fill the position straight away.

Some former Offaly players, All-Ireland winners from the 80s, questioned in the media whether we were good enough to win a second All-Ireland. That stung and motivated us at the same time. We did a huge amount of tough training and hurling in between 1994 and '98, with little to show for it. They were difficult years... we just couldn't get over the line.

The popular interpretation of Offaly hurlers during the 90s was that we were skilful players that were poorly disciplined.

It was overdone. Johnny Pilkington might go down to have a pint in the pub the night before he'd hurl in Croke Park. And he would have one or two... he wouldn't be telling you a lie. He could be there for three hours but he might have two pints. I often had a drink with him.

He liked to give that perception, *Jays, Pilkington was in the pub again last night.* Now he'd drink a few pints, but he wasn't what people thought he was. John Troy was the same. You didn't hurl like they did and be blackguarding yourself... you couldn't.

The way some people talked about us. *How the hell are these guys hurling like they are, if this is what they're at in their social life?*

It wasn't lost on us that people on the outside thought we weren't dedicated.

Of course players will lose form, that's only natural. But if you had a group of lads that played at the top level for a decade, committed to the cause of winning an All-Ireland for Offaly, you can't say they lack commitment.

When we were off in the winter, we'd socialise. We had great times out of it.

That's where you make really good friends as well.

You'd often hear the stories of the savage training Clare did under Ger Loughnane, or the work Liam Griffin had Wexford doing. Would we have won two All-Irelands in the 90s if we didn't train just as hard as them?

Some of the players gave an impression that they'd have their few pints and tip away at training. But you don't hurl at that standard we did, if you're that way inclined. We certainly let our hair down at times but in general we were minding ourselves… eating well and sleeping well.

We'd give it our all when we went to train. Any of those guys on the Offaly teams I hurled with, every time we went to Tullamore on a Tuesday or Thursday evening, the attitude was what was the point of going if you weren't going to give it your all?

We were especially vulnerable in 1996. Éamonn Cregan stayed on as manager for a fifth year. Maybe he was getting tired. Hurling's revolution years were in full flow at the tail end of the 90s… Wexford arrived as a major force under Liam Griffin and put us out of Leinster in 1996 and '97.

We'd beaten them the previous two years, but there was something different about them once they started rolling under Griffin. Earlier in 1996 they beat us in the National League quarter-final. When we met them in the Leinster final, they were confident. You could tell they were more up for it than we were. We were well in the game with 15 minutes to go.

I played well that day and grabbed a goal in the second-half. Only for good saves from Damien Fitzhenry, I'd have scored a couple more… he was a great goalie. I brought the ball in close to him a couple of times and pulled the trigger. For one of my opportunities, I made a lovely connection only for him to stop it with his body… he faced it up bravely and it went out for a '65'.

JOE

IF ANYTHING, I think we overtrained that year. We were so eager to get back on the horse again.

Liam Griffin had undoubtedly instilled toughness and mental strength in

Wexford. Liam Dunne was their backbone at centre-back. A hardy bit of stuff. For a small man he was mobile and a great stick man… Ger Cushe was a powerful full-back… Larry O'Gorman was very forceful and Adrian Fenlon was a quality midfielder.

Up front they had Martin Storey, he was always good for a few scores. His fellow half-forwards Larry Murphy and Rory McCarthy had great games in that Leinster final. They scored 0-12 between them, which was a surprise considering we felt Kevin Martin, Hubert Rigney and Brian Whelahan made up our strongest line. Tom Dempsey also had a great game in the corner.

My marker Rod Guiney was another big strong fit fella. Maybe not as good a hurler as the other lads but he was very athletic. And he wasn't afraid to let fly with his hurl, as I discovered during the second-half. By the time Wexford were lifting the Bob O'Keeffe Cup, I was lying in the Mater Hospital. During the second-half, I took a heavy knock to the head from Rod. A high ball came down between us and we both pulled… the end of his stroke caught my head and split me open… blood everywhere. I was badly concussed and couldn't recall much from the incident.

I was brought straight out the tunnel and into the back of an ambulance. As we were going up Jones' Road I could hear the crowd roaring. I knew things were going well for one team and I was trying to work out who?

★★★

JOHNNY

ON THAT DAY, Wexford were just on fire. They could shoot from anywhere and it would go over. They had enough heartache and their fair share of disappointments previous to that.

There were almost 45,000 at the match. Wexford had tremendous supporters and it created a brilliant atmosphere. I have good memories from that day, scoring four from play but anytime we raised the white flag, they seemed to respond straightaway.

They were knocking on the door for a good number of years. You look at the quality of the players they had. We picked them off by just being more economical in 1994 and '95. I had great time for the Wexford players because we always got on well with them off the field.

We socialised with them. It was brilliant in hindsight to see them go on to win the All-Ireland.

1997 STARTED OUT as a breath of fresh air.

The whole league structure was transformed as well, switching from the old system where we played three games before Christmas… now, we were playing five games on consecutive weekends from the start of March. It was brilliant.

Éamonn Cregan stepped down and Tipperary native John McIntyre took over. He was young and eager, even if he was inexperienced. He changed things around. He recalled Gary Cahill and Roy Mannion and it made the panel look a lot stronger. There was a great atmosphere in the camp. And we brought it right into the Tipperary game in the first round of the league.

It was the opening of MacDonagh Park in Nenagh and a huge crowd of around 15,000 turned out for it. For me, it was a game that summed up the class of Brian Whelahan. He was the best hurler I ever played with, without a doubt. He made us look good as forwards with the supply of ball he was able to give us. When Brian got the ball he'd read the run you were making and play it into your path. You didn't have to break stride. Other guys could come out of defence, burst past a lad and lump it down the field without looking.

He was so composed. He was a master at spreading the right diagonal passes. I usually played in front of him at No 10. I liked to drift across the half-forward line to pull my man out of position.

Early on against Tipp, Brian picks up the ball, I drift away from my marker George Frend towards the left-half forward channel. Brian spots me and drops it straight into my hand. I slot it over from 40 yards out. This happened on three other occasions. So four points I got arrived straight from the stick of Sid. He picked up the ball, spent half a second surveying the field… delivered it into my paw. I got the handy score and trotted back to my position.

I hit a couple of frees as well and we ended up winning by two. I was selected as Man of the Match but I could have just handed my award straight over to Brian. That's just an example of what he was capable of doing.

The greatest pass he ever gave me was in 1998, on the second day against Clare in Croke Park. He collected the ball about 80 yards out from goal. I'd moved into corner-forward and Brian hit a crossfield pass over the defender's head, straight into my hand. I had 10 yards of space and Davy Fitzgerald pulled off a great save to deny me a goal. It was the most unbelievable pass you could ever imagine. He had the vision to flight the ball perfectly and pick me out where I was, without having to break stride. It just showed the ability he had. We had great defenders but none were capable of that level of vision. That's a skill that not too many players would naturally have.

He'd be tailor-made for the modern game.

THE LATE START to the league gave us the chance to get a block of heavy physical training done early in January and February. We did eight weeks of solid work and it was the toughest training I can remember doing with Offaly.

We were in really good condition early in the year, which in some ways had us worried. *Can we sustain this? Can we keep it going?*

John McIntyre was bringing lads down that were a bit overweight and they were doing four or five consecutive nights of training. Other lads were on diets… it was all stuff we hadn't done before. If there was any downfall, we felt there was a lot of motivational talking done early in the year. We always liked to keep our powder dry for the summer months.

Something that always stuck with me was what he'd have us doing at the end of some training sessions. We'd be in the depths of February, with rain and sleet falling, and we'd finish off training with a warm down by jogging around the pitch in pairs.

He had us singing…

> *Who are we?*
> *We're Offaly.*
> *What are we?*
> *We're winners*

I never forgot it. We wouldn't be like that, that wouldn't be our character. It was like something you'd do in the army. One night, Martin Hanamy hit me an elbow into the ribs… 'Lord Jesus, I hope there's no one listening to us out over the hedge. They'll think we're mad'.

I could understand why he was trying to do it. But I don't think we needed that. We were a little bit embarrassed to be singing this at that time of the year. As the year went on, we seemed to lose a little bit of momentum coming into the championship... maybe John took on too much. He was doing the fitness, the coaching, the management... everything.

Consider the size of management teams now and how much goes into it... he was shouldering all that burden himself.

John came back in after and spent three great years with Offaly. He had a good career as a manager. I'd say he learned a good bit from that experience, as much as we did.

There's no doubt the commitment was there from the players in 1997. There was a huge effort put in. We had full turnouts for training sessions... there was nobody copping out.

★★★

JOE

I WAS APPOINTED captain. It was my first time being captain. I was previously offered the chance by Pat Joe Whelahan to skipper Offaly for the 1989 season. I was studying for my final accountancy exams and knew I was going to miss a few league games, so I turned it down.

In hindsight I should have accepted it, as we won Leinster that year. It's a massive honour captaining your county and I didn't think twice about accepting it in 1997.

The league that season was nearly too competitive to what we were used to. It meant that when summer came around it was like we were after playing four or five championship games already. Our poor showing traditionally in the league was usually down to the fact we didn't have the strength in depth. We were probably a bit lazy... we just wouldn't burst ourselves when we didn't have to.

When it came around to Leinster, we beat Meath in the first round and scraped over Laois in the quarter-final by a point. Then we fell to Wexford in the Leinster semi-final. In front of a huge crowd, there was very little in it. Billy had a great chance of a goal near the finish and Damien Fitzhenry made a brilliant save to deny us a draw.

BILLY

WEXFORD WERE HOPPING… reigning All-Ireland champions. You could see the buzz they had. They were just a little bit more geed up than we were and the better side in the grand scheme of things. The whole of Wexford was on a high and we were still a bit flat from 1995, even though it still came down to the last five minutes.

The county board decided to make a change of management at the end of the season. We had no say in that, nor were we asked for our thoughts. They were fairly ruthless. As a team, you only have a certain window of opportunity to produce. If a manager wasn't getting the results, then he got a bit of a quick knock, unfortunately for John.

One thing is for sure, by the time 1998 came around we'd developed that savage hunger to scale the mountain again.

II

St Brendan's Park

Clareen

Sean and Betty

The green Ford Anglia

Seir Kieran

Farmers first, hurlers...

A family labour force

Holidays in Coolderry

★★★

JOE

IT WAS ONE of those scorching hot August afternoons… perfect for championship hurling.

I was eight years old and wandering around St Brendan's Park in Birr trying to find a spot where I could see the green grass of the field. It was All-Ireland semi-final day in 1971 and the place was thronged with 15,000 Tipperary and Galway supporters.

Eventually I gave up my hunt and returned to my father behind the town goals. He lifted me up on his shoulders to watch the game. Babs Keating was Tipperary's star player and he had one of those unforgettable games for the winning team, finishing with 2-12. He scored one of the goals right in front of us.

Imagine an All-Ireland semi-final being played in Birr now… you couldn't even contemplate it.

Birr was the home of hurling. That's where the atmosphere was. Heading over there to take in a club or county hurling game on a Sunday was the weekly routine. The highlight of our week.

St Brendan's Park was a fortress for Offaly in those days. When the final whistle went after Offaly defeated Kilkenny there in the league a year earlier, I watched our goalkeeper Damien Martin jump up in the air and clench his fists. He was one of my idols. Around that time his father was doing some land reclamation works for us on the farm. I walked into the kitchen one day and could scarcely believe Damien Martin's father was sitting at our kitchen table.

My father was a hurling fanatic and it quickly rubbed off on us. He'd talk about it morning, noon and night. It was the topic of discussion with all of us in the house… it was bred into us from an early age. From the time I could walk, I was going to games with him. I brought a hurl with me everywhere I went.

In 1974 we were in Birr when Kilkenny beat Galway by 12 points in the All-Ireland semi-final. I can still see John Connolly coming off the pitch at the end of the game bleeding from his forehead. Eddie Keher scored 13 points that day. He landed two of his scores without even looking at the posts. Kilkenny went on to lift the Liam MacCarthy Cup. They had a great side… Keher, Pat Delaney, Kieran Purcell and Liam 'Chunky' O'Brien. All playing on our doorstep.

In my wildest dreams I didn't think I'd ever play in a game of that magnitude. Offaly were a million miles away from that stage. All-Ireland semi-finals and finals were for the big guns… Kilkenny, Tipperary, Cork… Galway.

I'd go home after those games in Birr and hurl in the yard, pretending I was Keher or Keating. But to think Offaly would actually get to those big days and actually start beating the traditional powerhouses? It was fantasy stuff.

Then they started to push back.

Towards the end of the 70s Offaly started to become a nuisance to the big teams. They were promoted from Division 2 of the league in 1977. In the top flight, they started competing and winning the odd game. In 1978, they beat Wexford, Cork and Galway. That was kind of the start. Those small steps eventually led to the breakthrough in the 80s.

★★★

JOHNNY

OUR PARENTS WERE solid people. You knew where you stood with them. Our father Sean was a native of Clareen and our mother Betty is from Coolderry. They got married in 1962 and had nine children… Joe, Seamus, Mary, Kieran, Billy, Sandra, myself, Patricia and Eilish.

Joe arrived in 1963. Billy came in 1969, and I was born in '71. Sandra arrived in between us… Patricia came five years after me, followed by Eilish, but I was the baby of the house for a good number of years. I used to always be plaguing my mother about having another baby.

And eventually she did. Even though I was still very young, when my two younger sisters came along I felt like I was a big fella in the house. I didn't realise at the time but it must have been a busy house. When you grow into something, you take it as normal. My father was a serious farmer and a great man to work. He wouldn't discourage you from going training but work was work… and sport was sport at the same time.

And he'd often get annoyed if you were going training and there was something left to be finished on the farm.

Or if he was in the middle of hay or turf and you said, 'I've to go training'. But he was consistent. There was nothing he'd love more than to see you hurling but he also had principles when it came to work.

My mother is an unbelievable woman. She was up at 6am every morning to milk the cows. She'd have the porridge made for breakfast and the lunches to bring with us to school. Everything was presented for us when she called us at 7.30am. We'd get up and in literally 10 minutes, we'd be out the door. Dinner was on the table the minute we'd come in every evening.

When we'd head off to watch matches, the whole family would go… be it Offaly games or county semi-finals and finals, we'd be there. It was a day out for everyone. We'd pack into an old green Ford Anglia. My mother would be up front and the rest of us would pile into the back. The car was so full that I'd have to lie sideways in the back window. That was my spot for quite a while, no matter where we went.

We had a blue Hillman Hunter after that. Every time we went anywhere the car was full. Eventually the older ones started to drift away at the top end and that created an extra bit of room.

My father would often regale us with stories about hurling in older times and games he went to when he was younger. He'd cycle down to Thurles to watch the greats in action. Tipperary's John Doyle and Jimmy Doyle were two that were frequently mentioned. He had great time for Limerick's Jack and Mick Mackey too.

Kilkenny and Wexford were the two big teams in Leinster. He'd always talk about Eddie Keher. He saw Christy Ring play a few times. From an Offaly perspective, Paddy Molloy was one of the most prominent Offaly hurlers in the

60s and 70s. We used to try and hold him up talking about hurling at dinner time for as long as we could. Because if we were doing that, we weren't out farming.

★★★

BILLY

CLAREEN SITS IN the shadow of the Slieve Blooms in Offaly hurling's heartland between Kinnitty and Birr. It's a rural area… we're the smallest parish in Offaly and second-smallest in Ireland. When we were growing up we had a shop, a post office, a church, a national school and a community hall, but no pub. The shop and post office are now closed.

About 90 percent of the people living there were farming households. You had the Connors down the lane from us. The Bergins next door, the Mulrooneys… the other Dooleys, the Coughlans, the Mooneys… the Kinahans. It just showed you how simple life was.

There was a great bond between the parents. There was no one looking any better than anyone else or looking for anything bigger in the world only to provide for their family and get the kids up and reared.

Our club is called Seir Kieran, but the team is known locally as Clareen. The hurling field was a place of contact with our neighbours… a playground for the kids. We had less than 400 people living in the area but Clareen were fortunate to contest 11 senior county finals between 1985 and 2000. The majority of those teams were backboned by those handful of families.

When we reached the county final in 1989, only two players on the team didn't have a brother playing alongside them. When we won our third title in 1996, my four brothers and I were on the starting team. It was a very proud day for our family.

From a young age we were always very active because of our farming duties. So when it came to moving to the hurling field we always had that bit of fitness. As a family, we were very united. We fought like cats and dogs when we were younger playing around the yard, but we were always unified when we went to hurl together.

When your mother and father are at home 24/7 it brings the family closer together, even if we didn't realise it at the time. Because everyone's in the one little circle.

My parents were very hard working people.

There was no fancy stuff but we always had enough. That's a credit to them. They ran a farm and raised nine children. Whichever of us wanted to go to college were put through it. We had a very happy childhood… everything was simple, we never worried about what anyone else had. It was about what we had ourselves. And if you're happy in what you have it counts a lot going forward in life.

From the age of six or seven we were out working on the farm. The whole lot of us would be up in the field turning hay. Our duties in the beginning might be bringing up bottles of water from a well for the older lads in the field. The hay would be gathered up with a tractor and buckrake. Then my uncles would come up and draw the hay, putting it into the shed.

My father sowed around seven acres of beet every year. So that had to be thinned first with hand hoes and we'd weed it after. We could be in the field for two or three weeks at that sort of work… we'd do it every day. We'd get up in the morning, do our few jobs around the yard and then get our breakfast and head on up to the field to work.

But there was never a huge panic on us. When we'd get to the headland after making our way across the field, my father might sit back into the ditch and have a smoke. We'd lie down as well… real relaxed aul' stuff. You'd get up then and go on again down the length of the drill, and maybe back up. He might have another half a cigarette… and we'd lie in the ditch again.

After that, we'd come down and my mother would have the dinner ready. We could go back up then and do another couple of drills. After eating my father might be a bit tired… sometimes he'd doze off, but we wouldn't make any noise to wake him up.

Most evenings in the summer, unless we were working at corn or making hay and it was going to rain, our father would be finished every evening by 6pm. For us it was great because we could always get to the hurling field then to do a bit of training or puck around. The evening was our own.

Come Autumn, we'd be out picking potatoes. The nine of us would go over to our neighbours… the Bergins, Connors or the Armstrongs. We'd be picking potatoes maybe every Saturday for a month, that'd be our job. You might get a pound or two if you were lucky. If not you'd get the dinner and they'd be over to you the next week picking our own potatoes, or over to another of the neighbours.

JOE

ONE TIME, WE were up in Armstrongs' farm picking potatoes. Har Armstrong, an old man, was picking away beside Johnny.

Next thing Johnny says to Har, 'What age are you Har?'

Har tells him his age.

'What age are you?' he says back to Johnny.

'I'm seven…today!'

Johnny was cute enough, he was hoping to get something for his birthday! His ploy worked. He got a bit extra for picking the spuds at the end of that day.

The Armstrongs were very decent people. When it was the turn for their potatoes to be picked, the field was always full for two reasons… the £2 they gave everybody for the day's work and the lovely dinner Mrs Armstrong would cook.

★★★

JOHNNY

WE LIVED UP a long lane so we were away from everything. It was quiet, but peaceful. There wouldn't be too many people passing by. In the earlier days, aside from school, it was only once a week where we ventured out the lane and went to Mass or shopping.

There were always jobs to be done and Saturdays were filled up with all sorts of work. We often got the odd day off school to work on the farm. Because we were a big family, we didn't go away on a summer holiday. Our parents never went away either. One summer we convinced the two of them that they needed the break… and they should head off somewhere. They agreed and decided to go to Galway for a couple of days.

Happy days, we can chill out and take it easy. We had all sorts of things planned but to our dismay, it was short-lived. They landed back home the following day.

'What happened?' we enquired.

Mammy explained that on the journey he was looking over every ditch into farmers' fields. Because the weather was so good, he got anxious that the corn at home might get overripe... he convinced himself that he needed to get home quickly to check it out. So they arrived back and we didn't end up cutting the corn for another two weeks.

He was just a home bird and never felt comfortable being away from home.

There was plenty of time for fun too. We had this old ass called Ned. Myself, Billy and our neighbour Martin Coffey would put a halter on him and venture down the lane. Ned never liked travelling far away from the house... he'd need some gentle encouragement to get moving. As soon as we'd turn for home, he'd take off with a mighty gallop. On occasion he'd surprise us by doing the buckaroo, followed by a sudden stop. We'd go flying out head first over the top of him. We'd dust ourselves off and hop back up.

Our neighbours would come up and we'd be putting halters on him and would pull things behind him. We'd head up to the woods a couple of fields across from us. We often spent a lot of our youth up there playing around with bows and arrows... our mother was happy enough to have us out of the house, out from under her feet.

All our neighbours had their own farms around the place. We'd often be moving cattle up and down between fields. We had some land in Cloghanmore, a nearby townland.

We'd run them along the roads. That involved blocking the gaps, jumping hedges... trying to get in front of the cattle. That's where there would be a bit of interaction with our neighbours. When we went herding, my father would be looking out over every ditch and wall... waiting to see someone so he could pull up for a chat. He loved meeting his uncle Tom Dooley in Breaghmore. That conversation always lasted a while.

We always had the hurls with us when we were herding. It was the one thing we brought with us no matter where we went. It filled in the gaps between whatever we were doing. Billy and I would puck the ball back and forth 30 yards apart as we made our way across the fields. I'd never walk out the backdoor without bringing my hurl with me.

JOE

AN OLD MAN called Will Young lived in a cottage next door to us. He used to love going to matches. Or perhaps it was more the day out he enjoyed. There was always a game on a Sunday and he'd ramble up to our house at around 11am and say to my father, 'Sean, we'll go to Birr today'.

'We will, Will.'

'There's a nice little minor match on before the senior game.'

'There is… is it worth looking at?'

'Ah… we might get in and have a look at that.'

That was code for they'd go early. There might not be a minor match but it would give them time for a couple of pints before the senior game. Because they knew they were on the clock after it ended and if they could fit in a couple of pints beforehand and a couple after, then they were happy enough.

I was always very close to my father.

Sunday was the only day of the week he'd go for a drink. Every Sunday night he'd head into Giltraps Pub in Kinnitty and I'd wait up for him to come home. Sport Scene was usually on the television so that kept me occupied until he arrived home at 10.30pm. Then he'd tell me all about the discussion that went on in Giltraps about whatever hurling was on that day. We could stay up until midnight chatting in the kitchen about hurling, while my mother was trying to sleep.

MY FATHER SAW us as a kind of labour force and he utilised it.

We did dry stock and suckler cows, we had sugar beet, corn, potatoes and vegetables. We had our own hens and pigs. We made our own milk, butter, bread, meat, eggs… the whole lot. So we were fairly self-sufficient.

He always said that work was number one. 'Sport is great, but you have to be able to get up and do a day's work… and you play your sport in the evening.'

We worked hard. Every day we came from school, we'd have jobs to do in the evening. Every Saturday we worked on the farm as well. There were no days where we were sitting in watching television, that just didn't happen.

Then every summer we'd go on holidays up to my mother's homeplace, which was Carrolls in Coolderry. It was more of a working holiday. They had a big farm and used to do a lot of corn there. We'd spend a few weeks up there when things got a bit quieter at home.

The hurling bloodline was rich on my mother's side. Her brothers Bill and Tom Carroll won a number of championships on the great Coolderry team of the late 50s and early 60s. Then my grandfather was Jim Carroll… known as big Jim. Himself and his brother Joe, my granduncle, were on the great Offaly team in the 1920s when they were winning junior All-Irelands.

Jim was only 17 when he played against Tipperary in the 1915 All-Ireland junior final. They lost that match, but Jim's brother Joe won junior titles in 1923 and '29. Jim got the Hall of Fame Award in Offaly in 1982. We've a great photograph at home of him with the award alongside Martin Furlong, who'd just won the Sam Maguire with Offaly and was named Footballer of the Year. It's a lovely one to have.

Tom Dooley, who was my father's uncle, won a Leinster Junior Championship in 1922. He scored two goals in the final against Kilkenny in Croke Park. No All-Ireland was played that year because of the Civil War.

He also played in the 1929 All-Ireland junior victory over Cork. There was plenty of hurling on my father's side too. He hurled with Clareen back in the day and his brothers Joe, Kieran, Billy and Tommy all did too. They won junior county titles with Seir Kieran in 1958 and '69. They added an intermediate crown with St Flannan's in 1956, when they were combined with Kinnitty. They were successful in their own right, but mainly due to a lack of numbers, Seir Kieran never won a senior title until we came along.

★★★

BILLY

WE'D GET OUR school holidays at the end of June. We'd head up to Coolderry then until we'd go back to school in September. They'd have beet to be thinned, straw to be stacked and drawn home, and sheep to be brought in.

But we'd always come back to Clareen to train during the week, be it at under-14 or under-16 on Tuesday and Friday evenings… myself and Johnny would cycle down to Clareen and back up to Carrolls after.

Our uncle Bill, who only passed away in February 2022, would tell us stories about Coolderry and championships they won. He was a very prominent hurler and played for Offaly alongside his brother Tom. They were big strong men. We were in awe of the big games they had played in, who they were hurling against and things that happened in those matches. He explained to us how he used to get fit for the championship. Early in the year they'd have their fields ploughed with horses. He'd always put on a heavy pair of boots and he'd run in the clay to strengthen his legs. When he'd get out onto grass then he'd be well able to move. We were listening to this thinking, *Is this lad alright?* But that's what they used to do.

Every Sunday morning and most evenings during the week, we'd go to the Connors' house to play a big game of hurling between all the youngsters living around the place. There could be 20 of us playing in a little corner of the field… all the Mulrooneys, Connors, Dooleys… and the Bergins as well.

★★★

JOE

THERE WERE FIVE lads in the Connors' family… Jimmy, Kieran, Paddy, Tom and Ger. They would all play, along with myself, Seamus and Kieran. In the later years, Johnny and Billy would join in.

Then we had Noel Bergin, Kieran Bergin, Michael and Paddy Mulrooney. We'd play in Connors' house morning, noon and night on a Sunday. We'd come home on a Sunday night black and blue from belts. It wouldn't be all hurling either… we played soccer when we got tired of the hurling.

★★★

BILLY

MYSELF AND JOHNNY were small enough at the time, so we'd usually get stuck in goals. We could have been killed with the shots that were flying at us. If we saved one, someone would come in, pushing us and the ball in. Their uncle, Jimmy Connors used to come out in the evening and play with us. We thought he was really old at that time but sure he was probably the age I am now. Sometimes he'd stand in goals and we'd have a fierce racket with him.

It was a great education. I don't mean this in a bad way, but we never got anything soft in life. If I got a belt of a ball or a kick off someone in Connors' field during those games, I didn't come home crying about it.

That wouldn't be mentioned. If you went to the field to hurl, it was like going to work... you don't bring it home with you. Whatever happened up there *happened*. That served me well in my hurling career and in life.

★★★

JOHNNY

OVER THE YEARS, people would often ask me how a family from such a small parish had three brothers play together in an All-Ireland winning team.

What it probably boiled down to was the thousands of hours of non-stop practice. It wouldn't be unusual for us to stand for two or three hours in the yard pucking balls back and forth at each other. Your first touch and ball control would have to improve.

'Yard hurlers' was an expression used years ago to describe hurlers who developed their skills on a farmyard. It's the same principle as 'street footballers'... soccer players who learned the game on the streets. In those days there were very few drills or ball work at underage training. Nowadays, it's probably gone too far the other way and youngsters aren't doing enough practice at home.

The farmyard was a better practice ground than money could buy. Every outhouse and shed had a gable end. From a young age, I was non-stop ball striking off my left and right. Behind the kitchen door, there was a stack of hurls and a bag of sliotars. If any of us went out to get a bag of turf, we brought one of each with us. We enjoyed nothing more than coming home from school and heading out to the back field for a puck around. Hitting the ball off both sides straight to the hand. We used the silage pit quite a lot for ball striking... and ground hurling was a big thing at the time. To be able to meet a ball and let fly on it without stopping was a useful skill to have.

Myself, Kieran and Billy used to play these games where we'd puck the ball off the gable end of the house and see who could catch it. Kieran was a big guy, 6'2"... Myself and Billy would be trying to compete with him for the high ball. Of course, he would be able to use his elbows to push us out of the way, but it sort of taught us how to compete with bigger guys. I'd get up and try to flick his hurl to move it out of the way to get the ball into my hand.

★★★

JOE

NOTHING WAS EXEMPT from being used for target practice. Not even our mother. Sometimes a few of us would be out pucking in the yard when she'd head from the house to the turf shed to fill up a bag of turf. We'd see her crossing the yard with the bag on her back. We had our target for a competition... a moving target. We'd stop whatever game we were playing and have a pot shot at her to see if we could hit the bag of turf. It's shocking really, not alone would we not help her but we were actually shooting balls at her. We were usually accurate enough to hit the bag without hitting her... usually. She'd laugh at the good of it anyway. She had a great sense of humour.

We had an outhouse door with a hatch in it that we used for shooting. We had tyres hanging and we'd see who could get the most shots through them. The games would be very competitive. Other times, we used the door of the cow shed as goals. Johnny was the youngest of the lads and the smallest... so naturally we'd put him in goals and bang sliotars at him. After a while they were sticking to his hurl. For a small lad he showed promise early on, he was plucky.

★★★

BILLY

WE HAD THESE little chickens that would roost on top of the chicken house. It sounds inhumane now, but they'd sit a few feet apart and we'd shoot the ball in between them. They'd fall asleep up there in the evenings and wouldn't even know we were shooting at them. They sat dead still, so all you had to do was get the ball in between them, but if you were even a little bit off… and there were a few times we were, the poor chickens would think they were after getting hit with a cannon ball!

Then we had an old bullock that came to an untimely end. He was being lined up for the freezer. He got his foot caught in some wire and ended up losing his foot. My father got his foot removed and had his whole ankle plastered up, so he made a full recovery. He came back to full health. He used to graze at the front of our house and at night he'd go back into the hay shed and lie down.

In the same shed we had a tyre hanging for shooting practice. We spent hours firing the ball through it. Then one night after we'd all gone to bed, the bullock put his head through the tyre and got it stuck. With the bad leg at the back he must have lost his balance. In an attempt to get himself free, he spun around and around in the tyre. It choked him during the night.

My father went down in the morning and the bullock was dead… taken out by the tyre we were after hanging to shoot the ball through. The roars from my father could be heard that morning. That was nearly a year's meat gone from the freezer. There wasn't a tyre put up for a long time again.

★★★

JOHNNY

MY FIRST HURLING idol was Eugene Coughlan. He was on the Offaly team that won Leinster in 1980, and the All-Ireland a year later. That was Offaly's first ever time to lift the Liam MacCarthy Cup.

In 1982 the footballers were crowned All-Ireland champions, preventing Kerry from doing the five in-a-row. There was a great buzz around the county, it was an incredible time to be growing up there. Eugene was an outstanding full-back. He marked all the top forwards in his day. We'd see him at Mass in Clareen and know he was after picking up the likes of Tony Doran, Jimmy Barry Murphy and John Connolly. You'd just want to get a look at him. Little did I know then I'd get a chance to play alongside him for so many years with the club.

Eugene, Joe Mooney, Noel Bergin and team secretary Tony Murphy brought the cup into us in Clareen National School. I don't think we realised the extent of what they had achieved.

That Offaly team definitely kick-started a massive interest in me, and I'd say most of my generation. When you see what that did for the county... first time winners in the sport!

Mark Corrigan and Pat Carroll were Offaly forwards that I loved getting a look at when they were playing in Birr. Pat Delaney was a flamboyant centre-back. Those guys were all massive players at the time.

You can't underestimate what something like that does for a county. You start to believe. *We can do this. Sure there's my neighbour Eugene doing the business on the big stage.*

OUR HURLING GAMES eventually drifted from the farmyard into the GAA field. National school was where it all happened. We had a little small pitch beside the school... It was running off the side of a mountain so it had an unmerciful slope. It's still there, but they've since put in a proper pitch beside it. Every day at lunchtime, it was our Croke Park.

There was no togging out. We went down in our jumper, shirt and trousers and played solid for half an hour every day. By the time we got back into the classroom, I'd have a big red face and I'd be pumping sweat.

We had a teacher called Damien White. He came from Clare and he was brilliant... he put an awful lot of work into hurling in the school. You'd have to give him a lot of credit for what he did to promote the game. All five lads in our family won Bord na Scoil titles in Clareen National School, which was a big deal at the time.

When Joe was in fifth class in 1974 he captained Clareen to the title... it was the first time Clareen ever won a school's competition. Our brother Seamus was on it too, along with Mick Coughlan, Paddy Connors, Mick Mulrooney... and a load of other lads that went on to win senior championships with Seir Kieran afterwards.

The strength of the teams depended on how many boys you had in your class. Kieran had a good class, there were seven or eight lads in it. When I was in fourth class and Billy was in sixth class we won a Bord na Scoil final against Lusmagh.

BILLY

THE DAY BEFORE that final, Damien White, the teacher, told us that we should be resting ourselves. We were testing cattle at home and we told him we wouldn't be in tomorrow, that we had a herd test at home and our father wanted us to bring in cattle.

'Jaysus, that's not a great idea!' Mr White said.

But we had no real choice in the matter. Joe, Seamus and Kieran were gone working at that stage so there were only the two of us left to get in these cattle. So we said we'd do as little running as we could. We were after cattle all day long, getting them into the yard. At that time there was no big facility where you'd get them all in together. You'd bring in one field of cows and then you'd go out and bring in the other field. So we finished that day around 3pm… and the match was at 6pm. The finals used to be played in the field around the back of the County Arms Hotel in Birr.

We came into the house and we were shattered. The amount of running we did chasing cattle all day! Our mother put myself and Johnny into a cold bath to try and take the pain out of our legs. We had a little bite to eat and then went on to Birr to play the final.

Turns out it didn't affect us too badly. I suppose when you're young, you don't worry about those things. We beat Lusmagh… and I played well that day… I scored 4-4. It was a record in a final at the time. Until Johnny came on two years later and scored 5-6 to beat me.

JOHNNY

WE BEAT LUSMAGH in that final two years later. It wouldn't be the last time I shared the field with John Troy. We generally were at opposite ends of the field when we came up against one another but, on this occasion, Mr White played me at centre-back to mark him.

He had so much skill at that age, it was hard to comprehend. He could make the ball talk. We had a right old battle. Both teams were well balanced. Every man, woman and child in both parishes was there, leaning in over the fence.

At the time, those finals seemed like the biggest occasions in the world to me. It felt like I was playing in an All-Ireland final. Some things you just never forget.

III

Presentation Brothers Birr

Bro Denis Minihane

Hammering young cats

Birr Community School

Croke Cup

Leinster minor champs

All-Ireland minor winners

Pat Joe

★★★

JOE

THE BUS PULLED in at the end of our lane and I hopped out. Gear-bag in one hand and hurley in the other. I said goodbye to the lads and strode up towards our house with my chest out. I was on cloud nine.

Hours earlier in Athy, Presentation Brothers College Birr under-14s had lifted the school's first ever Leinster colleges title. My parents weren't at the game. I couldn't wait to walk into the kitchen and tell the whole family that we were Leinster champions.

It was a watershed moment for me. Winning with the national school was great but then to win a Leinster colleges 'A' medal was another matter entirely. It was the first one ever for an Offaly school. The feeling of pride walking up the lane that evening is something I'll never forget.

I have a Leinster Colleges medal. This is big. We're on to something here.

When I started first year in the Presentation Brothers, I was on crutches with a broken leg after being hit by a car. I was lucky to be alive.

In July of 1975, I was on an errand for my mother. I cycled up to a watch fixer in Roscomroe, between Kinnitty and Roscrea, to drop off a watch. I was on my way back and about six miles from home near Aghancon, which is hilly country. I wasn't hugely familiar with the road. As I came up over the brow of a big hill, I met a fairly steep downward curve.

There was an S-bend on the road. I got around the first turn but when I came around the second one I was on the wrong side of the road. and there was a car coming the other way. I had no brakes on the bike and went straight into the car. Luckily enough, he wasn't coming at full pelt but I broke my leg all the same.

It was scary. I remember the initial impact but nothing after that. I was knocked out for a period of time. When I came to, the man who hit me asked me who I was? He brought me back down to our house and my father took me into Tullamore Hospital. They put my leg in a plaster... I was on crutches until October.

THE BROTHERS AS it was known, was a hurling-obsessed school. It was the perfect environment for me. I was a handy enough hurler and probably the best in Clareen at my own age group. But when I went into secondary school in Birr, that brought it to another level. All of a sudden, I was playing with the best lads from other parishes. We drew our playing pool from south Offaly clubs like Coolderry, Kinnitty, Clareen, Birr and Drumcullen... as well as some north Tipperary powers like Ballingarry, Lorrha and Rathcabbin.

We had some very talented players in our year. Ken Hogan was there... he went on to win two All-Irelands in goals for Tipperary... and Kinnitty forward Paddy Corrigan, who I lifted the Liam MacCarthy Cup alongside in 1985.

Another Kinnitty clubman Seamus Coughlan was there too. He hurled with Offaly at senior level... he tragically lost his life in a swimming accident in New York in 1989.

We also had the late Aidan 'Boo' Rosney from Birr. He was a brilliant prospect and a superb schools' player. He was cocky on the field, but in a good way. He tragically collapsed and died while training with the Offaly seniors in 1983... he collapsed during a Saturday morning training session in O'Connor Park.

I'll never forget that day. When he fell, there was nobody near him. At first we thought he was messing, but fairly quickly realised he was in bother. Joachim Kelly put him into the recovery position and an ambulance was called, but nothing could be done to save him. It was a disturbing experience and extremely tough on his family. I've no doubt he'd have starred on the successful Birr and Offaly sides in the 80s and 90s.

Pat O'Connor from Coolderry, who scored the crucial second goal in the 1994 All-Ireland final, was another teammate in school. We went unbeaten in the province over the five years I was in school, winning two under-14, a junior and two senior Leinster 'A' Championship medals. While Birr had won Leinster 'B' titles, they never won an 'A' final before that period.

Brother Denis Minihane was the man at the heart of it all. Hailing from football land in West Cork, he had coached Coláiste Chriost Rí with some success. But he grew up during Christy Ring's heyday and hurling enthralled him. A year after his arrival in Birr, he took over the Offaly senior hurling team. He stayed in that post for 12 years and led them to the Leinster final in 1969, where they lost narrowly to Kilkenny.

Bro Denis was a great promoter of the game. Some of the best hurlers Offaly ever produced passed under his tutelage. Everybody was tuned into the importance of hurling in the school. It was a hurling nursery really. Bro Cronin and Bro Thomas were two others who invested a lot of time into the game in the school, as did lay teachers John Joe Poole and Michael Queally, and in later years Padraig Horan and Frank Bergin.

Everyone had to play hurling, no matter what your ability was. Street leagues were set-up at the start of every year to establish the best players that went forward to represent the school. You needed a doctor's cert if you weren't going to play in the school league… you nearly had to be on crutches to be allowed to miss it.

The day after a colleges match, it was fairly normal for part of the class to be spent discussing hurling. Especially with the teachers that would be over the teams. All you'd have to do was ask them about it… someone would throw in a question.

'What did you think of the game yesterday, Sir?'

And it would take off. The whole class could be spent talking about the game. That was a regular ploy to get off class time.

THE TRAINING THAT time was all ground hurling… that was our style of play which is what we continued to do with Offaly after. We were learning it right from first year in secondary school. We trained regularly two evenings a week after school. When training finished, Bro Cronin would arrive with a big burco boiler of soup. He would put it into paper cups for us. It was gorgeous. We'd be starving by that time of the evening, and it kept us going until we got home.

I'd have to thumb a lift to get home. There were two or three guys that were serving their time as block-layers and the rush always was to get out thumbing before they left work.

WE LOST SUCCESSIVE All-Ireland Senior 'A' Colleges finals when I was in fifth and sixth year. The first one was to St Flannan's from Clare and the second one against North Monastery from Cork. We were well beaten in both. We were probably too much in awe of those teams.

North Mon was known as the cradle of Cork hurling. They had produced some household names in the past like Jack Lynch, Denis Coughlan, Con Murphy, Tom Cashman. In 1980 they had a great team with big names... Tony O'Sullivan and Tomás Mulcahy.

In late 1979, Birr Community School was created through the amalgamation of the Brothers' with the local vocational school and convent. Now we had 800 students in the school, but for the 1979-80 season we could only choose from the Presentation College selection of the Community School, which was about 200.

Even compared with the numbers they had in the other schools in the Leinster 'A' Championship... St Kieran's College, Kilkenny CBS and St Peter's, Wexford, we were much smaller. We were boxing well above our weight even to get that far. But it was disappointing we didn't win one of those All-Ireland finals.

We did enjoy great success in Leinster. Beating Kilkenny CBS by nine points to win our first Leinster senior title in 1979 was a major breakthrough. We knew Kilkenny had to be respected but we weren't afraid of them. To take down a Kilkenny school team was something we'd never done before at senior level... We got used to beating them during my time in the Brothers.

There was a bit of a change in the air after that.

The following year we hammered St Kieran's College in the Leinster semi-final. The final against St Peter's was played in Nowlan Park before a National League game and there was a good crowd at it. Pat O'Connor scored two goals that day, and I grabbed one.

I was small in school and a late developer. I usually played corner-forward... the small lad in the corner. I finished secondary school at 16, so I was nearly always the youngest on the team in those games.

The All-Ireland semi-final gave me the chance to play at Semple Stadium for the first time. We beat St Joseph's College, Garbally Park in a replay. It took place before Galway played Waterford in a National Hurling League game in Thurles. We were on the big stage on a good pitch and starting to get a taste of the big time. I scored two goals in the first-half and we went on to win.

It was a venue I was lucky to experience plenty of big days during my career. Little did I think that four years later I'd play in my first senior All-Ireland final there. In the twilight of my career in 1998, I probably had my best day in the Offaly jersey against Clare on that field. Thurles was a happy hunting ground for me.

The build-up to those games was colossal. The whole school would go. Beforehand, there was always cheerleader practice... Everyone would congregate in the school yard and practise the songs they were going to sing at the game.

You had a status in the school if you were on the senior team. We probably got away with a little bit more than the rest did. Those games brought serious pressure. I found them more pressurised than any others I played in before or after, be it with club or county. It was serious stuff for a young lad coming in from a rural parish that never had experienced it before.

★★★

BILLY

I STARTED AT Birr Community School in 1982. It was an eye opener for any young lad coming in from a small class in the country. The school was full of lads and girls from the town that were much wittier and wiser than us.

Only three lads from my class went there... myself, John Kinahan and Pat Gaffney. We were put into three different classes. We did entrance exams and were graded in accordance with how we performed. We were like bullocks going to the factory.

I struggled to get onto the hurling teams in Birr for a while. While my Seir Kieran teams were playing in 'B' and 'C' championships, there were lads in the school that had won under-14 and under-16 'A' championships with Birr.

Even though we were very good at our own level, when I went there I was boxing against a whole lot of lads that were similar or slightly better. It didn't put me off. I stayed at it and got stuck in. Bro Denis was principal by that stage. On the hurling front, he was more prominent when Joe was in the school. We had Padraig Horan, Joe Kane and Frank Bergin over us. Horan was the main man... he was a God to us. He played in the 1981 and '85 All-Ireland finals with Offaly and here he was training us, a senior colleges team, in '86.

It was a fair incentive for us to be playing under him. When Horan talked, you'd listen up. He'd know how to get your attention. Bro Denis took a back seat during my time there, but there was one incident where we got one of his famous motivational speeches.

Our senior team were after beating Garbally in the All-Ireland semi-final and a few of the townie lads went out in Birr that night. Word got out anyway, and Horan was vexed about it. They brought us into a little room and each of the management said a few words… about what was after happening and how it wasn't good enough, that sort of thing.

Then Bro Denis came in. He hadn't spoken to the team prior to that. He spoke for five minutes and the hair was standing on the back of my neck by the end of it. You could have heard a pin drop in the room. He just brought total reality back to us about the importance of what we were going to play in. Birr had lost three All-Ireland finals in the previous seven years. We were facing into another one against North Mon. I wasn't playing the previous year but I was in the crowd in Limerick when they beat us by 15 points in the final.

We retained five or six from that team… lads like Daithi Regan and Gary Cahill, and it was still fresh in Bro Denis' memory. He spoke about that heavy defeat 12 months earlier…

'And if we're going to allow two or three players on the team bring the whole thing down…'

He just hit all the right notes. Coming out of the room that night, everyone just said to themselves, *That's it now, we're going to have to drive on from here.* There was never another word about it. The following week, we went out in Portlaoise and beat North Mon by 15 points… a 30-point turnaround in 12 months. That showed the quality of players that were coming through. A load of us were too young to play in 1985, but by '86 they started to emerge… Declan and Johnny Pilkington, Joe Errity and Damien Geoghegan.

I started that final and scored 1-1, but it wasn't all plain sailing for me that year.

I HAD BEEN going well during our run to the Leinster title. I scored a goal in the final against St Kieran's. It was a big deal to win that game. It was Birr's third time to prevail in Leinster and the first in five years, since Joe was in school. We were gearing up for Galbally in the All-Ireland semi-final. We trained through the February mid-term break. During mid-term, a man down the road in Clareen was roofing a house and Jimmy Connors asked me if I'd go down and give him a hand. The pay was £10 a day, which was a lot of money at the time. I agreed to it without much hesitation.

The school was training during the day on Tuesday and Friday that week. I made the first session, but missed Friday because I was busy roofing. There were no mobile phones back then so I couldn't ring to say I wasn't going training. After playing well against St Kieran's, I probably thought I could afford to miss the odd session.

We trained again on Sunday morning and I knew by Horan he wasn't overly pleased that I hadn't turned up on Friday. So they picked the team the following week and left me off it. I was named among the substitutes. We went down to play Garbally in Ballinasloe on a rotten, wet day. Michael Duignan and Kieran Egan were hurling with them.

Sitting on the bench looking out onto the field, I was very disappointed. It's not a nice feeling when you think you should be playing, but it was my own fault. I couldn't argue with management and that actually made it harder. It stuck in my throat a little bit more. We were struggling with about 20 minutes to go, when they brought me in but we always looked like we were going to win the match. The following Tuesday we were back at training.

While we were pucking around beforehand, I spotted the giant figure of Horan walking towards me. He was a fairly intimidating fella when you were a young lad.

'If you want to play in the final, you don't miss any more training.'

He taught me a great lesson that day. I made the team at full-forward for the final against North Mon and we claimed a famous victory. It was a huge day for the school, our first ever Croke Cup victory. We'd been beaten in three finals before that, two when Joe was playing.

We never really doubted ourselves after that. For the next four years, Offaly won three minor All-Irelands. It was some injection into Offaly hurling.

★★★

JOHNNY

I HAVE ONLY happy memories of my time attending Birr Community School. It was a mixed school, which helped balance school work with the chance to meet and chat to a few girls. I considered myself quick on the uptake but I was never pushed too hard at home. Back then, there was no great emphasis on going to college. My results were reasonably good and I got a good pre-Leaving Cert when I was in sixth year. They were trending in the right direction.

Unfortunately, when April and May kicked in, county minor training was back. Hurling was up and running at full throttle. I took my eye off the ball with regards to my studies.

My results dipped slightly from the mocks to the leaving cert. That was obviously because I was gone to Birr three nights a week training with Offaly minors. Then again, it was never on the radar that I was going to college. In hindsight, I'd love to have had that opportunity. There were too many siblings in our house for us all to be pushing for college. It wasn't the done thing at the time anyway.

Education was important, but hurling was *everything*.

I was blessed to start secondary school in Birr at a time when a really talented crew of lads came along. Early on in my time there, I said to myself, *Jeez, you're in the right place at the right time.*

Sometimes in life, you can be a bit lucky. You're only as good as the teammates you have… and we were in a fortunate position that we had a side that could compete. From underage club hurling I had heard of lads like Brian Whelahan and the late Adrian Cahill, so now here was my chance to see what they were like and if I could compete with them.

Straightaway, I was measuring myself off everybody else. We had 150 in our year, around 75 lads. For the school leagues we had four regional teams of 15. I was captain of my team which was full of country lads… Kevin Kinahan was on it as well. There were a few town teams. Brian Whelahan was captain of his… Adrian Cahill was captain of another one.

So, we played these school league games against each other. This was the first opportunity the Clareen lads got to measure ourselves against 'A' teams. We were playing 'B' championship because we had such a small pick.

You could see immediately the talent the other lads had. The standards and skill levels jumped out. It was a great environment to be in. We didn't have any distractions. I wouldn't call football a distraction… there was no golf and no basketball, just hurling.

From first year, the whole way through, we played in about 10 Leinster finals and lost them all. It's unfortunate we didn't achieve any success. We were always the second best team in Leinster, behind St Kieran's of Kilkenny. They were a powerhouse at the time. They were massive, the pick and quality they had… DJ Carey, Pat O'Neill, Charlie Carter… who'd all go on to do big things with Kilkenny. We played them in Rathdowney in the under-14 Leinster final and Pat O'Neill togged out at centre-back.

He was about 6' 2" at that time and well built. I started at wing-forward but had to go in on him at one stage. I remember just looking up at this guy and wondering how in God's name I was going to mark him. He was still the same size when he played senior hurling with Kilkenny years later and while I had grown, he was still daunting to mark.

THE BIG GAMES in school, I didn't love them in the moment. I was full of all sorts of doubts, question marks and nervousness. There wouldn't be huge crowds at them but all our school friends would get on buses and they'd travel. They all seemed to be having the fun, they were out blowing whistles, waving flags and singing songs.

We were the ones in the melting pot and feeling the heat. I suppose that's sport really, in some ways you feel a bit jealous of the supporters who were able to go in and enjoy the occasion. There's a lot of nerves in a young fella when he gets on a bus to head off to play against a Kilkenny team and all his school friends are travelling to watch.

When the game gets going, it's fine. A lot of it is self-doubt and it's there until you build up a certain level of belief that you're actually good enough to be at this level.

★★★

JOE

OFFALY HURLING HAD no real history when I was growing up. When I was in school, no one would have dreamed of the county even winning a Leinster title.

Every Sunday morning after Mass in Clareen, people would stand around for a while outside talking about farming, the weather... and hurling. One Sunday in the late spring of 1980, I was outside the church chatting with a few lads. Someone said in jest, 'Maybe Offaly will win Leinster this year'. It was greeted with a laugh.

Even though Offaly had been going quite well in the league, no one could see a breakthrough coming. Little did we think that a few weeks later Offaly would beat Kilkenny to lift Leinster... and win an All-Ireland within another 12 months. The morning after that win over Kilkenny, my granduncle Tom Dooley admitted he never thought he'd live to see the day that Offaly would win a Leinster senior hurling title. He was nearly 80 by that stage.

What led to Offaly's rise in the early 80s? A few factors.

Offaly started to compete with the big guns in the National League. The interest in club hurling started to grow as it got stronger. St Rynagh's arrived with a great team... Coolderry and Kinnitty started to compete for county titles. That trio carved up the Offaly SHC between them from 1972 until we won our first championship in '88. Then you had the successful schools teams emerging in Birr.

There were good hurlers in the county and confidence was building. Padraig Horan, Johnny Flaherty and Damien Martin had been there for years. They were joined by Pat Fleury, Joachim Kelly, Paudie Delaney, Eugene Coughlan, Brendan Birmingham and Pat Carroll.

Younger talent also started to emerge... Ger Coughlan, Aidan Fogarty, Tom Conneely, Mark Corrigan, Liam Currams, Danny Owens and Paddy Kirwan. The team was full of character and leaders.

They served a long apprenticeship in Division 1 of the league from 1977. They were mixing it with the best and it was only a matter of time. Diarmuid Healy came in as coach in 1979 and he made all the difference. He instilled self-belief in everybody. By the time he left in 1986, Offaly had become a real force in hurling.

I PLAYED SOME underage hurling with the county, but I was never one of the main men on those teams. I made the Offaly minors in my last year in 1981. Padraig Horan was over us… we beat Antrim in the first round in Croke Park. I played corner-forward and scored two points. Kilkenny knocked us out that summer.

I was called up to the Offaly under-21s the following year. Liam Currams, Pat Cleary and Paddy Corrigan were on the squad too… and we made it to the Leinster final where Kilkenny gave us an unmerciful hiding… 5-20 to 2-6. I managed to score four points, although it counted for little.

Even though I wasn't setting the place on fire at underage level, I always believed I'd improve as I got bigger and older. I survived on my skill and hurling brain, whereas at underage level a lot of guys were excelling because of size and strength. It was only when I got a bit older and stretched out that I started to reach my potential. Between the ages of 17 and 19 I grew a few inches. I filled out too.

The big thing was I didn't drink or smoke. I lived for training and hurling. In truth, playing at adult level suited me because size was no longer an issue and it was a faster game. The higher the standard and the more talented players I was playing with, the better I liked it.

★★★

BILLY

SEVEN OR EIGHT of the Birr Community School team were on the Offaly side that beat Cork in the All-Ireland minor final later in 1986.

I came on at half-time in the final against Cork and the North Mon full-back that marked me picked me up for Cork. When the game was over I was chatting with him as we were heading over to the presentation. I asked him how many of the North Mon team were on the Cork side.

'I'm the only one on the panel.' And we were after playing them in the All-Ireland colleges final. From the school team, we had seven or eight playing and 11 on the Offaly panel altogether. North Mon had one player on the entire panel and we beat Cork in the final. I often thought about it after, we must have had a special little team to do that with what we had.

I WAS IN with the Offaly minors for a short while in 1985 when I was still under-16. I played a few games but wasn't kept on the panel. My first year to really get involved was in 1986. Pat Joe Whelahan, Brian's father, was over us and we were really strong. In addition to Birr Community School's success, Banagher Vocational Schools won an All-Ireland earlier that year as well… Roy Mannion, John Troy, Brendan Kelly and Ronnie Byrne were on it. They beat Kilcormac/Killoughey in the Offaly final, who contributed another handful of players.

When we put them all together, we had a serious Offaly minor panel. Joey Carroll and Brian Gath were also on the squad. They were two friends of mine in school who were from Kinnitty and Drumcullen. We had our own personal taxi to get to training sessions.

We all came from farming backgrounds and had no way of getting to training in Birr. We had one car in my house and my parents had enough to be doing in the evenings so they couldn't drop me in. Pat Joe arranged through the county board for a fella called Paul King to pick us up and bring us down training. He drove a big black Ford Cortina car.

He'd come to the house and pick me up, then he'd go down and pick up Brian and Joey, and then on to get Timmy Dooley in Killavilla. He'd bring us into Birr or wherever we were training, wait for the hour and a half and bring us back home again. You were looking at a 20 mile round trip. It was a great job. I'd come outside the door and there was a lad there waiting for me. It was like being a politician going around in it.

We beat Wexford in the Leinster final that year. I came on as a sub and scored a late goal in a game we won fairly comfortably. It was Offaly's first ever Leinster minor hurling title and the start of a great run of success for the county.

I felt that year I could have been on the team but it was a lesson for me as well. At the time I was disappointed I wasn't starting. We were after winning an All-Ireland with Birr, but so had the St Rynagh's lads with Banagher. There were no bad hurlers on the team. It was a toss-up for who Pat Joe would pick.

We played Galway in the 1986 All-Ireland minor semi-final in Thurles. We scored three goals and won it well… by six points. I didn't get a run-out in that game at all, which I was very disappointed with. If the game had been closer I would have had but it was just the way the match worked out.

The only time I couldn't sleep before a game was the night before the All-

Ireland final. I never slept a wink all night. I went off to bed at 10pm. If I woke up once I must have woken 100 times. And I wasn't even starting the next day. *Just the thought of getting up to Croke Park on All-Ireland final day.* I suppose the expectations were swirling around in my head. *Will I get a game? Will I play well if I come on?*

Maybe if I had been picked to start it might have been easier. I was generally nervous enough before games but once I went out on the field, I'd be fine. I wouldn't be one of these lads sitting calmly and chewing on gum. I'd be doing a lot of stretching and drinking water, going in and out to the toilet.

I was brought in at half-time in the final when the game was in the balance. I managed to score 1-1 and we won by three points. There was no feeling like it when the final whistle went. There's so much pressure built up to try and get you there. It's complete euphoria.

All of a sudden, I was after winning a schools and minor All-Ireland within the space of a few months. The three of us from Clareen were the first ones to bring All-Ireland minor medals back to the parish. We felt like we had arrived but we were never going to get too far ahead of ourselves.

Eugene Coughlan, Michael Coughlan, Joe Mooney and Joe had all won senior All-Irelands by that stage. So even they'd never let you get ahead of yourself.

I CAPTAINED THE school the following year in 1987. We reached the Leinster final but lost to St Kieran's. Johnny was on the team by that stage... Brian Whelahan, Johnny Pilkington and Joe Errity were there too.

We were coming off the back of an All-Ireland minor victory with Offaly and I was enjoying my hurling. I grabbed six points in the semi-final against St Peter's, and 1-7 against St Kieran's the next day. Johnny started at wing-back before he was moved up to the forwards and scored a goal.

They were very strong. DJ Carey came on for them in the second-half. He always had something special. If he got inside you and was within 10 yards of the goal, there wasn't a hope of stopping him. The ball was going to be in the net. Even though Kilkenny had a lot of strong hurlers at the time and we respected them, we didn't fear them. We always felt we were good enough to beat any Kilkenny team, be it with the school or county.

Going forward, it was a great thing that we had no fear of the bigger teams.

We beat Cork in the 1986 All-Ireland minor final, we beat Tipperary in the '87 one and Johnny's crew beat Clare in '89.

★★★

JOHNNY

I CAPTAINED THE senior team when I was in sixth year in 1989. We got to the Leinster final against St Kieran's. DJ Carey scored an early goal that day and even though we had a man sent-off, we battled back to draw it.

Brian Whelahan had been playing on the half-back line but they moved him up to full-forward as we chased the game, and he was fouled for a late penalty. I stuck it into the net and we went to a replay.

The replay sticks out in my mind for the wrong reasons. I scored a couple of frees in the second-half even though I wouldn't have been a renowned free-taker at the time. The management team just picked someone as we were going out the dressing-room door.

'Johnny, you take the frees today!'

It was that casual. I was playing up in the forwards and in the second-half I missed a couple of frees. They were quite close to the goal, around 25 yards out. They came at a crucial enough stage in the game and we ended up losing by five points. Being captain, I was so annoyed with myself for missing them. I wasn't the only one.

My father would normally never be critical of any of us after a game. When I came home I could tell he wasn't happy about something.

'Don't you ever take a 21-yard free again!'

I never forgot it… it didn't deter me either.

I can understand where he was coming from. We were in a position to win a game and your son stands up to take a free and he misses it from fairly close in front of the goal. I suppose he felt uncomfortable. I won't say he blamed me for losing the final, but I didn't help the situation. I played quite well on the day from general play but when you miss a free like that you feel like you've let people down. I had no prep done beforehand… no free taking practice.

In years after that, before any big match, I'd be practising three nights a week for an hour. Practising and *practising*. Without any practise, I had no confidence in what I was doing.

ONE OF THE most nerve-wracking experiences of my life was playing in an All-Ireland minor final at 15-years-old. When you play in an All-Ireland final in Croke Park at that age, you'll never be nervous again. Anytime I went into a game after that feeling edgy, I always reminded myself of that experience. It stayed with me for the rest of my playing career.

The year started out with my first call-up to an Offaly panel. I was brought into the under-16s in the spring of 1987. It was all fairly casual. Seir Kieran were asked to send in their two or three best players, so Kevin Kinahan and I went along. They picked a squad to head down to Nowlan Park to play a blitz.

We had a really strong team... John Troy, Hubert Rigney, Brian Whelahan and Adrian Cahill were all the same age as me. John, Brian and Adrian were already in training with the minors.

The blitz went very well, we played three games and won the Leinster title. They were very competitive matches. Kilkenny had two teams... Wexford and Dublin had their best sides out. So you knew if you were competing with them at that level, you were doing okay. We beat Kilkenny North in the final.

The following Monday night, Pat Joe Whelahan called out to the house looking for me. He invited me into the county minor squad... they were playing Kilkenny two weeks later in Croke Park in a Leinster final. They'd already beaten Wexford in the semi-final.

Funnily enough, the Leinster final had been delayed because the Croke Park pitch was damaged after a U2 concert. It allowed John, Brian and Adrian play in the under-16 blitz. Pat Joe obviously saw enough to call me up after the tournament. Sometimes things just work out in your favour.

So I started the Leinster minor final at wing-back having only come into the Offaly under-16 squad two weeks earlier. It all happened very fast. My only experience of playing in defence was earlier that year with the school's senior team. I lined out at wing-back during our run to the Leinster final.

On that Offaly side, we had three under-16s playing in the backline... Adrian Cahill was on the other wing and Brian Whelahan was behind me in the corner. And then another one, John Troy, was in goals. He played county minor for four years, having been sub goalkeeper for the 1986 All-Ireland win.

I loved playing wing-back but after that season I never got a chance to play there again. I enjoyed it because you're facing the ball. I always felt that playing in defence was a little bit more straightforward than in the forward line. Everything's out in front you.

Okay, you have your man marking job to do, but if you got the ball and you could just let it fly down the field. Whereas a forward has to be getting his head up and try shoot the ball over the bar or create a score. Unfortunately, I mustn't have been very good at it because I never got much of a chance after to play back there again!

Billy was on the team as well. He was a big player for us... he was in his last year at minor and played centre-forward. He was being marked by the best players on every team. He was always a great leader. He gave stability and was very clever with the ball. He was a serious minor at that stage.

To play on that team at 15 years old was a great opportunity. In my own head, I didn't feel that I was good enough to be there. *Is he just putting me in because Brian and Adrian are playing and we're all the same age?*

I had serious doubts. I was a bit younger than the other guys. The first game we played in Croke Park against Kilkenny, of all the days I've ever played at any level, it was the most nervous I've ever been.

I'd been in Croke Park so many times watching Offaly hurl and then, out of the blue, to be picked to start there for the minors, not having been on the panel two weeks before that. To be lining out wing-back, going over under the old Hogan Stand to me was daunting.

The stand went straight up unlike the new one that goes back at a slant. In the old Croke Park, everyone was looking right down on top of you. If you were playing wing-forward or wing-back, the crowd were so much closer to the pitch than they are with the new layout.

I remember going in under the big old concrete stand and the nerves were just tingling. I had so many things flashing around in my mind.

Will I play well? Am I good enough?

Will my uncles and aunties be at the match?

But anyway, the game went well and we won it thankfully.

BILLY

I ENJOYED THE 1987 All-Ireland campaign much more than '86 for a couple of reasons. I was starting on the team and Johnny was involved as well. There were five of us still there from the All-Ireland winning squad a year earlier.

Pad Joe Whelahan got most of us into fairly central positions. He made you feel more important than maybe you were, but he did it purposely because he needed us down the middle. Damien Geoghegan was full-back, Joe Errity was centre-back, Johnny Pilkington was midfield, I was centre-forward... we had Tomás Moylan and Declan Pilkington in the full-forward line. He knew that if we could win our battles there, the likes of Johnny, Adrian Cahill and Brian Whelahan would hold their corners as well. If the bigger lads were struggling it meant that the smaller lads were going to come under pressure.

We retained our Leinster title after beating Kilkenny in the final. I scored a goal and Declan Pilkington fired over nine points. We overcame Antrim in the semi-final to set-up a clash with Tipperary.

I was 18 playing that final. Johnny was the youngest of the four under-16s on our team but he more than held his own. I was on Conal Bonnar... the Tipp centre-back. He was a serious hurler. He was a big man at that time for a young lad... he had a pair of legs on him like tree trunks.

The first ball Bonnar got, he threw it up to clear it. I went in and blocked him down. But his hurl came through and hit the front of my helmet on my forehead. It was some stroke. I had a lump on my forehead like a golf ball. The physio came in to throw a drop of water on me and tell me I was alright. I hurled away and I did okay on him that day. I kept him out of the game and scored four points myself. Declan Pilkington was our main man with 2-8.

That game was close. It wasn't the sort where you could be smiling with 10 minutes to go knowing you had it. It was a very low-scoring affair that went right down to the wire.

★★★

JOHNNY

I FOUND THE All-Ireland final equally as daunting as the Leinster final. After that, I never felt that same level of pressure.

I played in another All-Ireland minor final in 1989. *Did I feel the tension?* Absolutely. But I was in my last year at minor and I was confident. I was playing senior with the club, I had won a Senior Championship medal with Clareen... I wasn't lacking in confidence. You have so many question marks hanging over you when you're 15 and you're playing against 18-year-olds.

I was on John Leahy that day and he was a powerful wing-forward. He had serious speed and I knew I couldn't keep up with him. I did everything in my power to use whatever cleverness, knick-knacks and little skills I had learned in the yard at home to try and get out of trouble... and get in a hook or block. It worked out for me that day.

You need to have a little bit of doubt, a bit of nervousness... a bit of fear. You get to a final and no matter what level it is, be it a county final or All-Ireland, there's always scenarios playing around in your mind.

Will the lad I'm marking show me up?

What if I have a bad game or let my family down?

But I never got it to the same extent as I did at that level. You build up a belief and a bit of confidence to know that you're good enough to be able to perform. But that doesn't mean you always will... You have to go through all those things.

I was waiting for this game to come up... thinking about it in every waking moment from the previous Monday. We travelled up the day of the match and pulled into Clane for a puck around. I had butterflies floating around in my stomach. I told the team doctor I wasn't feeling too well.

'I have a tablet that will sort you out.'

He handed me this small white tablet.

'Give it half an hour to work!'

I got back on the bus and started to feel better already. I asked him later that night what he'd given me. He said it was an Anadin tablet... it wouldn't have made one bit of difference but as long as I thought it would, that's all that mattered. It worked. There's so many things at play and once the game is over and it's won… it's like a complete release of pressure.

I felt nine foot tall coming out of Croke Park that day. That night we stayed in the Lucan Spa Hotel. There was nobody there, only the players. We were out just having a bit of fun. I drank my first ever pint in the hotel that night. A few pints of watery ale. I suppose peer pressure came into play, I probably didn't really want to drink but everyone was drinking and seemed to be having fun. So I had to join in as well.

I got back to the room that night. I was sharing with Brian Gath, a good friend of ours. I think I had three pints of ale and, of course, thought I was a great fella altogether. I couldn't get the key into the door. I just wasn't used to drinking.

I was a seasoned campaigner by the time the 1989 All-Ireland came around!

★★★

BILLY

WE WEREN'T SUPPOSED to be having a drink, but we snuck in a few pints that night. I wouldn't have been drinking in front of my father and mother anyway. It wouldn't be like now, where it would be seen as okay to do it. It probably wasn't a bad thing either… it always kept us fairly on the ball.

We had good times out of that. Johnny was young, really he was only a chap. I was heading for adult hurling at that stage but he was two years behind me. The townie guys went drinking again the next day, but that was unheard of for us.

My mother told me I was going back to school on Tuesday. So I went back anyway but the cup was only brought in there on Wednesday and I was back in school already at that stage. The rest of the lads hadn't even come back in yet, I was the first one.

★★★

JOHNNY

I PLAYED TWO more years with the minors after that. In 1988 we had lost a lot from the All-Ireland winning team… there were only a handful of us still around. We got back to the Leinster final but came up against an unbelievable Kilkenny outfit. They had a load of lads who were on the St Kieran's team that beat us in the Leinster colleges final a few months earlier, including DJ Carey and Charlie Carter. They beat us 2-16 to 0-6 and we made no bones about losing that game.

I was switched all over the place over the course of the hour. At different stages I ended up playing at half-back, midfield, half-forward... and full-forward. Kilkenny went on and beat Cork fairly handily in the All-Ireland final.

I don't think our 1989 squad overall was as good hurling-wise as the '87 team. In saying that, we did have eight players from that team who went on to represent Offaly at senior level for many years. Six in hurling and two in football, which is no bad return.

We won the Irish Press Cup again in 1989, Offaly's third in four years.

The crew that won the All-Ireland as under-16s in 1987 were now the senior players on the team. We had five or six very good hurling minors and the best of the footballers coming through the county as well. Fellas like Sean Grennan, a big strong centre-forward who turned out to be a great footballer for Offaly. Kevin Flynn and Niall Hand were talented dual players. Finbarr Cullen was at full-back, he went on to enjoy a super career and captained Offaly to a Leinster football title in 1997.

We comfortably beat Wexford and Dublin to get back to the Leinster final. It was the fourth straight year the Offaly minors and seniors both made the decider, which was a fair achievement. We drew our final with Kilkenny... 0-14 apiece.

I put that game down as one of my most enjoyable days ever in Croke Park. It's not often I can say I went out in Croke Park and everything seemed to just flow for me, but that day it did. I got four from play... and six from frees. We drew but were the better team on the day.

I came off the field that day and I felt like I was on a cloud. There was a good crowd coming in for the senior final afterwards and most of them were in place by the tail end of the minor game. I got a few good scores during the closing stages and I came off the pitch thinking to myself, *That was a really enjoyable game.* Those days are a dime a dozen.

We won the replay by 12 points in Portlaoise on a blistering hot Saturday evening. Adrian Cahill played unbelievably well that evening in midfield. Kevin

Flynn hit two goals for us. It was a great result because historically Kilkenny always seemed to get things right in replays. They were fancied to come through it.

We beat Clare by seven points in the All-Ireland final. They had Davy Fitzgerald in goals and Jamesie O'Connor came in as a sub. Things rolled for us that day. Niall Hand scored two goals. It was a massive bonus for us because we wouldn't have banked on that before the game started. The scoreline would suggest we won it handy but we didn't. It was a massive battle up until the end. We only pulled away in the last five minutes and got a few extra scores to get us over the line.

I always enjoyed the Monday after when the two senior and minor teams would meet up for the banquet dinner in the Burlington Hotel. You'd get a glimpse of the senior stars at the time…. like Joe Cooney and Nicky English. Get a few autographs.

Clare showed up fully suited with sponsored gold watches. We felt a little bit under-dressed and sheepish with our bottle green V neck jumpers, but no matter, we had the one thing that counted… the All-Ireland medal.

I MET SINÉAD the night we beat Down in the All-Ireland minor semi-final that year. The game was in Croke Park and we came back to the Spa Hotel afterwards for a bit of food.

She was there with her family, who went to all the GAA matches. She looked amazing and really caught my eye. She was a classmate of my teammates Sean Grennan and Kevin Flynn from Ferbane. They gave me an introduction and we got chatting. It was mentioned about going back to Melbas after. That was the nightclub in Birr where everyone went. She gave me a wink and a nod that she was going to be there. I was hoping I'd made an impression.

When she arrived at the nightclub, I was there with my schoolfriend Finbar O'Neill. I pointed her out to Finbar and I bet him £5 that I'd ask her out for a dance.

He took one look at her and said, 'You haven't a hope, Dooley.'

I did… she said yes, and as they say the rest is history. We've been together ever since. Years later I reminded Finbar about our wager. Needless to say, I never got the money!

Sinéad is from Ferbane and her family are big GAA stock. She played football and camogie back then. Her brother won football championships with Ferbane and her uncles before that.

We were together for four years before we got engaged in 1993. We bought a site in Tullamore in late 1994 and built a house. We got married in 1995 and have lived here ever since with our three children Jack, Emma and Hannah.

IV

Under-21s
Centenary year
Kirwan and Pat Carroll
Joachim and Horan
The gazelle
1985 victory

★★★

JOE

I WAS TWO years on the Offaly panel before I made my championship debut.

I was called in shortly after turning 18 following the 1981-82 National League. I'll never forget walking into the dressing-room for the first time… seeing Padraig Horan, Joachim Kelly, Pat Delaney and Pat Carroll sitting there.

It was a dream come true. I couldn't get enough of it. I was a bit over-awed by the craic they were having in the dressing-room… the mood was good. They were a close knit panel, which came as a surprise to me.

There was such rivalry between the clubs that you'd think these lads would hardly be talking to each other. That was my impression before I went in, but everybody mixed really well together. There was no such thing as only mixing with fellas from their own clubs. They crossed boundaries. If anything, the camaraderie was better than any club team.

Paddy Kirwan was the man with all the funny stories and dirty jokes. He had a repertoire of them. Pat Carroll was always up to some devilment.

Joachim and Padraig were the most vocal. They'd be cutting off one another. Everyone got on with the team secretary Tony Murphy. He often drove the team minibus to league games. When he'd pull in to give lads a toilet break on the way home, he'd start moving the bus before they could get back. The lads would be running after the bus while the rest of us were cracking up.

If there was a bit of mischief going on in the group, Tony would invariably be in the middle of it. He was there right up into the 2000s, when I was managing Offaly. Paudge Mulhare and Charlie Daly were selectors and great characters to have around the place.

The in-house games in training were like championship matches. Taking it easy wasn't in their nature... it wouldn't be tolerated, even for a fresh-faced teenager on the panel. It was full-blooded stuff.

Every night we'd finish with a sprint from the halfway line to the end line. That was the big one. Nobody could beat Liam Currams. He was like a gazelle. Later that year he won an All-Ireland with the Offaly footballers to add to his Celtic Cross in hurling from the year before. It was some achievement.

Diarmuid Healy had us constantly on the move in training. There was no standing around discussing tactics. We'd normally return in April and the intensity would ramp up as the summer went on.

I was disappointed not to get onto the field in the Leinster final that summer. We beat Laois after a replay and then Wexford, to set-up a meeting with Kilkenny. I was going very well in training, linking up particularly well with Johnny Flaherty. I felt I was close to making the starting team for the final. In those days, subs were only required if a fella picked up an injury. But management went with experience. In fairness, it was hard to argue with them sticking with the lads who delivered the All-Ireland the year before. Kilkenny beat us with a controversial late goal from Matt Ruth. Offaly's reign as Leinster and All-Ireland champions was over. The dressing-room afterwards was absolutely devastated.

Once Kilkenny got back on top of you, you might never get up again. We'd only won two Leinster titles in our history, so in my head there was a chance we might never even get to another final.

I PLAYED A couple of league games in 1983 before a broken hand I suffered in a club game ruled me out for most of the year. I was aiming to return for July, in time for the Leinster final if we made it that far. But the bone didn't set right and I had to have another operation to fix it. That ruled me out until the middle of September.

Kilkenny beat us in the Leinster final. They had a good side... they won back-to-back league and All-Irelands in 1982 and '83. The Offaly team of 1981 was starting to slip.

It took me until 1984 before I got a good run at it… Johnny Flaherty retired over the winter and left a place in the attack to be filled. I made my first start of the year in the final round of the league against Tipperary. It was a hot atmosphere over in Nenagh… there was a big crowd.

Despite the fact they beat us by five points, I did okay. I spent time marking John McIntyre and Dinny Cahill, and contributed two points. They kept me in the team for the quarter-final against Wexford at Croke Park… I marked John Conran and added a couple of scores. I felt like I was starting to establish myself on the team. Scores didn't come as easily in those days.

THEN CAME THE Centenary Cup, a competition organised to mark the 100-year anniversary of the foundation of the GAA. It was played in between the league and championship… and it helped kick-start my Offaly career. I shot 1-3 in our first round win over Westmeath in Mullingar and then we took out Kilkenny in the quarter-final at Croke Park. They were chasing a third All-Ireland in-a-row that year and it was our first time to beat them in three years.

In the semi-final against Cork, I scored two goals off Johnny Blake. He was Man of the Match in the All-Ireland final the year before. Cork turned the game around and beat us by two points in the end. They went on and accounted for Laois in the final. Personally, it was a promising start to the year.

Just as I was gearing up for my championship debut against Dublin, I was struck down with another injury. This time I damaged my thumb at training and was forced to sit out the opening round of Leinster against Dublin. I was going well in training and got back in time for the Leinster final against Wexford.

Wexford were flying high after dumping out Kilkenny in the other semi-final. The Cats were looking for their third successive title and a third All-Ireland to follow it, until a famous late goal from Tony Doran undid them. Wexford were fancied for the final, even if it had been seven years since they last reigned in the province.

I stayed with my aunt Maura Creaven in Terenure, in Dublin the night before, away from the hype down home. I was nervous. *Finally, my Senior Championship debut for Offaly.*

Wexford had plenty of big men and we tried to move the ball at lightning pace to keep away from them. It worked well… we squeezed over the line, 1-15 to 2-11.

I was marking Eamon Cleary, he was a big, strong corner-back and a very good hurler. He performed brilliantly the previous day against Kilkenny. Despite missing a couple of chances, I finished with two points. I was switched from the corner to midfield during the second-half to help break the Wexford dominance.

We enjoyed the celebrations. A big crowd turned out to welcome us home in Birr that night. We showed up late and our captain Pat Fleury apologised to the crowd. 'We had to stop along the way to watch the game on TV and see how good it was.' In those days the games weren't televised live so the only time we could watch it back was on *The Sunday Game* at night.

The 80s team was full of natural leaders and characters. They were all headstrong. Damien Martin would go through you for a shortcut rather than let a ball go past them in goals.

We had a brilliant hurling full-back in Eugene Coughlan. He was our best player and one of the top hurlers in the country.

Pat Fleury was a great leader... Paudie Delaney was a fantastic reader of the game at centre-back. Ger Coughlan for his size was a brilliant hurler. Aidan Fogarty could hurl corner-back or wing-back... he was a great man to catch a ball. Joachim Kelly had a great presence in the dressing-room and was always super fit.

Danny Owens was there for years as well and gave great service. Brendan Keeshan was another good one... Tom Conneely was a lovely hurler, naturally gifted... he was always fit and could strike off both sides.

In the forward line, Padraig Horan was a savage leader. Pat Carroll was a fiercely determined hurler and a great Offaly man. The Corrigans, Paddy and Mark, had bags of skill and were real sharpshooters. Pat Cleary was a great goal poacher.

Brendan Bermingham was another fiercely underrated hurler. He played centre-forward and was a team player. Paddy Kirwan could do spectacular things like the long range frees he scored against Laois in 1981 and Wexford in '82. Declan Fogarty was also a really clever player.

WE ROLLED ON to face Galway. On the morning of the game, I pucked around with Eugene Coughlan at the crossroads in Clareen while we waited for the bus to pick us up.

I was 20-years-old and heading off to play in an All-Ireland semi-final in

Thurles. It was dream stuff. The game didn't start out great for me. I was put through on goal in the early stages and tried to place the ball instead of smashing it. It rolled wide… a bad miss, but I kept my head.

I finished with 2-3 from play. My first goal was a crisp strike where I doubled on a dropping ball on the edge of the square shortly before half-time. Not long after the restart, Mark Corrigan's shot struck the upright and Padraig Horan belted it back across the goal, setting me up for a simple finish from a tight angle. In truth, I left a few more scores behind me. I could have finished with 3-5. I missed as much as I scored because I was raw, but I was creating the chances. One of my abiding memories of that game is the commentary by Michael O'Hehir, who heaped great praise on me that day.

Fellas stood up all over the field. Padraig Horan was beside me at full-forward and he helped himself to 2-2. Joachim Kelly ran the show at midfield and ensured we had a steady supply of ball. Pat Carroll and Sylvie Linnane had a great battle. We ended up winning by 12 points against a good Galway team that were All-Ireland champions only four years earlier.

It was the day that made my name on the national stage. I was a marked man from that point on.

The week of a big game, I'd think about nothing else beforehand. It was a long time before county teams were working with sports psychologists. We had to figure out the mental preparation ourselves.

Over the years I fine-tuned my approach to big games, so that by the time Friday came around, I was relaxed knowing that I was tuned in and ready for what was to come. I'd try to visualise nearly every conceivable type of scenario that might happen on the day. Even things like a ball hitting the goalpost… that I'd be alert for it. Alert for their puck-outs, watching for everything. Playing against top class defenders, you might only get one chance in a game and you have to take it. I'd psych myself up to be aggressive, to contest every ball and leave everything on the pitch.

If you don't have that mental work done, it won't just happen for you on the day. It's a very important part of preparation, especially for the bigger games. Diarmuid Healy's team talks helped too. He was a brilliant motivational speaker and he knew how to get people going. That team had other great speakers too, fellas like Pat Fleury, Pat Carroll and Padraig Horan. They'd all have their say as well, in the dressing-room and on the training field.

It was all about not letting the team down, letting yourself or your family down. The stuff being said hasn't changed over the years, even if it's a bit more tactical now.

THERE WAS A massive build-up nationally to the All-Ireland final. Because it was the GAA's centenary year, it was staged in Thurles, where the association was established 100 years earlier.

There was a huge media circus around it and, after how well I'd played in the semi-final, I was in the middle of it. There were big crowds at training. I felt a lot of pressure on my shoulders in the run-in. In hindsight, all the attention didn't help me.

Everyone was looking to interview me… the new kid on the block. Newspaper articles were written about me and it was all new. *Was I too young to deal with it all?* I definitely felt afterwards that I should have been protected a bit more by team management. Given it was my first All-Ireland I shouldn't have been talking to anybody, just focusing on the game.

Myself, Billy and Johnny did an interview for the RTÉ Guide before the 1995 final. That probably didn't help either. They're all things you can do without before games. Sometimes it's not that easy to say no.

As a player if you do an interview and on the day of a big game, when you open the paper and there's a big spread about you, of course that will affect you. For some people it won't, but for others it does.

We lost that All-Ireland final to Cork. It was a very tough pill to swallow. In truth, it lingered for a good while after.

On the day, Cork were by far the better team. It was a game laced with mistakes from both teams. We were well in it at half-time, just a point behind. The third quarter killed us. Cork fired 1-6 and we failed to score during that period. I missed a half-goal chance in the first-half and then had a golden opportunity early in the second period. I didn't strike it well and Ger Cunningham made a good save.

I was marking Denis Mulcahy… he was a great hurler; very strong, fast and experienced. Being the youngest player on the field, I was never going to get anything easy off him.

Unlike the Galway match, the supply line into the full-forward line dried up considerably. There wasn't much ball coming into my corner. A switch to centre-forward or wing-forward might have helped bring me into the game. We struggled around the middle of the field and all over really… apart from at full-back, where Eugene Coughlan held the great Jimmy Barry Murphy scoreless. He deservedly picked up his first All Star that winter on the back of that achievement.

After going scoreless, I was replaced by Paddy Kirwan near the end. As I trudged off the field, a wave of disappointment washed over me.

I've let the team, myself… my family down.

The centenary All-Ireland, played at the newly refurbished Semple Stadium… it was built up to be such a great occasion and then things went so badly for us on the day, and for me personally.

But that's the way it goes, you have good days and bad days. You have to just get on with it. But being honest, it probably took a couple of years to get over it. It stuck with me a lot longer than it should have. Even when we lifted the Liam MacCarthy Cup in 1985, I struggled for form on the back of the disappointment on how that game went.

As a team, we didn't feel our window to win an All-Ireland had closed. Damien Martin was 37 and Padraig Horan was 34, but he didn't drink or smoke so he wasn't going anywhere. Joachim Kelly, Eugene Coughlan and all those lads were still under 30. Then there was an infusion of younger fellas like myself, Pat Cleary, Paddy Corrigan and Declan Fogarty coming through that kept us strong.

I'D MOVED AWAY from home a few years by this stage.. After my Leaving Cert, I did a year boarding in Multyfarnham Agricultural College. Football was the big game there… Tom Daly, a brother of the Galway footballer Val, was over the team and he roped me in.

We used to train twice a day, in the early mornings and the afternoons. We enjoyed a great year and won the All-Ireland Agricultural colleges football competition. That was a nice way to start and finish my football career.

Shortly before I was called into the Offaly senior panel in 1982 I got a job in the ESB head office on Fitzwilliam Street in Dublin as a clerical officer. I lived with my aunt Maura before moving into a flat in Rathmines. The Garda club on South Circular Road is where I first met my wife Marie, soon after the 1984

All-Ireland final. It was a great haunt for all the country people in Dublin. She is from Cork city and was working as a student nurse in St Michael's Hospital in Dun Laoghaire. She was living in Foxrock.

She loved going out and dancing. We clicked from day one.

I was out with my flatmate Declan Scally that night. I borrowed his car, a Fiat Bambino, to drop Marie and her friend Sinéad Reedy home. The brakes weren't hectic. It was a wet night and I had to pump the brakes at red lights. I'm not sure what Marie made of it, but it didn't put her off.

While Marie had a level of interest in hurling, Sinéad was from Birr and gave her the full lowdown on me after I left. We arranged to meet again the following week. I brought Declan's car again and parked it outside the National Ballroom in Parnell Square. When we came back out to go home, the car was gone. Stolen. We reported it to the Gardai and it was recovered a few days later.

Marie and I never looked back. By 1986 we were married.

I MISSED THE pre-Christmas 1984-85 league games through injury... pulled ankle ligaments.

Matt Connor's crash happened on Christmas Day in 1984. He was only 25 but was already arguably Offaly's greatest ever footballer. He was a three-time All Star and drove the county to the All-Ireland SFC crown two years earlier. It was a huge blow to everybody in Offaly and a shocking tragedy for him. We played a game in his honour the following May in O'Connor Park.

We were determined to make up for losing the final in 1984, but it was a long road back to September. As Leinster champions we got a bye to the semi-final where we faced Kilkenny. Liam Fennelly was on fire for the Cats that day and buried two goals. I set up Mark Corrigan for a goal in the first-half but we dug ourselves into a hole. Ten minutes into the second-half we were nine points down. It was looking like we were going to have a very short summer.

Then we produced a great comeback.

Paddy Corrigan raised a green flag from a speculative free that ended up in the net. Joachim Kelly drifted into the edge of the square and pulled on a dropping high ball. Another goal. Kilkenny were rattled. As we approached injury-time, Paddy Corrigan sent over a free to haul us level. We had all the momentum and were awarded a late '65' with the game on the line.

Paddy's effort dropped short into a crowded square. It broke to Kieran Brennan and as he collected it, the whole field opened up in front of him. We were caught with too many men forward. I was the nearest one to him. I had to go with him as there was no one else close.

He threw it up on his hurl and tore off down the field. He was capable of running the whole way and scoring a point. He was in the army and was extremely fit. He was playing brilliantly at the time for Kilkenny and had scored four points already that day.

He ran and ran, and I gave chase. My tongue was hanging when he threw the ball up to shoot. I hooked him. The crowd gave a huge roar.

As soon as the ball spilled, Ger Coughlan whipped it back down the field. The referee blew the full-time whistle. I was more known for scoring but I often think that run to chase after Kieran on that day was one of the small steps on the path to All-Ireland victory that September.

We beat Kilkenny by six in the replay, which was only our second win over them in the championship. It was also the second year in-a-row they failed to reach the Leinster final. It was the first time since 1948 that neither Wexford nor Kilkenny reached the Leinster final. Laois had a very good team and they knocked out Wexford in the other semi-final.

They didn't fear us and had given us their fill of it in recent years. In the run into that game, Diarmuid Healy kept repeating his mantra.

'Laois have never played us in a final. We're a different team in a final.'

On the day we got off to a great start. We got a couple of goals early on and we won easily enough, 5-15 to 0-17. Even though we were scoring freely, I only contributed a point that day. After lifting the cup, Pat Fleury brought it down to Matt Connor in the stand. It was a lovely gesture.

WE WERE GETTING onto the bus outside the Athletic Grounds in Armagh after beating Antrim in the All-Ireland semi-final. Pat Carroll sat down beside me at the back.

We were second cousins. My mother is a Carroll… she's a first cousin of his father, Jack Carroll. He dropped his head down and put it between his two hands.

'I have to get myself sorted,' he said. 'I can't continue on the way I'm going.'

Even though we won fairly comfortably, he hadn't played that well and he wasn't happy with himself. He'd been getting headaches at home. He was taking painkillers, but things weren't improving. He went for scans the following week and the news wasn't good.

Within a week he was in hospital in Dublin getting treated for a brain tumour. The Antrim game turned out to be his last appearance for Offaly.

He was too sick to make the panel for the final.

That motivated the team even further. We were trying to win it for Pat as well as for ourselves and the Offaly supporters, having lost the previous year. One of the reasons we won the second game against Kilkenny was because Diarmuid Healy put Pat marking Ger Henderson. The tactic was to stop Henderson hurling and he did a great job.

Pat was a brilliant man for the big day. He could be playing poorly in training but he'd always be able to find good form the day of the game. He was one of the key drivers of that team, he was captain in 1982 and '83 as well. The team's mantra was always... 'I can and I will.'

Pat lived that.

★★★

BILLY

BECAUSE WE WERE related to Pat, I was always inclined to look out for him. He was my favourite club hurler of all time. He was an iron man. I saw him winning matches for Coolderry on his own. He was a serious hurler. His son Brian had a great career with Offaly and he's been one of Coolderry's main players for almost two decades. At 38, he's still as good a club hurler as there is in the county.

Pat was such a whole-hearted player. He got more belts in the 1981 All-Ireland against Galway... but it didn't deter him. He stayed doing what he did. When he was going for goal he only needed an inch to go through... he had that sort of mentality.

Some of the points I saw him scoring in Birr... off on the wing and maybe out near the middle of the field. He'd cover the whole place.

He was taken out as a young man.

The day we won the 1986 Leinster colleges final in Rathdowney, we were in the dressing-room at half-time. Our manager Padraig Horan was called out and when he came back in we knew by him that something was after happening.

We won the match, but he came in after the game told us that his friend Pat Carroll had died during half-time. It was very sad news.

★★★

JOE

'FARMERS ARE DEPRESSED and they need a lift.'

It had been a really wet summer and Diarmuid Healy was using every possible angle to get us going for the final.

Everything about the build-up to the 1985 final was managed better than the year before. We got sucked into the hype 12 months earlier. This time was a much more subdued lead-in to the game. That's the beauty of experience.

YOU HAVE TO be joking.

I can only shake my head in frustration. There's 15 minutes to go and I'm after hand-passing our third goal to put us five points up against Galway.

Or so I thought.

Referee George Ryan comes in and disallows the goal for a square ball. In my view, it was a perfectly legitimate goal. Pat Cleary floated a high crossfield ball inside. Just as he was about to strike it, I glanced behind me to make sure I was outside the square. And I was. I jumped and fetched it over Ollie Kilkenny's head… I landed in the square, but started my jump from outside it. I slipped Ollie's grasp and handpassed it into the net, as you were allowed to do in those days.

I thought I was finally after getting off the mark in an All-Ireland final. Then George Ryan arrived on the scene and instructed the umpires to disallow the goal. Con Houlihan wrote in Monday's paper that I was in the square, but by Thursday he had changed his mind after a video review. *Joe caught the ball outside the little box, his impetus carried him inside the line; then he palmed the ball to the front of the net,* he wrote. Whatever Con said was right.

He was a brilliant journalist.

Maybe if we were a couple of points behind, the referee would have allowed it, I don't know.

It was a strange sort of game. At stages in the first-half it looked like Galway might hammer us. They had stars all over the field... Conor Hayes, Sylvie Linnane, Pete Finnerty and Tony Keady in defence. Brendan Lynksey, Joe Cooney, Noel Lane and PJ Molloy up front. They missed a load of chances with their powerful running game. Somehow, we hung in there.

That Offaly team was mentally strong. Defensively we were solid. We still had five of the six backs from the 1981 All-Ireland final. Joachim Kelly was a good man to protect the defence from the middle of the field.

They were all big men and had great ability to hook, block and tackle without fouling the man.

We were never going to win two or three in-a-row. But we were always in with a chance of winning one. It was an all-round team effort that got us over the line that day. Pat Cleary scored a goal after pouncing on a mishit free from Paddy Corrigan. We were taking any chance we got, in contrast to Galway at the far end. As the game wore on we grew into it.

Pat Cleary got another goal shortly after half-time to put a bit of daylight between the teams. PJ Molloy struck a great goal for Galway to get them back into it, but after my goal was disallowed, Padraig Horan put over a fine point near the end.

We held on.

My form had dipped that season. My confidence was still a bit shattered after the 1984 All-Ireland. I was still contributing and in that 1985 final I set up a few scores and was happy with my overall contribution. But I felt I should have been doing more. When the final whistle went, I just got smothered by the crowd rushing onto the field. Mick Murphy of Clareen got to me first. He went on to be chairman of Seir Kieran and used to always make a beeline for me after those matches.

To win an All-Ireland was a dream come through. I had just turned 21 so I was very young. It nearly passed me by, to be honest.

I met my parents outside the dressing-rooms under the Hogan Stand afterwards. It was a special moment. They'd always wait there for a quick word after every big game. I'd never even taken a drink before the night of the final. I had my first pint of Smithwicks… and I've drank a good few of them since!

It was unbelievable for all my family and relatives. I looked up to my grandfather and granduncles who all played in All-Ireland junior finals. To actually know that you've won a senior All-Ireland… it's hard to describe the emotions. Especially after the pain of losing a year earlier.

Coming back to Birr and Tullamore for the homecomings, it was brilliant to see the excitement on people's faces. Then we went to Clareen with the cup. Now I was joining Eugene Coughlan in bringing Liam MacCarthy back to the parish. There were four of us on the panel… Joe Mooney and Mick Coughlan were there too.

The joy it brought to people… you can't describe it really. When you win it, you're the best in Ireland. Everyone knows that. You're gone into the history books. You're on the pub walls and the pictures in houses. It brings it to a different level. You feel that and the euphoria and just a sense of achievement. It's the pinnacle.

It was tradition for the two teams to meet up for lunch on the Monday in The Burlington Hotel… it doesn't happen anymore. After lunch, the cup was brought over to Pat Carroll in St Vincent's Hospital.

It was emotional for the players, especially for the lads that played with him from the time he started out… Pat Fleury, Pat Kirwan, Tom Conneely and those fellas. Pat and Tom were very close. He passed away six months later.

We headed to Heuston Station then to get the train down. You're arriving home with the cup and everybody's on such a high. The big thing at the time was to get the Monday papers and read about the game.

Maybe we were making sure it actually did happen!

Funnily enough, a lot of the 80s team weren't drinkers. Padraig Horan, Damien Martin, Mark Corrigan and Brendan Bermingham didn't drink. Paddy Kirwan and Ger Coughlan drank very little. Aidan Fogarty might drink a short, but that would be it.

The 90s side were a different kettle of fish.

BILLY

I PLAYED THREE years at under-21 level and never won an All-Ireland medal. At county level, it's the only one I didn't capture. I have regrets at not winning one, but I also felt that down the road it probably wasn't the worst thing for our group.

I felt our hunger to win a senior All-Ireland was multiplied by not winning an under-21. The Offaly team of the 90s were backboned by lads who'd won two minor All-Irelands. John Troy won three. Johnny played four years at under-21... he has three Leinsters, but didn't win an All-Ireland either. Waterford and Galway beat them, and he was on the team against Tipp that beat us in '89. I only played in the one under-21 All-Ireland final. But it was probably the one that we could have won. We hurled fierce well that day but didn't win it.

We lost the Leinster final to Kilkenny in 1988 but beat them at the same stage in '89. We had a good few from the Birr college team and our successful minor sides... we had players coming off three All-Ireland minor winning teams, and yet Tipperary defeated us in the final. And their group hadn't won a minor.

1989 was our biggest chance to win an under-21 All-Ireland. That was our best team. The core of our team was John Troy, Brian Whelahan, Brian Hennessy, Brendan Kelly, Roy Mannion, Johnny Pilkington, Daithi Regan, Michael Duignan, Declan Pilkington, myself and Johnny. They got a run of goals from their full-forward Dan Quirke. It was just one of those days, everything he touched turned to gold. He finished with 3-2 in a two-point victory.

For us, facing the Premier was like a red rag to a bull. When they beat Offaly in the 1988 National League final, the Rathcabbin and Lorrha lads marched down the middle of Birr Community School on the Monday morning. They waved Tipp flags and sang *Slievenamon*. That didn't sit too well with us.

Over 30,000 people crammed into O'Moore Park in Portlaoise for the final. We were held back in the dressing-room for half an hour because the crowd couldn't get in the gate.

We raced into a 2-3 to 0-5 after 15 minutes, but from there they passed us by. In the period before half-time, they outscored us by 3-5 to 0-1... with Quirke doing most of the damage. We lost Damien Geoghegan to a red card yet managed to fight back to within two points on a couple of occasions in the second-half.

JOHNNY

THE DEFEAT WAS tough to take but my only consolation was that we had won a minor the week before. That eased my disappointment somewhat. I had an All-Ireland medal in my pocket. It was harder on the older guys, the likes of Daithi Regan, Mike Duignan, Damien Geoghegan and Billy. I knew I was going to probably get a few more chances.

As it turned out, that was my best one.

We did win Leinster earlier in the summer which gave Offaly an historic senior, under-21 and minor treble.

The final against Kilkenny was another scorching day.

On the way to the match I wasn't feeling too well. Struck down by a tummy bug. I was picked to start wing-forward but management decided to hold me in reserve. Kilkenny went a point or two up in the second half and it was hanging in the balance. I got the call to come on with 20 minutes to go. Our captain Michael had been taking the frees up to that point and was going well on them. He took them for the minors three years earlier.

I had been on them for the minors and under-21s all during that season. Shortly after I arrived onto the field we were awarded a free. Given he had four scored already, I assumed Mike was going to take it.

He often slags me about this. Mike and I were both jogging towards it when management shouted at me to take it. It showed the type of character and team player he was that he never made an issue out of it.

He just went back to his position. When I think back, it was a big ask for a youngster of 17 to be taking on that level of responsibility when there were lads three years older on the team. I managed to send over the couple of placed balls I took.

As it transpired, we won the game by seven points. It's always one that sticks out in my mind.

★★★

BILLY

WE MET A Kilkenny under-21 side with a score to settle in 1990. They put us out in the Leinster semi-final. DJ Carey scored two goals and we were well beaten on the day. I was named captain but ended up missing the campaign after tearing ankle ligaments in training.

It happened in Birr. Brian Hennessy was marking me in a training game. The ball was at the far end of the field and I was keeping him honest by moving over and back across the goals. All of a sudden, I got my foot caught in the grass and went over on it. CRACK... I knew straightaway when I heard that sound I was in bother. I was brought to hospital in Tullamore and put in a big cast for six weeks. That ruled me out for the campaign. Kilkenny went on and won the All-Ireland.

★★★

JOHNNY

WE MADE IT back to the All-Ireland final in 1991. We enjoyed a fairly straightforward run through Leinster, although we needed a replay to overcome Wexford in the semi-final. I missed both those games with an injured finger and returned for the four-point Leinster final win over Kilkenny.

It was a great result considering they were short just two of their All-Ireland winning side from the year before. Kevin Kinahan was the big addition to our team that year... he came in and added stability in the full-back line. Before long, he'd be the rock at the heart of the senior team's defence. John Troy had moved out into attack and minor goalie Damien Franks replaced him in the nets.

We cruised through the All-Ireland semi-final against Antrim. As a result, we went into the final against Galway a little bit underprepared. I don't think our minds were fully on the game.

We thought we were better than we were... I think even management did. Training was fairly slack and easy going. Everything was being taken for granted. We got walloped 2-17 to 1-9 and deserved it, to be fair.

IF 1989 WAS our best chance, then '92 was the most disappointing. We came again with a really strong team, full of All-Ireland winning minors from three years earlier. Our defence was strengthened with the introduction of Kevin Martin.

Myself and Brian Whelahan were established at senior level with Offaly by this stage. We won our third Leinster under-21 medal, seeing off Kilkenny by two points in the decider.

Next came Galway in the last four of the All-Ireland series. Having lost to them in the final the previous year, we were well riled up for it. I had a good day in front of the posts and we overpowered them all over the field. We ran out 3-17 to 1-5 winners. At one stage in the second-half, Galway were awarded a penalty.

Their goalkeeper Kevin Devine came up-field to take it and our wing-forward John Troy went back into goals. He made a good save and immediately picked me out with a brilliant pass. I fed Mark Gallagher who finished into an empty net. The Galway crowd started clearing out of the Gaelic Grounds after that.

The final pitted us against a Waterford outfit we wouldn't have been overly familiar with, though they did have future All Stars in Tony Browne, Fergal Hartley and Paul Flynn.

We drew the first game 0-16 to 4-4. It was a most unusual hour of hurling. By half-time, only midfielder Johnny Brenner had scored for the Deise. Their forwards didn't score a point between them in the whole game. We should have won it but couldn't keep the goals out. Sean Daly scored three goals from full-forward for them, and Paul Flynn grabbed another one. Brian Whelahan broke forward for a late equalising score to send us to a replay.

A huge crowd of 21,000 crammed into Nowlan Park for the replay. It was an electrifying atmosphere and a great occasion to be involved in. We didn't realise it at the time but the crowds that were travelling for underage games were almost unheard of. You'd know going down to the match that nearly every man, woman and child in Offaly was attending. Even still, Waterford's support probably doubled ours.

It was a complete turnaround. This time we couldn't raise white flags and relied on goals. We led by three at half-time but didn't score for the entire second-half. We missed chances and had 1-1 disallowed. Went down by 0-12 to 2-3. Another chance missed.

V

Here's... Billy and Johnny

Paudge Mulhare

86-90...and dropped

Four Dooleys appear

Faughs call

Leathered in Boston

★★★

JOE

SOME GAMES LEAVE you scratching your head, wondering how you managed to lose.

I never saw our All-Ireland semi-final defeat to Antrim in 1989 as one of those, even if many described it as the shock of the 80s. That was unfair on Antrim.

They had a very good team and they had beaten us twice in the league that year... including in a relegation play-off to send us down to Division 2. Our preparation was hampered somewhat with the news that our wing-back Ger Coughlan lost his brother Seamus in a drowning accident in New York the week of the game. Seamus was part of our squad in 1987... he was only 28 when he died.

It was a huge shock to us all. Ger played in that semi-final, and we all had huge respect for his decision to tog out. We wore black armbands as a tribute to Seamus.

When the final whistle sounded, sending them into their first All-Ireland final since 1943, you could tell Antrim players themselves were somewhat stunned at the result. They probably didn't expect it but they had a very good team... the Donnellys, Naughtons, Ciaran Barr, Dominic McKinley, Olcan McFetridge... they were all fine hurlers. Crucially, they didn't fear us. Maybe if it was a Kilkenny or Cork jersey they might not have had the belief, but they always upped their game when they played us.

We probably did underestimate them. We had chances in the first-half to put them away. We left them hanging in and, before we knew it, they got on top and beat us deservedly. Aidan McCarry and Olcan McFetridge scored 4-7 between them. You can't ship 4-15 and expect to make an All-Ireland final.

Recognising the scale of what they had achieved, we formed a guard of honour and applauded them into their dressing-room.

It was seen as a generous gesture by the Offaly team. The credit must go to Mick Spain, he was a selector with the team from Drumcullen… it was his idea. I was standing in the corner of the pitch near the entrance to the Hogan Stand dressing-rooms when the final whistle sounded. I was nearly gone down the tunnel but Mick had the vision to see that Antrim were after creating history. He was standing in that corner, still carrying a few hurls.

'Lads, we should form a guard of honour. It's the sporting thing to do.'

That's how it happened. They were a bit like ourselves… a small county trying to make the breakthrough. Maybe not every county would have given them a guard of honour, but we did.

THE OFFALY TEAM of the 80s started to break up after the 1986 season.

There were some signs of decay from the All-Ireland winning team of a year earlier. Paddy Corrigan's nine-point haul guided us past Laois and into the Leinster final, but the concession of four goals to our neighbours was concerning. We shipped another four goals against Kilkenny, three of them in the first-half… and lost by 11. We never looked like winning.

A *Simple Minds* concert took place in Croke Park a week before and as a result the pitch wasn't in great condition. Afterwards, Diarmuid Healy stepped down as manager. His seven years in charge brought unprecedented success to the county… four Leinster titles and two All-Irelands.

We lost a few veterans that winter… Pat Fleury, Damien Martin and Padraig Horan retired. It was the end of an era. We entered a period of transition. The youngsters emerging from the successful underage sides of the late 80s would need another couple of years before they properly broke through.

Georgie Leahy, another Kilkenny native, took over for the next two seasons. I enjoyed working with him. He was as honest as the day is long and would call it straight. At the start of the year, the county board chairman asked him what he'd like us to have to eat after training.

'Meat sandwiches!'

He was a great big man and he didn't want any lettuce, chicken or egg... or anything like that... just beef sandwiches.

But he was great. Everybody liked Georgie. We did reasonably well in 1987, making it back to our eighth Leinster final in-a-row, but Kilkenny beat us again. We led by six at the interval, but wilted after that. A hail of points from Ger Fennelly gunned us down.

1988 WAS A big year for me. My form had been so-so in 1986 and '87... then I started to feel things turn. I finished it with an All Star nomination.

Several of the young lads from the 1986 minor All-Ireland winning side broke onto the panel. They gave us a good bounce just when we needed it. Michael Duignan came straight into the starting fifteen. Declan Pilkington was around the panel too. John Miller wasn't on that minor side but he arrived in and nailed down a starting spot at corner-back.

Georgie Leahy made some tactical tweaks. He moved Eugene Coughlan up to full-forward and brought Paudie Delaney to No 11. Both had played full and centre-back all their lives. Georgie's idea was to introduce a bit of power up front. It was left-field thinking that paid off.

While we were never a team that took the National League too seriously, we enjoyed a great run in it that season and reached the final. I missed the early part of the league due to injury and accountancy exams. I came off the bench in the quarter-final win over Galway. A knee injury to Danny Owens paved the way for me to start the semi-final against Wexford. I made the most of my chance.

We were trailing by two in the dying minutes when I scored a goal to put us through. Eugene Coughlan created it with a lovely back-handed pass. Tipperary beat us well in the final, denying us the county's first ever league title. They were coming with a good team... they were strong and fast. All in all, it was a very positive league campaign for us. We brought that momentum into the championship. A three-point win over Dublin set-up a final showdown with Wexford.

Wexford knocked Kilkenny out in the other semi-final. In the final, similar to 1984, we tried to move the ball quickly. We always felt that Wexford would find it hard to manage fast ground hurling, because they were usually very strong in the air.

My first goal that day was as sweet a ground strike as I ever hit... it could have gone anywhere. The game wasn't on long when goalkeeper Paul Nolan mishit his puck-out into the path of Eugene Coughlan, who whipped it back across the 21-yard line. I pulled first time and it flew into the corner of the net.

I raised my second green flag after Michael Duignan's point attempt dropped short and broke off Nolan's stick. I pounced and flashed it home. We ran out 3-12 to 1-14 winners and were back on top in Leinster again.

While we were good enough to win a Leinster, an All-Ireland title was a step too far. We were very much a team in transition. Our journey ended in the All-Ireland semi-final, where Galway beat us well. At the end of that season, Georgie Leahy stepped down and Pat Joe Whelahan took charge.

ALTHOUGH I WAS fairly lucky with injuries throughout my career, I did have some troubles with my back in the late 80s. I put out a disc around 1987 and it caused me some bother for three or four years after that. I was getting sciatica pain in my lower back, particularly after training. I still played away, we weren't told to sit out for a few weeks like you would be nowadays. It was tough for those few years because I wasn't fully fit. I just got on with it, but it definitely affected my performances. Eventually I went to Paddy Kelly, a brilliant spinologist from Wicklow who had a clinic in Portlaoise. He sorted me out.

In the 1989 Leinster semi-final I suffered a fractured jaw. I was having a good game up to that point and had 1-3 to my name. I went past my marker Cyril Duggan when he swung his hurl around and accidentally connected with my cheekbone. I finished the match, but missed the next few weeks of training and didn't get picked for the Leinster final against Kilkenny. I was disappointed not to start but ready to come in.

Daithi Regan got injured early in the game and I replaced him. I scored three points against the team managed by our old boss Diarmuid Healy. We beat them by 3-15 to 4-7 in a cracking game. That was Offaly's 10th Leinster final in-a-row... some going, when you think we haven't been to one since 2004.

It would be four years before I'd line out in a provincial decider again.

IN MAY 1990, the new Offaly manager Paudge Mulhare phoned the house with bad news.

'We're leaving you off the panel for the championship,' he informed me.

'That's fine Paudge. If that's what you want to do, then that's what you want to do.'

That was the end of it.

Dropped from the Offaly panel… it was like a death in the family. I had a fall-out with team management that year over my availability. It was tough watching the lads lift the Leinster title that summer and not being involved. When you're so conditioned to being part of it, you really miss it when, all of a sudden, the show rolls on without you.

I was never one to clash with managers. It wasn't my style. The man in the bainisteoir bib never really bothered me. I always concentrated on my own game. My priorities were being fit, having my head right and making sure I was on the team. Even when the drama with Babs Keating happened in 1998, I didn't give any opinion, nor was I asked for one, because the lads knew better.

The issue was my back troubles had flared up again. I was getting treatment from Paddy Kelly in Portlaoise. I played a couple of league games and then missed a few weeks training through injury. My body wasn't right and I was doing myself no justice by forcing myself to keep playing through it.

In those days the Walsh Cup took place in between the league and championship. We were due to play Kilkenny in the semi-final in May. I hadn't been training consistently with my back and I wasn't seeing eye-to-eye with Paudge because of that. When I didn't turn up to the game, all of a sudden it became a big deal. Things weren't going great in general. *Was he waiting for an opportunity to make an example of me?* I don't know. I wouldn't have been fit to play and, anyway, it turned out Kilkenny played a B team that day.

Incredibly, the year started out with four of the family on the panel.

Kieran was there since the mid-80s and Billy was called up on the back of our 1988 county title victory. Johnny was added to the squad in early 1990.

The four of us featured in the same game for Offaly on one occasion… a February league clash against Clare in Ennis. Johnny, Billy and I started, with Kieran coming on as a substitute. By the time the summer came around, none of us were involved. I think Kieran and Billy had already left the panel by the time I was dropped. Johnny spent the summer hurling in Boston.

As Offaly progressed, they tried to persuade Johnny and Billy to rejoin the squad, but not me. At that stage the year was over… and they didn't return.

★★★

BILLY

IT TOOK ME a while to really believe I was good enough to be in with the seniors. I didn't grow much from when I was minor, so I went from being one of the bigger lads to one of the smallest.

There were still a lot of good hurlers involved when I joined, lads with All-Ireland medals in their back pockets. The older players welcomed the influx of youngsters that joined the squad around them. But they didn't want to lose their place on the team either.

It was good for us because even though we won trophies at minor and under-21 level, they had done the business at the elite level of the game. They kept our feet firmly on the ground during that period. We learned what it took to play senior hurling for Offaly and how to conduct ourselves.

During the 1991 National League, when Mark Corrigan came off near the end of games, I was usually the one that replaced him. That was sort of the regime that year. He was coming towards the end of his career, but was still hanging in there.

He was a great player. I was a huge admirer of his. His skill level was incredible and he'd pop up anywhere for a score... a real sharpshooter.

I PLAYED A handful of league games in 1990... and left the panel before the summer. I moved to Dublin in March and I was living the good life that year, which didn't help my hurling.

After school, I worked in a factory in Birr that made materials for buses and trains. I did four years there, and then in 1990 it went bust. It closed up almost overnight and I was left without a job. I was tipping along for a while not doing a whole lot, apart from helping out on the farm at home.

Work was scarce. There was a fair recession going on at that time.

I wasn't overly educated. I did my Leaving Cert and got on alright in it, but I was never going to college. My father always said to us that if you're a good worker you'll always figure out something. There will never be a bother on you. And that's the way it was.

I was put in contact with Éamonn Rea, an All-Ireland winner with Limerick in 1973. He passed away in late 2021. He was chairman of the Faughs club in Dublin and he ran a well-known pub near Heuston Station that was popular with hurling supporters heading to Croke Park. I rang him anyway and went to Dublin to meet him. The agreement was that if it worked out I'd join Faughs at the end of the year. In the meantime he was to get me a job up there.

So I started off in Dairygold on the Long Mile Road. It was a grand spot to work.

FIONA IS FROM Kinnitty parish. It's gas... she has four brothers and a sister, but she was the only one who had any great interest in hurling. Her father John Maher was the very same... he came from a big family and was the only one who was hurling mad. So, Fiona used to go with him to all the matches. 'I first met her in the County Arms the night after the 1987 All-Ireland final. She was after attending the homecoming with John that evening. We were very compatible and had similar interests... we just connected straightaway.'

John hardly missed an All-Ireland for as long as he was alive. For 50 years, whether it be football or hurling, he managed to get a ticket. He was a great GAA man and we always got on well. He'd go to all my games... Whether I was hurling in Birr or Dublin, he'd be there.

He had a couple of brothers living in Clareen so he always had an interest in Seir Kieran as well.

Fiona did a secretarial course in Limerick after school. Then she got a job in Trinity College, working as a secretary. So she lived in Dublin for four years. After I got the job with Dairygold, I moved in with her and a friend of hers in Rathmines. After six months I switched jobs to Musgraves Cash and Carry. Éamonn Rea gave me long enough to get used to the place. I went out and hurled a couple of challenge games with Faughs. I was tempted to join them.

That October the gun came to my head... *was I going to sign with Faughs or what?* Seir Kieran was always at the back of my mind. I was travelling home on weekends and still hurling with them that year. *Was I prepared to leave my club behind? Would I get any work if I moved back home?*

Fortunately, Seamus had just moved home from England. He was starting his own gig in construction and he told me he'd have full-time work for me from

January if I came back home. So that's what I did. I worked with him for the next seven years.

★★★

JOHNNY

JOE'S FALLING OUT with Paudge Mulhare didn't affect me too much.

Not long after linking up with the seniors, I scored five points on my debut against Laois in February 1990. I started midfield alongside Johnny Pilkington. Then the disagreement happened with Joe, and I suppose we'd be stubborn and clannish enough. There was a decision made that we wouldn't make ourselves available either.

I don't think I was too upset with that decision because I was still only on my first year out of minor. And more importantly, I was planning on going to Boston for the summer. That was occupying my mind… there was plenty of time to hurl with Offaly.

THE KILMACUD SEVENS helped pave the way for my summer in Boston.

I went up to Dublin with a group of lads from home one weekend. An Offaly contingent in Dublin had a team entered in the Kilmacud tournament. Some of their mates heard I was there and asked if I'd tog out for it the following morning.

'I've no gear, no boots, no hurl… nothing.'

'Don't worry Johnny, we'll sort you out!' So I went anyway and played. I got on fairly well…despite the hangover! After the blitz was over, a fella by the name of Jerry McGrath approached me. He was from Tipp and was home from Boston to see them play in the All-Ireland.

'Would you be interested in travelling out to Boston next summer? We'd love to have you out.'

'Sure give me a shout next spring… and we'll see!'

I gave him our home number and thought no more of it for six months. Sure enough, the phone call arrived the following spring and flights were arranged. Best thing I ever did.

Ger Connors, a club mate of mine was supposed to travel as well but he pulled out at the last minute. So that left me on my own. I was only 18, which was young to be heading off. America seemed much further away back then.

IT STARTED OFF with a bang.

The flight to Boston was my first time on a plane. It was all fairly rushed. I had to go up to Dublin that morning to pick up my passport and visa which were ready for collection. Then I headed straight to the airport.

We flew to New York initially and there were thunderstorms so the connecting flight was delayed for two hours. Eventually, we got going in the thunder and lightning. For a young lad who hadn't flown before, it was a big ordeal.

The rules in Boston GAA dictated that I had to be registered to the club by midnight on June 1... the day I was due to arrive. Because of the delay to my flight, I was now under serious pressure to make the deadline. If I didn't get there in time, I was ineligible to play in the championship... my big summer would be ruined and I might have had to return home.

So my flight lands on the runway in Boston and I'm chauffeur-driven straight to what I presumed was going to be some sort of registration office. I hop out of the car and we enter a Nixes Bar, a little old Irish bar with a galvanised roof. It's like a scene out of a mafia movie.

I'm hunted into this little small room around the back of the pub to sign a piece of paper. At 11.45pm I sign up for the Tipperary club. Once the paperwork was signed, we moved back out into the bar for a few welcoming drinks. They were salt of the earth and couldn't have been more welcoming.

They put me up in a house with two cousins... John was from Kerry and Mick was American. Both were about five years older than me. To say they were fond of the good times would be an understatement. It was full throttle every night. If they weren't hitting the town, they were downing cans by the dozen at home. I used to even participate myself occasionally. I was sleeping on the couch in the living room. It was one hell of a summer. In the seven weeks, no cutlery or cup was ever used. We were living on takeaways.

I got a job working as a carpenter with a retired Garda.

Things were fairly relaxed. The fella I was working with was a bit of a character. I'm not sure what his background in carpentry was but he seemed to depend a lot on reading manuals to get by. He used to go drinking every Friday and Saturday evening. He missed most Mondays. I'd be waiting outside the house for him to pick me up but he'd fail to show. I'd join him sometimes, and the odd evening I'd have to duck off after a few hours and head to training.

So that was interesting!

He took one job building a sun decking on the penthouse of a $5 million 10-storey apartment block. We cut a hole in the ceiling to facilitate access for the new stairs to the decking. The temperature was in the mid-90s and I had to drag every bit of material up this tiny fire escape. I also had to bring all the waste materials down.

He was sitting above reading a DIY book on how to build stairs. I was more than a bit amused as to how he kept winning these contracts, but everything seemed to work out in the long term. My carpentry knowledge I had learned in Ireland came in handy. Another job saw us tasked with removing bees and repairing soffit and fascia boards… he gave me this spray and had me walking across the roof to spray into the hive.

'After you spray, run as fast as you can… because they'll attack!' he warned me. 'But they'll only travel so far… before turning back!'

I took his advice. The only problem was, when I took off across the roof, there was no sign of the bees turning back. I had to jump clean off the roof onto the lawn. Luckily, it wasn't too high. Health and safety was low on the priority list!

Even though I was enjoying myself, I was working it off every evening when we went training.

I NEVER MINDED getting rough treatment on the field.

I always gave as good as I got. Every defender that came over would try to lay down a marker. They'd arrive over and give me a shoulder or start yapping in my ear. I never minded that. It said more about them than it did about me. Because that would only make me more determined. I think playing hurling, you have to be a bit stubborn. When I was on a lad and he started annoying me I'd think, *I'm going to show you.*

It's man-on-man. You have to stand up and fight your corner. Even if he got the better of me, my mindset would be, *Okay he might have got me this time but I'll get him next time.*

That's part and parcel of the game. It's a manly sport. Nowadays you can't touch anyone anymore. That time you let fly, there were a lot more strokes being pulled and hurls being broken. You hardly ever see a hurl being broken now.

That's not saying it was right either. The only time I can remember off the ball stuff going too far was in the county final in Boston that summer. The game out there was of a high standard but it could get lawless at times. The refereeing was terrible. Of course, I was young, inexperienced and possibly thinking that after winning a minor the year before I was going to get away with things… I was leathered. There were lads hopping off me constantly and I had no protection from the ref.

What I liked most was how after games, beers would be handed out in the dressing-rooms. We'd all sit there and chill for an hour… having a laugh and a bit of craic. The early games were low-key and, by and large, the referee had control of them.

Cork came second behind us in our group and got through to play us in the final. Of course, we were fairly confident heading into it after walloping them earlier. *They can't improve that much.*

But unbeknownst to us, they were after flying out three or four county players on the morning of the final. I was marking this red haired guy. He was a citóg. For the whole game I was getting the handle of his hurl into the ribs and back. It never stopped… I was absolutely dogged. My ribs were black and blue for a week afterwards.

It was the worst mauling I ever got in a game of hurling. I was hit everywhere I turned and to make things worse, we lost the game by a point. It was devastating.

To go from beating them by 20 points to losing to them six weeks later… needless to say the whole team was down in the dumps. It ended the summer on a downer. We had our few drinks that night and I flew back the following Tuesday. If we had won that we would have gone to the North American finals two weeks later.

I'd have stayed on for that but once we lost, I flew home. Then on Wednesday, word came through that we had been awarded the game. The county players they flew out were illegal. They broke the rules. Boston County Board officials had a meeting about it and kicked Cork out of the championship. So we were declared Boston champions. The club asked me if I'd fly out to Chicago to play in the North Americans, but I didn't. Once I was home, I was *home* and that was it.

VI

Jack Lynch

Seir Kieran... the early years

In at... 16

Kieran and Seamus

Marie's courage

The Boss at 24

Victory in '88

The loss of '89

★★★

JOE

BEFORE WE EVER won a championship with Seir Kieran, I had discussions with the famous Glen Rovers club in Cork about joining them. The former Taoiseach Jack Lynch even did his best to make the move happen!

After three years with the ESB in Dublin, I got a promotion to Rhode power station as a level two clerical officer. I was there for a couple of years when a level three position became available in the Inniscarra power station outside Cork city. If a higher position was advertised in the company you were expected to show ambition and apply for it, which I did.

My application was merely a box-ticking exercise. A move to Cork wouldn't have suited. Marie and I were newly married and had just moved into a house in Ballinagar, near Tullamore. Shane was only 12-months-old, and Marie was expecting Aideen.

Somehow, word got out in Cork that I had applied for the job. I got a phone call from Denis Coughlan, the famous Cork hurler and footballer. He was managing Glen Rovers and asked if I got the job in Cork would I consider joining them?

'Sure, I'll think about it.'

I agreed to meet them. I met Denis, and Cork hurlers Pat Horgan and Johnny Buckley. We spoke about what hurling with Glen Rovers would be like. They were knocking on the door at the time in the Cork championship. They also had Tomás Mulcahy, John Fitzgibbon and young Christy Ring playing for them.

I left the meeting without making any firm commitment either way.

They spoke to Jack Lynch, the former Taoiseach who was also a great Glen Rovers man. He won six All-Irelands in-a-row between hurling and football with the Rebels during a legendary playing career and retained a keen interest in the game. Lynch wrote to Paddy Moriarty, the ESB's chief executive and brother of RTÉ Micheál Ó Muircheartaigh, letting him know that I'd applied for the job and asking if he could put in a word for me.

Almost straightaway, I was summoned to Dublin to meet the former Dublin footballer and manager Kevin Heffernan. He was the ESB's HR manager. We met a number of times after at ESB events. He was a great man.

I explained my story… that I had just applied for this job because it was expected of me. The ESB in its wisdom decided not to offer it to me, or perhaps because I wasn't the best candidate. They did the right thing by me. And somebody had to tell Jack Lynch that they weren't going to grant him his request. I don't know who did, but it wasn't me anyway! I was chuffed that he had written a letter on my behalf.

I'd been a huge admirer of his, because of what he achieved both on the sporting field and in politics. He's buried in St Finbarr's graveyard in Cork, just 25 metres away from where Marie's parents John and Mary Moriarty are buried. Any time we visit their grave, I'd always go over and say hello to Jack.

Glen Rovers won the county championship without me in 1989, the year after I was possibly going to transfer to them. It's a good thing I stayed, because Seir Kieran won the first county title in our history in 1988. I wouldn't have missed that for the world.

WHEN I WAS young, the Kinnitty club tried to persuade me to play with them. Our home place is located in the Kinnitty parish, but we were always determined to hurl with Seir Kieran. Our father lined out with them, and we went to school in Clareen.

Father Madden was the Kinnitty parish priest and he looked after their underage teams. He drove a Volkswagen Beetle… it had a distinctive sound. On the occasions he called up to the house to convince me to join Kinnitty, I bolted into the field to hide when I heard his car coming. Eventually he gave up his chase.

I started training with the Clareen seniors when I was 14. That was the way back then. We had an under-14 team, but you might only have a game or two all season. Our only outlet to get regular hurling training was to go in with the senior team. I made my championship debut against Ballyskenagh in 1980, when I was 16… and I got turned upside down by Paddy Kirwan with a shoulder. No prisoners were taken in club hurling, no matter what age you were.

As a club, we had never won an Offaly Senior Hurling Championship. We had only reached two finals, in 1939 and '52 and lost both. For 30 years after that, we didn't come close to another one. The club had a decent record in intermediate and junior ranks, but struggled to have 15 strong players because of the size of the parish.

Our close neighbours Kinnitty and Coolderry, were the dominant senior hurling sides in the 70s and 80s, along with St Rynagh's. Coolderry knocked us out in 1982 and again in '83 when Pat Carroll scored the winner at the end of extra-time in a replay.

I missed it with a broken hand.

Then we started to turn a corner. Some of the youngsters from our games down in Connors' field started to emerge at senior level. We were an improving side. The Coughlans, Dooleys, Connors and Mulrooneys backboned the team. I had two brothers on it. Kieran started at midfield and Seamus was alongside me on the half-forward line.

Including myself, there were five of us on the Offaly panel… Eugene Coughlan, Michael Coughlan, Noel Bergin and Joe Mooney were there too. Kieran Mooney, a great club and county player, had just retired.

We started to get competitive. We made the county semi-final in 1984, when St Rynagh's narrowly beat us. The feeling grew in the camp that we weren't far away. We reached the club's first county final in 35 years in '85 after beating Coolderry. I was our free-taker and had a good day in front of the posts. I scored nine points, four from frees.

It was a huge win for the club. I don't think we had ever beaten them before in the championship.

An experienced Kinnitty outfit, seeking their third title in-a-row hammered us in the final. With the Corrigans, Johnny Flaherty, Paudie Delaney and Ger Coughlan all hurling well, it looked like their dominance would continue for another few years.

After Lusmagh knocked us out in 1986, we got back on track in '87. Two years after they brushed us aside in the final, we managed to get revenge on Kinnitty in the semi-final. The wheel was slowly turning in Offaly club hurling.

All five of the brothers were involved for the final against St Rynagh's, although just two were starting. Billy was 17 and playing in goals. With work very scarce, Kieran and Seamus had both emigrated… Kieran was in New York for the summer and Seamus had moved to Cheltenham in England.

When we got to the county final, they both came home a few days beforehand to strengthen the panel. They were on the bench alongside Johnny, who was only 15.

Kieran badly hurt his ankle in the final and fortunately for us, didn't return to New York.

★★★

JOHNNY

I PLAYED A few league games for the seniors that year but our run to the All-Ireland minor final with Offaly meant I didn't see much game-time in the championship. We were a point or two down with 20 minutes to go in the final, when a shout came in my direction.

'Johnny, get ready to go in!' I looked across the bench. My older brothers Seamus and Kieran were still sitting there.

'No, I'm not going in… unless those lads are first!'

I felt it was an insult to them for me, at 15 years of age, to be brought in first. It wasn't a pre-orchestrated family position. That was just my mentality. I had respect for the two lads. I knew what both of them were capable of. Kieran was 20… he was a serious hurler who played senior with Offaly. At 22, Seamus was as strong as an ox… he'd go through a stone wall for the team. They were both in their prime.

So my instinct was not to go in, and I refused to. Whether it was right or wrong, we'll never know. We were only beaten by two points.

Who knows, I could have made a difference.

JOE

IT WAS HUGELY disappointing to lose our second county final in three years.

For the 1988 season I took over as player-manager. Eugene Coughlan was over us in 1987 and wasn't putting his name forward for the next season. I went along to the club AGM at the beginning of 1988 and was asked if I'd take on the job of training the team. After a bit of persuasion I agreed to it.

It was called a trainer at the time, as opposed to the manager, but it was the same thing. I was doing everything. I'd been on the scene a good while at that stage and even though I was only 24, I was among those driving it on during games and training sessions. I had plenty of help too. I brought Liam Corcoran, Michael Murphy and Johnny Breslin on board as selectors… Three great hurling men. Liam's sons have continued the tradition and they all hurl now with Coolderry.

Michael and Johnny have both since passed away. Michael later served as chairman of the club. Johnny was another brilliant clubman and he helped in any way he could, often by fixing hurls. I can honestly say we left no stone unturned to try to win that championship. I was balancing a lot of stuff off the field as well.

WE HAD A fierce tough year at home. Our daughter Aideen was very sick when she was born on May 11.

Marie has a rhesus negative blood type which meant that her body was producing antibodies that can destroy the baby's blood cells. So we knew Aideen was going to be sick when she was born. She arrived a month premature, because if she was let go the full-term, she might have been too sick because her blood was getting infected.

Aideen spent several weeks in intensive care. She was in hospital most of her first three months and had a good few blood transfusions during that time. She was what's called a blue baby, where she came out with her skin that colour. It happens when there's not enough oxygen in the baby's blood when it's born. She was also a very floppy baby, meaning she couldn't control any of her movements for a period.

We'd get her home for a few days at a time and then she wouldn't take her food and we'd have to bring her back in. So they were a tough few months for both of us, but especially for Marie. We were up and down to the Coombe Hospital in Dublin every second day. I was hurling with Offaly, managing the club and we had Shane at home to mind as well. There was a lot going on.

Eventually, Aideen started to get stronger. The morning of our All-Ireland semi-final against Galway in early August, we had an appointment with Dr Elizabeth Griffin to discuss bringing her home from hospital. Dr Griffin was a brilliant consultant who looked after Aideen from day one. She had agreed Aideen could come home. She arrived to meet us a little bit later than planned. During the course of the conversation I said I'd have to excuse myself as I had to be in Croke Park to play a match.

Dr Griffin gave me an unmerciful dressing down to more or less say, *Get your priorities right.* I'll never forget it. Sometimes there's more to life than hurling.

Once we got Aideen home that weekend, she never looked back.

NIAMH ARRIVED TWO years later on November 29, 1990. And with that rhesus condition Marie had, every child you have gets progressively worse.

So Marie was brought in six weeks early. Niamh only weighed two pounds and four ounces when she was born. She was very, *very* sick. And she was anointed on the evening she was born. We weren't sure if she was going to make it. When she first arrived, everything seemed to be okay. I went away for a few hours to get some sleep, unaware of what was about to transpire. When I came back, it was pandemonium. She had taken a turn and things weren't looking good.

The priest was called and all the doctors were there helping out. It was very much touch and go for the next few hours. Niamh was brought down to the intensive care unit, and Marie and I went into the hospital oratory to say a few prayers that she would pull through.

Niamh survived, but as a result of what happened she had a number of complications. She had a heart problem and premature lung disease as her lungs weren't fully developed. We had to sign a form allowing doctors to administer a drug that wasn't even available in Ireland at the time. It was to help develop her lungs because she wasn't able to breathe on her own. She had to have a number of blood transfusions.

After a couple of weeks, she had a grade three brain haemorrhage. She slipped into a coma. Myself, Marie, Shane and Aideen went to see her on Christmas Day. She was lying there in the incubator and there was absolutely no movement from her… no life whatsoever. Looking at her lying there and being completely helpless, it broke our hearts.

We used to call up every second day. We'd ring every other day and the news was always the same… no change. Then the nurses rang from the ward on New Year's Day to say there was some change in her medical readings. That was great news. Thanks be to God, she just gradually came back out of the coma.

But it wasn't looking great for a couple of weeks. She came home from hospital in March 1991, after being in hospital for four months. A lot of her time was spent in intensive care. She was a miracle child really… she went through so much.

While Shane's birth was straightforward and he was healthy from the start, it was very, *very* tough after the two girls were born. Fortunately, both of them came out of it and had no side effects.

Thinking back, we put down some hard days.

★★★

BILLY

IN CLAREEN, WE were always led to be competitive. From a young age, it was drilled into us that it's an honour to wear the black and amber jersey. *When you put it on, remember you're representing your club.* Every time you put on that jersey you should appreciate it.

I'm a firm believer that's the way it should be. You don't put the jersey on to make up numbers or think it's great just to be hurling. It's about representing your club and your family. You should respect that.

We never hurled like we were a small parish. We never had an inferiority complex when it came to playing the bigger teams. You'll win nothing if you think that way. I always felt we were well able to box above our weight. At the same time, we had plenty of lads involved with Offaly. Then, you had us young lads coming through that were getting recognition at county level. When we won our first county final, there were nine or 10 of us who had worn the Offaly jersey at some stage.

Then, the other handful of lads on it… you'd get it hard to get a score off them in training. They were that dogged and thick, they wanted to be on the team as well.

I made my senior club debut in the forwards in 1986 and then found myself between the posts for the opening round of the championship in '87. The idea was that if you were a reasonably good hurler and young, sometimes the best place to put you is in goals. It's probably still the case.

In the meantime, we won the minor All-Ireland and I played centre-forward with Offaly against Tipperary in Croke Park. When I arrived back to club hurling in September, I was still standing in goals when we hurled. I probably should have been playing out the field by then. I was 17 and definitely could have contributed in the forward line for the 1987 final. Liam Coughlan was an exceptionally good goalie and he was playing wing-forward that day.

Liam would have been better than me in the goal and I'd have been better out the field. In a two point loss, a little switch like that could have made all the difference. When Joe took over in 1988 one of his first moves was to swap us. Straightaway, it improved the team.

He started to put his team together from early on and anyone who didn't train… didn't play. He was only 24, still very young and had a young family at home. He made some commitment to come up to Clareen to train us.

In hindsight, that sacrifice probably won us the county final. An awful lot of the lads recognised the effort he was making. Here we were living all around the hurling field and Jesus, if we couldn't make our way up there with the commitment he was giving… there'd be something seriously wrong.

When Joe was asked to train us at that AGM, he didn't hesitate. And when he took it on, he took it seriously.

★★★

JOE

THE WEEK BEFORE we played Kinnitty in the 1988 semi-final, the aul' lad arrived home from his weekly night out in Giltraps. He said he'd overheard one of the Kinnitty players saying they'd have no trouble getting over Clareen… 'They are only a crowd of young lads!'

Needless to say, that resulted in us frothing at the mouth. He knew how to get us going. I doubt if anybody said anything of the sort. It was just his way of making sure we were well motivated.

As well as moving Billy to corner-forward, Johnny came into the team at wing-forward. There was no nepotism at play. He might only have been 16 but he was without a doubt good enough to start. He was starting to show real promise. He'd won a minor All-Ireland in 1987 at 15. In the county semi-final he was marking Ger Coughlan who was a great Offaly hurler and Johnny more than held his own. He scored two goals in a 5-9 to 2-10 victory that backed up our win the previous year.

★★★

BILLY

THAT GOT US into the final against St Rynagh's, who we'd already played twice in the championship. They defeated us in the group stage before we beat them in a three-way play-off to decide what two teams advanced from the group.

I put that county final down as one of my favourite games. I scored 2-4, 1-2 from play and the same from frees. I wasn't often a free-taker throughout my career, but I was on them all that season.

For my first goal, I took a free and tried to put it over the bar. The ball dipped just as it approached the goals and landed under the crossbar. It was one of a few things that worked out for us that day. If the keeper had caught that ball and we lost the game, I could have been hung out to dry for not scoring a point. But you need luck to win matches.

The game ebbed and flowed. Michael Mulrooney scored our second goal of the opening half... we were all chipping in. Johnny scored four good points off Roy Mannion... Joe added a few scores.

In the second-half Rynagh's went ahead, but I got on the end of a ball and stuck it in the net to put us back in front by a point. We finished off with a couple of more scores to claim our first ever county title. The four of us played well on the day.

Kieran had a storming game at midfield and ended up winning Man of the

Match. We were 101 years in existence and to win our first county senior hurling championship was special.

We'd never won an 'A' title in Offaly before.

★★★

JOE

I WAS EMOTIONAL and drained after the final whistle. Relief was the main emotion, that we'd gotten over the line. The season wouldn't have wanted to have run on for much longer because it was a tough year on a lot of fronts.

When you're on the field celebrating a win like that, you see what it means to the older people in the club... men like Seamus Mulrooney, John Coughlan, Chris Connors... our father, and uncles Joe, Billy and Kieran. All the people who brought us to games over the years.

Tony Murphy did a lot of work at underage level in the parish. There was a cohort of people like Michael Connolly, Sean Dooley and Tim Mulrooney, who all played in their day and kept the thing going when they looked after underage teams.

What we did would never have been achieved unless they kept it going. They spoke about memories of great games of the past, great teams and players. That gets passed on from generation to generation.

★★★

JOHNNY

IT'S UNBELIEVABLE TO think back on it now but, at the time, I didn't realise what it meant to the older people in the parish. It was my first year hurling senior with Clareen and we won a championship, the first in the history of the club.

It's probably the club's greatest day ever. It's still remembered that way. I was only 16, and I hadn't been trying for years and years to win a championship, like all the more experienced and retired players were.

Eugene and Tony Murphy had just opened up the Sportsman's Bar down on

Main Street in Birr. All the Clareen crowd went back there that night. I'd love to turn back the clock now, and see what it really meant to people because I didn't fully appreciate it.

I remember old men coming in and grabbing and hugging me in the excitement of the win. You'd be thinking, *Jaysus, you're going to choke me, will you let me go.* I did enjoy it. There's no doubt about it... I had the fun and craic with the rest of them.

I'd say our parents and all the older folk in Clareen never thought it would happen.

★★★

JOE

WE MADE IT back to the final in 1989 after beating Birr in the semi-final. We played Lusmagh in what was a unique occasion, the two smallest parishes in the county meeting in the senior final. We had about 380 people living in our parish, and Lusmagh's population was marginally higher at 470.

Unlike in 1988, when we had all the neutral support, Lusmagh had it this time. Funnily enough, you do feel the things on the field when you're trying to get over the line. Near the end of the game we were a point up when I received a pass from Michael Mulrooney. The goal was half-on... I had enough time to weigh up my options. *Should I go for it or take my point?*

I decided to pop it over. Jim Troy was in goals and at the top of his game.

We're two points ahead... *they'll need three to beat us!!*

Lo and behold John Kelly, Lord have mercy on him, popped up with an injury-time goal to steal it for Lusmagh. It was a crushing blow.

★★★

BILLY

PEOPLE ALWAYS SAY you remember things you should have done, not the things you did.

There's one incident from that match that still crosses my mind from time to time. Not long before John Kelly's goal, I had the chance to extend our lead. Rather than putting the ball over the bar, I went for goal.

Their full-back Tom Kelly pulled off a great block out of nowhere. Had I taken a point… we might have at least drawn the game. I always regretted not putting it over.

When you make a little mistake like that you learn from it.

That defeat didn't hit me as hard as some of the older lads. We had won the county title the previous year. I had a couple of minor All-Ireland medals and we won a Leinster under-21 earlier that season. Success was coming fairly regularly and I was taking things a little bit for granted.

When we came back into the dressing-room, Eugene Coughlan was sitting beside me. He's 13 years older than I am. He was crying… not openly sobbing, but you'd know by the man he was upset.

'It'll be alright Eugene, we'll win it again next year!'

'Now is now… next year is a long way away!' he replied.

That was the first time the penny dropped with me. After everything he'd won in his career, that was his attitude. I thought to myself, *I may get into the real world here. This is not going to go on forever.*

Any time after that, when we weren't successful, it had a much greater effect on me.

★★★

JOHNNY

WE ALL ARRANGED to meet up in Dooly's Hotel that night for a few drinks with family members, girlfriends and wives. It was a very sombre, low-key affair. I can remember it as clearly as if it was yesterday.

It's much more painful when you're the favourites and you just don't get the job done.

I can still see John Kelly's strike flying through all those legs and nestling in the corner of the net.

We had opportunities to close out the game and didn't take them. If you leave a team hanging in long enough that's what happens. You pay the price. That's no disrespect to Lusmagh… they deserved their county title as much as we did the year before.

It started a run of us losing county finals by small margins before we'd eventually get to taste that winning feeling again.

VII

Horan
Sacrificing Saturday nights??
Rod Stewart
'We'll start two of them...'
Cats' claws
Cue Éamonn Cregan
The lightbulb moment

★★★

JOE

IN 1991, PADRAIG Horan replaced Paudge Mulhare as Offaly manager. That ended my exile from the squad. Johnny had returned from America and was called in, as was Billy. It was the first full season with the three of us on the panel.

In his first team meeting, Horan told us there would be no more smoking, drinking and going out on Saturday nights during the season. That prompted a couple of players to stand up and say they weren't going to sacrifice all their Saturday nights.

Horan went on. He gave out about lads being down the town in Banagher drinking and talking s***e.

Banagher being his local town, John Troy took offence.

'I might have been drinking, but I wasn't talking any s***e,' he said.

It wasn't a massive commitment. During the league, we mostly trained one night during the week and had a game on the weekends. For a team that never took the league terribly seriously, we won it for the first time in Offaly's history that year.

Horan blooded a lot of youngsters from our string of successful underage sides and it started to bear fruit. In the league quarter-final, we defied the pre-match predictions to beat Waterford after extra-time in Thurles. It's a game that really stands out... that was the day the penny dropped for me. You could see the cavalry was coming.

Brian Whelahan was only a young fella and he hurled a blinder... Johnny scored four points... Declan Pilkington, Johnny Pilkington, John Troy, Shane McGuckian and Hubert Rigney... they all came of age against Waterford. The transition from the team of the 80s to the 90s side was well underway.

Daithi Regan missed the game with a 'flu and Michael Duignan was playing with the Offaly footballers. Both played key roles in the semi-final and final. We beat Tipperary in a low-scoring semi-final in Limerick. To defeat them in a knockout match in any competition was sweet... another milestone for the group. Their manager Babs Keating came into our dressing-room to say a few words. After he left, we sang a rendition of *Slievenamon*.

That wasn't being disrespectful to Tipp, it was a compliment to them that we were so ecstatic after beating them. Funnily enough, Tipperary had a serious team meeting after that game it probably turned their year around. They went on to lift the Liam MacCarthy that September. Maybe losing to us was the kick in the arse they needed.

★★★

BILLY

WE BEAT WEXFORD 2-6 to 0-10 in the final in Croke Park. Daithi Regan scored two goals. I came on at half-time... I was after putting in a hard winter to get back up to fitness.

My diet was poor when I was living in Dublin. I was eating whatever was convenient. I put on over a stone in weight. I was home one weekend early in the year and sitting in the kitchen... it was my first time back in a couple of months. My father took one look at me.

'Jesus, what are you eating?'

He even knew by me when I walked in the door. I wasn't long having a word with myself... *It's time to sort things out here.*

I had a short window of opportunity to break through for Offaly. From working with Horan with the school, I knew he wouldn't accept anything less than 100 percent commitment. I started to do a bit of running myself in Bushy Park in the evenings.

JOHNNY

IT TOOK US a few years to figure out that you can't be successful and win at a higher level unless you look after yourself off the pitch. There's a time to socialise and enjoy yourself. There's also a time when you have to be serious and knuckle down.

We were on a roll and Padraig had his own way of training. He was very easy to deal with, a great motivator but there wasn't much fitness and stamina running. It was more enjoyable, training was all about playing games.

Padraig wasn't a socialiser himself and never drank. Maybe he didn't realise the extent of what he was dealing with. The night before we played Waterford in that league quarter-final I went down to visit Sinéad in Ferbane. On the way, I pulled up in Cloghan and had four pints. Two of the pubs were called the Caman Inn and the Wheel Inn. I always found it hard to pass them with names like that. My attitude was fairly lax… mind you, I felt great the next day. I didn't suffer from any side-effects and ended up scoring four points from play.

I'd never have done that in later times… not in a million years. But we were young and inexperienced and thought we could do what we liked. We did have quite a number of characters in our team. I'm not pointing the fingers at anyone else… we all knew how to enjoy ourselves and we didn't always go by the rulebook.

When we won the league, we took our eye off the ball. We were young lads, and living life a little bit more than we should have been. Management didn't nail us down either. That's not to say it's their fault but we just didn't seem to be properly tuned in.

The week before we played Dublin in the first round of Leinster, Billy and I went down to Athlone for a night with Sinéad and Fiona. We stayed over, went to the local nightclub Bozos and then went back to Sinéad's brother Liam's house for a party. It went on late into the night.

We travelled back to Tullamore the next day. We went training and just tried to get through the session because we weren't in great shape. It was a poor session… everybody just seemed flat. The following week, we were making our championship debuts in Croke Park. Padraig said to the squad after training,

'Lads put away your hurl for the week. Don't even pick it up and we'll see you next Sunday for the match.'

We didn't meet up at all the week of the game. He believed in keeping a fresh mind. He wanted us chomping at the bit and mad for action at the weekend. That was our prep. Then the day before the Dublin game, the four of us had tickets for Rod Stewart.

★★★

BILLY

WE ASKED HORAN if it would be possible for us to go to the concert. Obviously we weren't going to be drinking. He gave us the green light.

We were staying in Rathmines and our house was full of people. We walked across to the concert in the RDS. From the time we left, we were seven hours on our feet, between walking there, standing at the concert… and then walking back across to Rathmines.

We got up the next day and our legs were like lead. It was like we were after walking a marathon. 40,000 people in this place pushing and shoving. To make matters worse we were eating stuff we shouldn't have been that day as well.

If you said it now to a manager, I'm not sure how well it would go down.

We went across to the Lucan Spa Hotel and met up with the team before the game. It would be unheard of for that to happen now. Not that we did anything wrong but we were on our feet for seven hours the day before instead of conserving our energy.

It was a good concert though. Rod Stewart was top class.

★★★

JOHNNY

NEEDLESS TO SAY it wasn't great preparation for a first round Leinster Championship match. If you were doing that nowadays, you wouldn't last too long in the game.

As it transpired, I scored 1-7 and had one of my better games for Offaly... Billy added a couple of points. Dublin were the better team on the day though and beat us by two points. It was the first time Offaly failed to reach the Leinster final in 12 years.

Maybe winning the league made us a bit complacent. Being young and inexperienced, we were taking things a little bit for granted. Having said all that, Dublin hurled very well on the day... they came out as underdogs and tore into us. They had good fitness levels. Our one night a week training earlier in the year caught up with us, without a doubt.

It was a bitter pill to swallow. Our season was gone.

★★★

BILLY

EVEN IF THE year was unsuccessful, it was great to finally get to play in the same Offaly forward line as Joe and Johnny. It's always a big ask to have three brothers in the one forward line... especially in a county like Offaly, where we had so many quality players and a lot of talent coming through. What tended to happen was they'd say, *We'll leave off one. We'll start two... and bring one off and bring in one.*

But to squeeze in three and hold down those positions on a regular basis was difficult. In the early days, if we lost a game by a narrow margin and all three of us started, the easy criticism was, *Why did they start the three of them?*

Johnny was our free-taker and was a certainty to be picked consistently. Joe was there for a decade at that stage... they were always going to be the first two selected. I had no problem with that. Where I would have had an issue was, if I was being left off the team when I felt I was good enough.

It took a few years before management saw that I was good enough to be starting as well. I don't blame anyone for that. In fairness to Éamonn Cregan, he was the first one that started the three of us regularly in the one attack. And by the time 1994 came around, I definitely felt I was good enough to be on the team.

I had a great understanding with the two lads. Johnny played at No 10... Joe was on the far wing at 12, and I played in my corner. We'd already developed chemistry from playing together for years at club level.

Everyone on the forward line in my mind was treated exactly the same. Whether it was Michael Duignan, Daithi Regan or John Troy… the ball always went to the fella in the best position. Even though there were three of us in the forward line, that didn't change. But we had that innate understanding. Johnny and Joe knew my patterns and runs. They knew the ball I liked to receive. If Joe got the ball, Johnny would always be moving… he knew to make his way diagonally across the forward line if he got his head up.

★★★

JOE

AFTER LOSING TO Dublin in the 1991 Leinster semi-final, Kilkenny dumped us out at the same stage in 1992 and '93. It might have seemed like we were drifting, but the Cats were a good outfit and went on to win the All-Ireland both years. It was very frustrating watching them go all the way. We led them both years at half-time and failed to close it out in the second-half. We were probably still in transition. We weren't fit enough to stay with them for 70 minutes… we didn't train hard enough.

★★★

BILLY

IN 1992 WE were flying it during the first-half. We raced into a six-point lead and ended up losing by six. Kilkenny got an unmerciful run on us at the tail end of the game. Our fitness levels cost us. We just weren't able to sustain 70 minutes in Croke Park and we weren't at peak fitness levels. There was a myth at that time that you couldn't sustain form from early in the year right through the summer. *If you get fit too early in the year you're going to run out of steam by August.*

We tended to be fairly lethargic in the league. Even going over to Birr on a wet day, you wouldn't be looking forward to it… I don't think anyone does. But we got through the spring and had that six week lead-in to the championship…

that's when we really got revved up. When the extra few pounds were lost… when the ground firmed up was when we hit our stride as a team.

Losing to Kilkenny in 1992, our summer was cut short by June. Any concerns we had over a lack of fitness well and truly ended when Éamonn Cregan took over for the 1993 season.

★★★

JOHNNY

ÉAMONN CREGAN NEVER got close to any of the players. He always kept his distance. He was stern and confident in himself. He had played at a high level with Limerick and won an All-Ireland in 1973. He was very clear in his thinking of how he wanted the game to be played. He had a strict vision of how he wanted us to behave and train. I'd say he got a bit of a shock when he first arrived.

We had developed a lot of bad habits and weren't the easiest bunch in the world to lead. He almost walked before it even started.

In early 1993, only 12 players showed up to a training session in Birr. It was one of those wet, miserable nights you wouldn't put the dog out in. I was after getting a procedure on my knee, so I didn't tog out. I arrived up to look at training. I could see Éamonn out on the field. Even from a distance I knew he wasn't pleased.

He'd always blow the whistle at 7.30pm on the dot for training to start. God help anyone who arrived onto the pitch after that. They'd be doing extra laps, press-ups… you name it. On this particular night, there weren't any stragglers coming from the dressing-room. He was furious with the lack of numbers. He walked off the field, packed his bags, got into his car and drove back to Limerick. As far as we were concerned, that was the end of it. He was stepping down. Tony Murphy came over to us. 'Lads, this is shocking!' he said, shaking his head.

Tony was right. It was disrespectful not to have the numbers there.

Panels were smaller back then, we might only have had 23 or 24. A number of absentees might have been for legitimate reasons but there was an awful lot that just didn't bother. For only 12 lads to show up for county training…. you could understand his frustration. Thankfully he was coaxed back.

He almost walked another year when only a handful of players showed up for a challenge match in Waterford. The county board were in the habit of arranging one annually on the June Bank Holiday weekend, which was fine except they'd also have a round of club championship fixed for the same weekend.

We were about to get into our cars after playing Birr in Tullamore on Sunday afternoon and head for Waterford straight afterwards. We were beaten fairly badly by Birr, and coming off the pitch a few of us were chatting to Daithi Regan. 'Did you hear the match is off this evening?' he said.

I didn't ask too many questions as to how he knew this. Maybe I just didn't want to know the answer. The truth was I didn't need much convincing either.

'Is it?' I replied. 'That's great!'

Having already played a game, I was looking for any excuse not to travel. There were no mobiles back then, so we took Daithi's word for it. We ploughed on into town for a few pints. The night went from there. It later transpired the match wasn't called off. A handful of the lads travelled part of the way down and pulled in somewhere for a few refreshments. They didn't go any further. It didn't wash too well with Éamonn. He insisted he wouldn't return after that episode either. But he was cajoled into coming back. I think he mellowed over the years.

WE KNEW FROM his first meeting when he spoke that this guy meant business. He was the boss and you never questioned him… he didn't like that. It took place in the Birr Community School gym. He laid down what he felt we needed. He did say something that I found curious and I'm not sure how well it went down with certain members of the panel.

'I won All Stars… when All Stars were *All Stars*!'

Johnny Pilkington, Martin Hanamy and Brian Whelahan were the only players in the room with All Stars. Maybe it was his way of keeping us all grounded. I thought it was a strange thing to say. I don't know if there's one All Star better than any other one.

I'm not so sure if he loved us, or cared for us that much. He was very driven and had huge ambition to succeed. Whatever it took to get there, he was going to do it. He looked at it like a business.

I don't ever remember him telling me how to play the game… what way I should be running or who I should be picking up. There was no information given on anything like that. But by God, you knew what you had to do as regards winning your position and keeping the ball moving.

It was all about simplicity. His theory on hurling was to keep it open, keep out of the rucks and keep the ball moving. Ground hurling was our thing, even before he came in. He was a big believer in it as well. A lot of our training was spent doing drills on ground hurling and stuff that would be unheard of nowadays.

He took it as a given as far as being so professional himself, and being a non-drinker, that once you hit summer-time, that you have enough respect for your body not to be doing any messing. He wouldn't have put drinking bans on us. But he would have expected us all to be behaving ourselves and which we would generally once we got to the championship.

But the training was so tough, you'd be found out straightaway if you weren't behaving yourself, because you'll be seen at the end of the group when you're doing a 20-minute stamina run.

★★★

JOE

ÉAMONN WAS STRICT on discipline, and timekeeping. He placed a huge emphasis on physical fitness.

We weren't fit enough to last 70 minutes of championship hurling and that's what was killing us. When you're not working hard enough and not feeling the pain in training, you're inclined to maybe drink an extra pint or two. But if the training is tough enough, and you feel like you're going to go somewhere and you're going to win something, fellas make extra sacrifices.

Éamonn's right hand man and fitness coach was Derry O'Donovan. They were a proper duo.

They had us in a gym in Ferbane in January… it was the first time most of us had ever seen the inside of one. The only ones dabbling at that kind of stuff were Kevin Kinahan and Kevin Martin. Derry really came into his own with the fitness work on the field. He had spent time with Arsenal when he was younger and was really into the science of good training. We started to move away from laps. He brought in this multi-sprint stamina running where we'd be going for 20 minutes without stopping. It was 20 seconds on, 20 off… sprinting and jogging, sprinting and jogging. It was really intense.

Derry had a lovely way about him. He'd be absolutely killing us and he'd be there smiling away.

★★★

JOHNNY

NOW WE WERE down to fighting weight. We just felt like we were so well prepared. We were ready for anything on match day then because you had all the hard work done. Whereas if you come in soft and you haven't done the hard work when you hit into a heavy championship match, you'll capitulate with 15 minutes to go. Your mind is weak and soft.

Our sessions were bordering on two hours. It was non-stop from the minute you'd go onto the pitch. It was so well organised and structured. They used to love running us the Tuesday night after a match. That would be a mule of a session. Whatever badness you might have had in your system from the Sunday or Monday was out.

We'd dread it.

★★★

JOE

ONE NIGHT AT training in Tullamore we were doing these runs with Derry O'Donovan. Johnny Pilkington wasn't bothering his arse.

A few of us called him out in front of the group. For the next run, all we saw was white smoke. He was gone like a rocket. Just more or less to say, *I can do it when I want to do it. Ye look after yourselves.* That was the way he was.

He liked to portray a certain image but at the back of it Johnny was a very serious man about his hurling. A year after he retired he gave up smoking, which was typical of Johnny. But there was no better man to step up when the game was in the melting pot.

★★★

JOHNNY

CERTAIN GUYS HAD strengths when it comes to running. Sid was more of a sprinter. I would have considered myself reasonably fit… I'd be in the middle to upper half of the distance running. I'd always be on the inside trying to cut the corner. Every half yard counted. I suppose I was trying to save myself the embarrassment of not being the one lagging behind.

I'd love to be playing in the round-robin provincial format they have nowadays. We wasted so much time training. We trained like dogs. We did heavy slogging for three weeks, and then had a week to sharpen up. We were wasting so much energy running around a field, when we could have been playing more competitive games. The system was just wrong, you got one chance. For my first eight years with Offaly, it was straight knockout. The backdoor was introduced in 1997, but you still had to reach a provincial final to get a second chance.

We had a very good team from 1991 to '93 and we were gone out of the championship after one game.

★★★

BILLY

WHILE ÉAMONN KEPT his distance, Derry was our best friend. He still is to this day. He's a very nice man. He came on holidays with us with his wife Joan a couple of years ago when we went on our 25-year team reunion holiday. He had tragedy in his life as well, he lost his son Shane in a fire accident at home after he was involved with us. It took an awful lot out of him, Joan and all the family. We went down to the funeral and did a guard of honour for them.

That Offaly team has a WhatsApp group and Derry is part of it. But Éamonn Cregan was different… you never really got to know what he was really thinking.

1993 WAS A stop-start year for all the three of us. Johnny missed the league after having a knee operation over the winter.

At least he got to return for the championship.

A couple of bruising rounds of club games before the summer saw the season cut short for myself and Joe for very different reasons.

Joe shipped a heavy belt against Kilcormac/Killoughey. He suffered a fractured eye socket and broken cheekbone. It was a bad injury. He had to undergo surgery in Dublin and it kept him sidelined for a few months. When he returned for the club later that year, he was wearing a face guard for protection... although it was quickly discarded.

I had the misfortune of being slapped with a three-month suspension by my own county board that ruled me out for the rest of Offaly's season. It was unbelievable.

We played Coolderry in a league semi-final in Kinnitty. A bit of a row broke out and a good crew of players got involved. Some Offaly players were in the middle of it. It started between myself and David Dooley... we threw a few strokes at one another. Mick Coughlan and John Miller arrived on the scene. What happened wasn't anything out of the ordinary in the game back then. The four of us were on the county panel and were actually friends, believe it or not. It was just a heat of the moment thing. It didn't seem like a big deal... until referee Martin 'Dinger' Walsh came in and sent the four of us off.

Straightaway, we realised the seriousness of the matter.

'Offaly are hurling in two weeks' time!' I reasoned with Dinger.

'You're off now... OFF!' he replied.

We presumed this would be rectified by the county board. We lost the game and went back training away with Offaly. We thought nothing more of it until we were notified that the four of us got a 12-week ban each for striking... 12 WEEKS!

We went to the county board then to see what could be done, but by then it was too late. There was nothing they could do once the sentence was handed out. It couldn't be reversed because it went down in the referee's report as striking. It was an awful blunder on the county board's behalf or even the management that it wasn't looked into. They must have presumed, *The boys got put off, they'll probably get two weeks or a month.* By the time the verdict was delivered it was too late to do anything about it.

It was a lost year for the four of us.

Offaly were already depleted heading into the Leinster semi-final. Joe, Kevin

Kinahan, Pat Temple and Hubert Rigney all sat out the Kilkenny defeat through injury. I could have made a difference... and so could Mick Coughlan and John Miller, they were in their prime.

CREGAN WAS AT the helm and it was the first time we were doing serious training. They brought in a professional set-up. We started to eat better, we were training more often, with more intensity. Everything was done to a plan when we went down to train in Birr. We weren't wondering what drill we were going to do next. At the same time, all the talk about this golden generation in Offaly quietened. For the first time in our careers, we weren't winning much.

When 1994 came around our attitude had changed hugely from '91. In the beginning the feeling was, *This is going to happen eventually*. When it wasn't happening, the pressure started to mount. Questions were being asked of us around the county. Even some retired players were starting to doubt us. *Are these guys good enough?*

I hadn't nailed down a place on the starting team coming into the 1994 season. I only came off the bench in the closing stages against Kilkenny in 1992. I missed 1993 through suspension. Eventually, Cregan saw that I was good enough to start in the forward line alongside Johnny and Joe.

★★★

JOHNNY

BY 1994, WE were at a make or break stage. Things were looking like they were going to slip by us. There was a lightbulb moment there with the whole squad. Myself, Brian Whelahan, John Troy, Kevin Kinahan, Hubert Rigney and Kevin Martin were hitting 23... Mike Duignan, Daithi Regan and those lads were hitting 26. They were well into their mid-twenties. So if we didn't do something at that stage, when were we going to do it?

We felt the previous two years we gave Kilkenny a good game, but didn't take our chance. Those couple of weeks leading up to facing them in 1994, we could sense that there was something happening... and, if we didn't beat Kilkenny, Éamon Cregan mightn't have been there the following year.

VIII

Frees...
And goals
Troy wizardry
1994
Low to the left

★★★

JOHNNY

ON A MISERABLE Sunday in November 1999, I was lining out for Leinster against Connacht in the Railway Cup. I never refused an invitation for the Railway Cup if I was called in. We got all the gear for the day out and it was always a great honour to be asked to represent your province. I played in it a good number of years and lost a few finals. It was one medal that eluded me throughout my career.

Among the Kilkenny contingent on the team that day was a young Henry Shefflin, who was coming off the back of his first season with the senior team.

Already, he was hitting frees for Kilkenny.

There was no mention of who was going to take the frees by the Leinster management but I presumed that responsibility would be mine. I was around a lot longer than Henry and was still hitting them for Offaly.

And plus, we were playing in Birr. As soon as the first free is called, who makes a beeline for the ball only Henry. He jogs out towards it from corner-forward. I'm a bit closer to it so I get there just ahead of him. I get my body over it.

I put my stamp on it and show I'm taking ownership for the day. That is that. I score that one, add a few more and hold onto it for the day. I think no more of it.

A few weeks later, we're at the All Stars banquet in The Burlington Hotel. It's late into the night, around 3am, and I find myself in conversation with a few Kilkenny lads… Michael Kavanagh, James McGarry and Noel Hickey. That Railway Cup game comes up.

They start slagging me... 'Jaysus, you have some neck, Dooley. How dare you!'... 'You have some cheek taking frees ahead of our Henry.'

Winding me up just to see what I was going to say. I knew what they were at. I thought about it for a second and bit back.

'Right, right. Well, I'll tell you what... whenever Henry has a few All-Ireland medals, I'll let him hit a free.'

Little did I know what would transpire. He has 10 of them now! But at the time he hadn't any.

I LIKED THE pressure of taking frees. I think most free-takers probably do. They want to be the one who takes on the shot to save the game or win it.

I bounced back from the disappointment of missing those close-range frees for the school in the Leinster final. By the summer, I was hitting them for the Offaly minors and under-21s as a 17-year-old. In October, I was on placed balls for Clareen in the senior county final.

In the 1991 championship, I took over free-taking duties for the Offaly senior team. Aside from the 1998 season, when I was coming back from injury, I was on them for the rest of my career. If I could convert seven or eight out of 10, I saw it as a good day's work. Nowadays, the standard is even higher because the balls and hurls are better. They're popping over '65s', which used to be a bit of a struggle.

Of course doubts cross your mind when you're standing over a free. *What if I have an off day? Am I going to miss the one that will cost us?* Over the years, I learned to deal with it. You try to drown out the noise of the crowd as best you can. Take a few deep breaths to get your heart-rate down.

I had a '65' to level the 1998 county final against St Rynagh's. It had been a real tough, low-scoring battle. Dinger Walsh, the referee, handed me the ball.

'Now it's the last puck of the game. It either has to go over... or the game is over!'

Was it trying to put me off? Maybe he was, but it didn't faze me. I had scored nine out of nine placed balls already that day. Every ball I hit seemed to be coming off the sweet spot. A Rynagh's player came up in front of me waving his hurl. I didn't even see him. I struck it as sweetly as I've ever hit a ball. Without sounding arrogant, I knew I was going to score before I even took it. It's not often I could say that. It went over and we won the replay.

There were other days when I didn't feel like that. I was a little less sure of myself. Maybe I started off with a low-percentage free from a tight angle or into a tricky wind. Miss that and it can play on your mind. I worked hard on them. I didn't practise so much early in the year, but once we got to the latter stages of the championship I'd be up in the field two or three evenings a week. I always preferred to work on my own. I'd practise from all different distances and angles. When I stood over them I'd visualise myself taking a big free in Croke Park. On match days then I'd pretend I was back on the training pitch.

You have to keep your percentages up when you're practising. The worst thing you can do is stay too long. I might only do 20 minutes… and head home.

Your routine is everything when it comes to taking frees. You keep it the same no matter what, be it in the first minute or last minute… be it out on the wing or in front of the posts. Then you fully concentrate on the jab lift and the strike. Once you have a system that works… stick with it.

My own technique worked for me. I had a fairly distinctive style. I'm right handed… I'd hold the hurl on the bás in my left hand. It gives you control. If you can grab the hurl down fairly low near the bás and you drop the hand to the back of it as you raise it, you're literally jabbing the ball when the hurl is level to the ground. There's no fear of the ball not coming up.

You have to eliminate the possibility of a mistake. The other thing I had was, I used to take a step forward before shooting. Nicky English used to do it as well, he'd jab the ball, hold it on the hurl for maybe a split second… step forward and then strike it moving forward. It gives you a chance to settle, when the ball comes up, you've that split second just to hold it and then you let it up to strike.

BILLY

SINCE I WAS young, I was always conscious of how a goal could lift a team.

Playing at corner-forward, I felt I'd get two or three chances in every game. Not every forward did, but I was often the one playing nearest the goals.

I had to develop patience as well. I was always willing to hang around in there as much as I could, but you're only as good as the ball that's coming in.

We had exceptional hurlers. When John Troy, Michael Duignan, Declan

Pilkington, Kevin Martin were in possession, I knew it was coming in fast. Johnny and Joe were always quick to get their heads up. Brian Whelahan would see you behind a wall and so would Johnny Pilkington.

Brian was on the same side of the field as me. He could puck the ball off left or right, he was the sort of lad who could go down the line with the ball. On the opposite wing was Kevin Martin, who was equally as good for delivering it in. Johnny Pilkington was exceptional in the middle of the field because he never held onto it. He'd let it go. We always had the mantra that goals win games.

I HAD MY best year for Offaly in front of goals in 1994. I managed to hit the net in every game on our run to the All-Ireland final.

We played Kilkenny in the Leinster semi-final and from January, that game was our only focus. They were going for their third All-Ireland in-a-row. There was no way we could let them beat us for a third straight year. We got ourselves into a really good frame of mind for that day in Croke Park.

Éamonn Cregan made a few important tweaks to the team. Into the defence arrived Kevin Martin and Kevin Kinahan, who did a great job on DJ Carey. John Troy was given a new home at centre-forward. Having Troy at No 11 was a corner-forward's dream. He was a genius with the ball.

If the ball came to him on the ground or the air, I knew that more often than not, it would be coming my way. Midway through the second-half he picked up a ball on the '45', took one look up and picked out my run inside. I moved it on to Joe and he dispatched past Michael Walsh.

In the opening period, I scored my first goal of the championship from 30 metres out. I actually didn't mean it. And this is the first time I've admitted it!

Declan Pilkington got the ball in the corner and scanned outside. I had a bit of time to take a look at the posts and went to go for a point. It was too far out to go for goal. I didn't connect with it properly and it ended up dropping into the top corner. We played some brilliant hurling that day and ran out 2-16 to 3-9 winners. I finished with 1-2. Us three brothers shot 2-10 in total. We were all hitting form at the right time.

MY GOAL IN the Leinster final defeat of Wexford certainly wasn't a fluke. Once again, John Troy was at the heart of it.

I can still visualise it. Johnny caught it on the wing over Sean Flood. He pucked it up in the air down the flank towards John Troy. I was standing around the D... my marker John O'Connor left me and moved over towards him to try cut out the pass. I was 15 metres away and didn't call for that ball, but instinctively John knew the man was coming and that I was free inside. Without looking or taking a touch, he volleyed a first time pass into me. It was like a stroke you'd see Roger Federer play at the net. I took a touch and shot for goal. A Wexford defender managed to half-hook me as I was shooting. Sometimes when you're half-hooked, if you do still connect with the ball it's the very same as putting twice the strike into it. When that happens you often get more power in the ball. The goalie never saw it fly past him.

With referees letting things go a bit more back then, if you took on your man to go for goal you earned it. You knew that when you got the ball. That was the decision you had to make... whether you were willing to take a little bit of hardship to get in with it or not. If you managed to get away from the defender you were in the goalkeeper's full line of fire. Even if he couldn't get near the ball, he'd get to you and make sure you felt it.

In the All-Ireland semi-final against Galway, their goalkeeper Richard Burke left me in a heap on the ground after I finished past him. Johnny Pilkington played a ball down the wing. I tipped it on to Pat Connors and continued my run around the back of the defence. He rose it and hand passed back into my path. I soloed in along the end line and could see Declan Pilkington standing at the back post. But the corner-back sprinted back to cut off that option.

Burke rushed out and I batted it low past him, just before he made contact. It narrowly went over his shoulder and I got the full impact into my chest.

★★★

JOE

BILLY'S KNACK FOR scoring goals was extremely valuable for the team. Almost any game we went to play in the 90s, he was our go-to inside man for goals. In 1998, I had marked Frank Lohan in the first two Clare games and Billy came on as a sub on the second day. He scored a crucial goal to bring us back into the tie. But when we went to play on the third day, Ger Loughnane shifted Frank across to mark Billy because they felt that he was a bigger threat for goals. That freed me up then to get away from Frank. He was probably the best corner-back of the 90s.

Billy was a marked man going into the 1994 final. When he was fouled for Johnny's late free against Limerick, I'd say the corner-back Joe O'Connor was warned not to let him in… to foul him rather than let him go past him for a certain goal.

Billy could win his own ball, whether it came in high or low. He had speed… he went straight for goal if the chance arose. Above all else, he was brave.

★★★

BILLY

I ALWAYS FELT that if there was a goal chance, I needed to go and take it. If it doesn't work, it doesn't work. I never liked bottling it and saying, *I'll put this over the bar and I'll get in with the next one.* That's a bit of a cop out.

Late in the 1994 All-Ireland, Johnny sent the ball in and I fetched it ahead of Joe O'Connor about 25 metres out. I had enough space to take my score. If I had put that over the bar, there were still four points in it. Limerick would have seen it out.

Johnny Pilkington was to my right… John Troy was to my left. They both turned and moved away, creating space in front of goals. I only had one thing on my mind. A point was no good to us with five minutes left. We needed a spark. I turned Joe O'Connor and he pulled me down. Johnny did the rest.

★★★

JOHNNY

WHEN WE AWARDED awarded that free, I stood over it to make it look like I was going for a point. Normally, if I was going for goal, I'd step back from it a little bit and jab lift it. But I wanted to have an element of surprise. The way Joe

Quaid was lining up it looked like he was expecting me to go for a goal anyway.

If it didn't go in, our chances of winning would have reduced considerably. I mightn't have been too popular with our manager. I did look over to try and get a visual on what instructions were coming from the line, if any. There didn't seem to be a lot. I didn't see Éamonn. Derry just pointed for what I assumed was to just tap it over the bar. I didn't feel like we were in a position where we were going to win a game if I took the point. We weren't hurling at all well enough to pull it back five points in that time. I was a bit disgusted with how the overall day had gone and decided to give it a go. By then… it was do or die.

Of course, there were doubts in my mind… considering the circumstances, the time on the clock and where it was. Going for goal from a 20 metre free, at the best of times it's probably less than 50/50 that you'll convert… maybe nearer to 40/60 or even 30/70.

You don't have time to consider the doubts. You just make your mind up and go for it. You can't second guess yourself. You put your head down and pick whatever side you're going to, hit as hard as you can… and hope for the best, really.

Anyone who tells you any different is lying.

I knew I was gonna go low. I didn't want to risk putting it high because the hurls are all held at head height. So I hit it low and aimed for the left.

When there's that many bodies, you're not going to get specifics into which leg you're going to hit it through. You just aim for the left corner and give it your best shot.

Thankfully, it rattled the net.

IX

Boom time
Galway... by 6!
A nine year itch
Lights, cameras... Dooleys!
Bike crash!!!!
Last five minutes... BANG, BANG!
Johnny
Connors
Billy's three

★★★

BILLY

THINGS SEEMED TO run smoothly for us that summer in '94. The new Offaly jerseys had come out and there was a bit of flamboyance to that team. After we won Leinster, it was an uplifting time. The country was going well, the economy was starting to boom.

A lot of lads were finally after winning our first provincial medals and starting to experience a run in the championship. We could enjoy the benefits of some success. We celebrated beating Wexford with a session on Sunday and Monday. They were a brilliant couple of days out.

However, we switched back on fairly quickly again.

We were well aware that winning Leinster wasn't much good to us unless we went further. At the end of the day, you're judged on what you do at the tail-end of the championship. By the time we returned to training on Tuesday night, it was parked. Any fella that wasn't focused was set straight fairly quick by Éamonn Cregan.

★★★

JOE

WE BEAT GALWAY by six points in the All-Ireland semi-final. They were tough opponents. They were beaten by Kilkenny in the final the year before. They still had a lot of their team from the late 80s… Joe Cooney, Pete Finnerty, Gerry McInerney, Michael Coleman.

Our youth really told. Fellas were coming of age. We had a young team apart from myself and Jim Troy in goals. Martin Hanamy was a few years behind us. But all the rest of the lads were 25 or under.

We were just on a roll.

You could feel it in the camp.

★★★

BILLY

WE WERE LIVING from week to week. There was such excitement around the place before the final… they were craving success in Offaly. It had been nine years since we reached an All-Ireland.

You had all the flags and the bunting around the place. Supporters could still watch the training sessions and there were huge numbers coming along. Training ran like clockwork.

It was high tempo stuff and everyone was fighting for places.

Éamonn Cregan never took his foot off the pedal. He relentlessly drove us on. He had his own experiences of losing in 1980 and was determined we wouldn't suffer the same fate. He drilled it into our heads about the need to be focused and to stay tuned in.

Once you finish training the Sunday before the All-Ireland, it's like waiting for a bomb to go off. *This is coming now and you better get yourself ready for it.*

I was fairly nervous as the days ticked down to the final. I was lucky enough my father always had something on the farm to do on a Saturday, so it helped keep my mind occupied the day before. I made sure to get a good bit of work done to tire myself out. That meant I'd get a good night's sleep. You wake up then on the morning of the game and whatever happens, *happens.*

We were slight favourites because of the teams we'd beaten. There was an expectation on us.

Limerick came in a little more at ease with it.

★★★

JOHNNY

WE DEFINITELY FELT the national spotlight on the three of us coming into the All-Ireland final.

The media look for an angle to write about… something that's a bit different. Because Joe, Billy and I were grabbing some of the headlines by playing in the same forward line, we had a flurry of requests for interviews.

Perhaps we were too accommodating. It was in the days when players were open to everybody and you nearly felt you couldn't say no to people. Looking back, I wouldn't say a ban should have been put on us… however, less media work avoids the possibility of saying something that might give the opposition an edge.

You'd be out doing your day job and your phone would be going off in your pocket. You'd answer and talk away to some journalist… next thing, there's a big article in some newspaper. That's the way it was done in those days.

One day the RTÉ cameras and Ger Canning came up to our home house to record a piece with the family. The *Irish Independent* did a spread on us as well. We embraced and enjoyed it. Sometimes you can get too caught up in wondering if it affects your performance.

We did interviews and we weren't saying anything out of the way… just being respectful to the opposition. But too many cameras, limelight and all that sort of thing leading into a match can be more than a bit of a distraction. If we had it all to do again I don't think we should have been allowed to be that accessible to the media.

★★★

JOE

THE WEEKEND AFTER the semi-final and three weeks before the final, I had an accident that left my participation in the final in jeopardy.

In the build-up to an All-Ireland, I tried to fill my weekends without doing anything too stressful. On a Saturday morning I went for a short cycle down the road from the house. I had Aideen on the crossbar. She was six. We were freewheeling down a small hill and her legs were dangling in front of the bike... one of them got caught in the spokes of the front wheel.

That flipped the bike and we were thrown out over the crossbar. I caught her with my hand and put out my other hand to break the fall. Thankfully, Aideen was okay, although she got a big fright.

Initially, I thought I was okay. But fairly quickly I realised I was in bother. My wrist was throbbing in pain. I had broken bones in my hand before after taking belts playing hurling and I knew something was wrong. An X-ray in Tullamore hospital that afternoon confirmed a broken scaphoid bone in my wrist. It's a common injury sustained by jockeys when they fall off horses.

I couldn't believe my luck. *I'm going to miss the biggest game of the year. That's the whole year gone. This is a disaster.*

The consultant, Dr Frank Thompson had no choice but to put a plaster on my wrist. After a bit of persuading, and against his recommendation, he agreed that he'd take it off in two weeks. It was on the provision that I'd put it back on after the final. I had no problem with that.

After he removed it, I got my wrist strapped up and went out onto my local pitch in Ballinagar to test it out. I could hardly hold the hurl properly... I couldn't hit the ball 10 yards. My mind was racing. *Am I going to be able to play?*

We had training the following morning, a week out from the All-Ireland. I called into our team doctor Dr Brendan Lee. He strapped up my wrist into a position that allowed me to strike a ball with minimal wrist movement. He gave me some painkillers and told me that by the following week I'd be fine once we did the same thing, that I wouldn't feel anything on the day of the game with adrenaline flowing.

I held the hurl with my left hand so I was lucky it wasn't my hand-holding hurl.

We managed to keep it under wraps and it didn't get out to the media. I just did the running over that three-week period in training. I did no hurling, aside from a few pucks the week of the game to satisfy the selectors that I'd be okay.

Coming into the final, I had a very simple approach: *I need to get myself involved in the game early. Forget about the wrist.*

I knew from experience that finals can pass you by very quickly.

I was lucky that we were awarded a penalty in the first few minutes. After

Joe Quaid saved Johnny's strike with his foot, I was the first person in to send home the rebound. While we were taking our chances up front, Limerick seemed to have turned up more for the game than we did. Damien Quigley got two excellent goals in the first-half. That cancelled out my goal and it gave them that bit of breathing space.

Éamonn Cregan had a fair cut off us at half-time. He didn't show any mercy. We went in six down and weren't hurling well.

★★★

BILLY

WE WEREN'T HURLING anywhere near our potential. We were underperforming. They took control in the second quarter, dominating until the break.

We got back into the game after half-time and cut Limerick's lead down to two. They popped over a couple of scores to give them some daylight again... I thought the game had slipped away from us. When Gary Kirby pointed a free with six minutes to go to put them five points up, Martin Hanamy told him it was time to get his speech ready.

'I think so!' Kirby replied.

They were that close to sealing it. When I won that free, it looked like it was going to be a consolation score... until the goal went in. It turned from there.

★★★

JOHNNY

THE WHOLE DAY was just petering out, going nowhere and I wasn't having my best game. I was getting on the ball but felt I wasn't doing what I wanted to do. I wasn't contributing as much as I would have liked.

Those last five minutes were electrifying. It was like an out of body experience. Everything I touched seemed to go nicely. It was the same for Billy, John Troy and Brian Whelahan. It went from one extreme to the other. You didn't have time to think about winning because for most of the game, you were nearly thinking about losing it.

Then… BANG… BANG!!!!

My goal went in but we were still two points down. I often think, *If I didn't go for goal and instead took the point, would we have won the match?*

We still could have won by four points. But I do think the first goal kick-started the whole comeback. As a collective, we got this burst of energy we didn't think we had in our bodies beforehand.

★★★

BILLY

BEFORE WE KNEW it, Joe Quaid had the ball pucked out again. Johnny Pilkington collected and launched it straight back into the full-forward line. Pat Connors moved across in front of me. I had to let him off because he was on a mission to get there first.

I expected him to rise it but he pulled first time… back of the net!

Not in my lifetime could I have forecast what happened after that. I arrowed over three points on top of the two I had already scored.

Nearly everywhere I stood the ball came to me. It seemed to follow me around no matter where I went. I scored those three from the Cusack Stand almost on the sideline… two off my left, and one off my right. I had two wides as well during that period.

I can still see those points in my mind's eye… Johnny Pilkington and John Troy playing them across. It was a lovely warm day and it was like being above on the hurling field at Clareen… a ball just comes floating across to you, you put out your hurl to control it and fire it over.

I could have nearly pucked the ball the other way and it would have gone over the bar. That's the sort of luck that came our way. It was really, really enjoyable. The crowd never really got to settle from the time Johnny's goal went in until the match was over.

I ran into Johnny shortly after the whistle blew. It's an unbelievable feeling to have your brothers on the field with you when you win an All-Ireland. The way it ended up was very special for myself, Joe and Johnny. We scored 2-11 out of 3-16. It was a fair tally for one household.

★★★

JOHNNY

TO SEE A game finishing out like that… to score 2-5 in five minutes, it's unheard of. For it to happen on All-Ireland final day, it just couldn't be better.

Because there's no comeback when you rally that late… there's no way back.

It irks me when people say we stole the All-Ireland. It wasn't like we won it by a point… we had six to spare.

Okay, Limerick made mistakes but we still had to rattle off five points from play as well in that length of time.

The ball hopped for us, there's no point denying it. The beauty of it was we could enjoy the last couple of minutes when we knew the game was as good as over and we couldn't be caught.

All of a sudden, the final whistle went and we were being carried off the field. When the game ends, it becomes a bit of a rushed blur. You don't get much time to yourself.

The pitch was just mental.

The crowd come racing on, you're carried across and the head is pulled off you.

Then you're into the dressing room and that's absolutely mayhem, it's full and you have nowhere to turn. We met our parents outside the dressing-room, they had big smiles from ear to ear.

They were loving it.

It's hard to comprehend what must have been going through their minds for the previous two hours. Their relief must have been greater than ours. You hardly get time to soak it all in. I remember the satisfaction of getting to the hotel, booking into the room and having a few drinks there with Sinéad and my parents. *The Sunday Game* was live from the hotel.

The pain of losing is so bad, when you win you have to really enjoy it. Because you just don't know when it's going to happen again. You're thinking about what it means to your own parish, your family, your brothers and sisters.

★★★

BILLY

THE PRESSURE WAS off… it was a release. We could have a few pints and enjoy ourselves.

We had the homecoming to look forward to the following day. We got up the next morning and walked down to Doheny and Nesbitt. It was nearly the nicest part. The sun was shining. We were sitting outside having a few large ciders. It was just perfect.

We got the train home from Heuston Station. There was a band playing there and we all danced merrily on the platform to the *Siege of Ennis* as we waited to board. We had a few beers and the singing continued all the way back.

On the train, Johnny Pilkington gave a live commentary of the game. He's very good at it, he went through the final five minutes and threw in all his own thoughts into the process. We had a great night in Birr and it was onto Banagher and Cloghan the next night for our captain Martin Hanamy. On Wednesday night we had our own homecoming in Clareen… going out to our own little parish and seeing what it meant to your own people was special. They were so proud that there were four lads from Clareen on the team.

★★★

JOE

WHEN WE GOT back to Birr an overexcited supporter shook my sore hand and the pain in my wrist lifted me out of it.

The best day we had was on Thursday. We all met up in Tullamore and didn't have any official places to be. Paddy McCormack, the former Offaly footballer known as the Iron Man from Rhode, treated us all to a steak dinner and a few drinks in his bar. It was the day where we could really sit back and enjoy a special moment in time. It was nine years since my first All-Ireland victory in 1985. Back then I was very young. I appreciated it all the more. Our kids were old enough to remember it too, which added to it.

BILLY

I SENSED ÉAMONN Cregan was quieter in the dressing room before that game than other big occasions. I've no doubt that was to do with who we were playing. But I never felt him reneging on us during the lead-up to it. Cregan and Derry ensured we had top class preparation coming up to it. He must have been torn after the final whistle. He was entitled to be upset that it was Limerick we beat.

Finally leading us to the Holy Grail but doing it against his native county, that can't have been easy. He had Pat McLoughney, Paudge Mulhare and Mick Spain in his backroom team… all true Offaly men.

★★★

JOHNNY

IT WASN'T LONG before 1995 came around and we had to refocus again. There was no question about Éamonn Cregan staying on, even though his post-match interview didn't go down well with some supporters.

Obviously, he was disappointed for his own people. I felt he could have shown a little bit more excitement for us on the day. But then again, it's hard to know what was going through his mind. He was after beating his own county, he hurled with them for 18 years. Maybe he felt he blocked the path for them to end their long wait for an All-Ireland. I just thought he could have been a bit happier for us as a group of players for what we achieved.

I'm sure he got great satisfaction out of it. He had spent time coaching Limerick and Clare before he got to us, but we were the first county where he achieved any sort of national success. As a manager, we gave him the most success he ever had at that level, in senior county management.

I'm sure he went home and was quietly satisfied… but we didn't see much of him after. He came back with us on the Monday night and we didn't see him again until the team holiday. That's just the way he was, he wouldn't have been one for the limelight or socialising.

HE WAS A great man to find an angle to drive us on.

Straightaway in 1995 his message was… 'You don't want to be a one trick pony. You have to back it up. You have to show what you're made of….'

The feeling out there was that we'd stolen an All-Ireland from Limerick. We came in at the last minute and won it. The best team didn't prevail. We had to prove ourselves now. We had a reasonable National League and it made it to the semi-final despite being without the Birr contingent. They were in the middle of a run to the All-Ireland club title on St Patrick's Day.

Kilkenny beat us 4-8 to 0-14 as DJ Carey scored a hat-trick. They went on to beat Clare by nine points in the final. Straightaway we were being written off. The narrative was that 'Kilkenny are back!' All of a sudden, they were favourites to win Leinster and the All-Ireland.

We were shelved. The vibe among the hurling fraternity was… *Offaly are happy with their All-Ireland. They're going to be a burnt out force for this year.* That got our dander up a little bit.

SINÉAD I GOT married in June 1995, the week before we played Wexford in the Leinster semi-final. It was a busy time. We bought a site in Tullamore seven months earlier and were building a house. I was doing it myself by direct labour and managing the whole job from start to finish.

At that time, I was working in Dublin with Waterways Ireland. I was on the road at 6.30am and not getting home until 7.10pm. Training was at 7.30pm, so I had to head straight there. We were trying to build a house and with a wedding coming up which Sinéad managed to organise completely on her own without any assistance from me. We had a lot going on.

We just got the house built and moved into a concrete shell. It was nice to have our home, somewhere that you could call your own. We had tons of work still to do. On the evenings I wasn't with Offaly, I could be trying to finish a few rooms and building the garage until midnight.

In fairness to Sinéad, she understood how hectic things were and wasn't too hard on me during the hurling season. So I was putting in massive hours, but I did what I had to.

Then the day we got married, our house got robbed!

It was announced on the radio that our wedding was taking place and listeners were sending in good wishes. Someone listening in obviously knew where we lived and realised there would be no one home. There's a big window in our living room. They broke in and took some of our weddings gifts.

I got a phone call during the reception from the Gardai to say there was after being a break-in at the house. It was something you could do without on your wedding day. To add insult to injury, our home insurance didn't cover anything as we hadn't spent a night in the house yet, so technically we didn't live there.

A good lot of the Offaly team were at the wedding and, needless to say, we had a good day out even though we were playing Wexford the following Sunday in the championship. We had a great wedding. I've often said that when you're really fit and you're in good form, a few pints are no harm.

From that Monday onwards, I minded myself all week. We honeymooned up in Donegal for a few days. Even though we were away, my mind was focused. I spent most of the week on some GAA field in Donegal taking frees. Sinéad was brilliant. She would be behind the goals pucking balls back to me. It probably wasn't much of a honeymoon for her.

Sinéad is 100 percent GAA. We had a great week up there. We made up for it later in the year… we got away when we went on a team holiday to the Canaries.

We beat a strong Wexford outfit. Liam Griffin had just taken them over. It was the first Leinster Championship match broadcast live on TV… a baking hot Saturday evening.

I got Man of the Match, so at least it showed I held it together on my first week of marriage.

JOE

ÉAMONN CREGAN TOOK particular pleasure in beating Kilkenny. I don't know why, it probably went back to his playing days. To be able to retain Leinster and beat Kilkenny for the second straight year was brilliant.

That sense of being disrespected motivated us a lot… going into the Leinster final as underdogs despite being All-Ireland champions stung. We seemed to be a team that got the best out of ourselves when we had a cause. And we had a serious cause for that game.

Éamonn was spitting fire in the dressing-room beforehand.

'Get in their faces, bring the game to them and give nobody a free puck anywhere!' He gave his final rally call before we went out.

'Whoever blinks first today will lose this game… AND IT WON'T BE US!' he bellowed.

★★★

BILLY

THE WEATHER CONDITIONS were atrocious. With dark skies above, it was a sweltering humid day. Just as we were due to come out onto the field, a monsoon started.

We were led out by Johnny Pilkington, who had assumed the captaincy from Martin Hanamy that year. We got as far as the field and the heavens opened up. Torrential rain was coming down in buckets… thunder and lightning, the works.

Kilkenny were due out ahead of us but there was no sign of them. Unwilling to stand there getting soaked to our skins, we retreated to the dressing-rooms. The start of the game was delayed by a few minutes.

We changed our jerseys and waited inside for the downpour to ease off. Our view was that Kilkenny had left us out in the rain to get saturated. It only added fuel to our fire.

It really riled up Brian Whelahan… he went berserk in the dressing room. As it turned out, they did come out ahead of us and had taken shelter in the dugouts.

★★★

JOHNNY

THE WEATHER MADE for very slippy and dangerous conditions. It was a tense, low scoring game… We led by 0-5 to 0-3 at half-time. It was end-to-end stuff, full of physicality and hits.

I had my nose broken in the first-half. I won a ball out on the wing and went to step inside Willie O'Connor. As I did he cracked me on top of the nose with the heel of the hurl. You'd think he had a sword in his hand the way he was swishing it around. I was lying by the sideline with blood pumping everywhere. The old Hogan Stand was looking right down on top of me. I was right out underneath the crowd. By the time our doctor Brendan Lee got over, I was saturated in blood... it wouldn't stop pouring.

Brendan started shoving cotton wool up my nose. *What's he at here? Sure that's it... I'm done.* In my head I thought I wasn't going to be able to play on. He kept jamming up more cotton wool and I couldn't breathe.

'Brendan what's the story here? Is that my game over?'

'What do you mean... what's the story? You're going back in!'

'I'm going back in? Sure I can't breathe!'

'Can't you breathe through your f***ing mouth?'

So I spent the rest of the game with my nose jammed up with cotton wool, breathing through my mouth. When I went back in, I stared at Willie. *I'm going to get you back before this game is out.*

I'd always have it in the back of my head that if a lad got me, I'd try and return the favour in some way before the game was over. I waited for my chance. It's always sweeter if you don't make it look blatant or like you're intentionally trying to hurt them.

Fifteen minutes later, I dropped back to help out the defence. Hubert Rigney pulled on a ball in my direction. In the corner of my eye I could see Willie was coming up behind me... it bounced perfectly.

On the half-turn, I let fly and connected, leathering the hurl off Willie's leg with my follow through. No free was awarded. I made eye contact with Willie. No words were exchanged. It was like a gentleman's agreement. We were even.

We ploughed on. We romped home in the second-half and gave Kilkenny a fair trimming, winning by 2-16 to 2-5.

Billy was only after returning from an ankle injury and fired over five points. Daithi Regan and Pat O'Connor scored a goal apiece during the second-half. After having a tough time on him in the league semi-final, Kevin Kinahan did a great job restricting DJ Carey. He scored a late goal, but by that stage the game was long over.

X

Clareen

Final heartache

... and more heartache!!!

Gerry Kirwan's promise

Hanamy and Johnny

THE JOY OF '95

Rynagh's downed

Back-to-Back

Coughlan's goodbye

2000... the last stand

★★★

JOE

IF YOU WERE starting out again and someone said, 'Here's four county medals… or you can give them back and see how many you can win?' *What would you do?*

It's a question Mick Coughlan often asks me.

My answer? I'd take the four medals. Clareen had never won one before we started out. I played in 13 senior county finals, including two replays. We lost some by a point and two points, and we won a few narrowly as well. It was a great journey.

The championship was extremely competitive back then. Birr were regularly reaching club All-Irelands and St Rynagh's had a very strong side. We endured a few lean years after our maiden win of 1988. For a while we were wondering if we'd win a second title. We lost three finals by a total of four points between 1989 and '94.

The year after Lusmagh pipped us in the 1989 final, St Rynagh's scored a goal with the last puck to put us out in the quarter-final…. they went on to win the title. I missed that season with Offaly and didn't have a great year for the club either. My back was giving me problems and I wasn't playing well.

We made it back to the county final in 1991. Birr beat us 1-12 to 1-11. We led for most of the game and they scored a goal three minutes from time to draw level. They were awarded a '65' in stoppage-time. Paddy Kirwan, who transferred to Birr from Ballyskenagh, came out from goals and stuck it over.

St Rynagh's were county champions in 1992 and '93. They knocked us out in the '92 quarter-final. In '93, we lost to Lusmagh in a play-off and failed to advance from the group. It was starting to look like we wouldn't add another title.

Gerry Kirwan, a fine hurler and excellent referee in his day, took over as trainer in 1994. We got our act together that year and returned to the county final. I was still nursing a broken wrist from my cycling accident before the All-Ireland final. I got the plaster taken off and had it strapped up for the club semi-final and final. In a mud bath, Birr scraped over us in the decider by 0-8 to 0-6... another crushing blow. That was my fifth county final to lose. I hated losing, absolutely despised it.

★★★

JOHNNY

THOSE DEFEATS WERE hard to take. Now, the teams that beat us deserved to win as much as we would have deserved but it doesn't make it any easier when you lose. You start to question yourself. *Are we ever going to get a second title?*

For me, winning the second one meant more to me than the first one, because I had felt all the pain of losing finals in the intervening years. I was still only 23. I'd lost four finals and won one. It was at a stage where we either start winning now or forget about it and finish up with one medal.

We had a great track record of getting into finals... we very rarely lost semi-finals through all those years. I think we only lost one semi-final in my 16 years playing senior. Winning and losing finals often come down to small margins, very simple things where if you got a lucky break and a goal goes in... that could be enough to swing it for you.

When we won in 1995 we got a bit of luck that we didn't get the previous year. Then we bounced on and added a couple more.

Birr were a bit of a bogey side for us. They always seemed to get the upper-hand. If we could get Birr out of the championship we felt our chances improved straightaway. That's where St Rynagh's came into play. They had a good habit of being able to knock out Birr and we could get one over them.

When you're in a small area like Clareen, you don't have a conveyor belt of talent coming through. We had the same team for 10 years, give or take two or three positional moves, or a couple of lads coming in and out. So for a decade you're playing with the same team.

BILLY

AFTER LOSING THAT 1994 final, the team headed across the road from St Brendan's Park into the County Arms for some food.

I walked in with Fiona, Johnny and Sinéad. As we entered, there was a big porch where we dropped off our bags and hurls. A man I knew approached me. Only weeks earlier he was clapping me on the back in Croke Park after we won the All-Ireland.

'You wouldn't think ye boys were hurling with Offaly this year, would ye? That was some disgrace.'

I looked at this lad thinking, *Does he want a box in the jaw or what?*

I thought it was the most hurtful thing someone could ever say to a player who's just lost a county final. It put a fair sting in the tail. We just ignored him and walked by… some people have no cop-on.

It's heart-breaking when you get beaten by such a small margin. The only positive is that it leaves a glimmer of hope. Gerry Kirwan rammed home that message afterwards.

'Lads, we're not far away. I've one year done with ye… I can guarantee you within three years we'll have two county finals won!'

It's a funny story about how Gerry Kirwan came to be our manager.

A native of Ballyskenagh, he hurled for Offaly in the 60s. He wasn't known for training teams… he made his name as a referee and took charge of a number of All-Ireland finals.

No one ever upset him when he was refereeing. I saw him officiating county finals in Birr between Kinnitty and St Rynagh's which were slaughter battles. St Rynagh's often had four lads sent off in those games in the early 80s. But no one ever frightened Gerry Kirwan or tried to bully him out of dishing out red cards.

Johnny Breslin was working in the baking factory in Roscrea with Gerry in

1993. Johnny and Mick Coughlan were on the Seir Kieran committee that were busy looking for a new manager at the end of that year. Back then, bringing in an outsider wasn't the done thing. The committee had meeting after meeting, trying to find someone local to train the team.

Johnny Breslin had a funny way of talking. Every meeting he would tell them, 'Well Gerry Kirwan says he wants to train ye and no one else will do it. Will ye not give him a chance?'

They had a meeting once a week for almost two months. Johnny Breslin made the case for Gerry every time. His pleas were ignored. He was going back to Gerry telling him the answer was no and they were still looking for someone. It didn't deter either of them.

Eventually, seven weeks in someone said, 'For f**k sake will ye give it to Gerry Kirwan and see how he gets on.'

★★★

JOE

GERRY KIRWAN MADE a big difference, he was an excellent trainer. He was a great man to get us fit and disciplined. He had three things he used to keep espousing… discipline, determination and work-rate.

He didn't want to be reading the paper the following week where the opposing team scored 10 points from frees. He also trained us hard. At the end of every session we finished off with a 10-minute run which got more competitive as the year went on and lads got fitter.

He constantly told us before games: 'You don't aim to play as well as the lad beside you, you aim to play to the very best of your own ability.'

It was aimed at us as county players. I thought it was a very good standard for him to set. There can be no cop out by the county players or anyone else for that matter. And his philosophy meant that whether it was the Dooleys, Kevin Kinahan, Eugene or Mick Coughlan, the county men had to be playing better on the law of averages than the non-county man.

Going into 1995, I was appointed captain. It gave me a huge lift.

We decided as a team we'd had enough of the hard luck stories and were going to do everything in our power not to let it happen anymore. We went all out. We had a welcome injection of youth that freshened up the team… James Coakley, Damien Murphy, Paul Scully broke onto the starting fifteen. Having said all that, we needed a win over Tullamore in late May to stay in the championship.

We'd lost our first group game to Coolderry, and beat Kinnitty in round two. It came down to a straight shootout between ourselves and Tullamore for a place in the knock-out stages. We went into that game down Noel Bergin, plus Kieran and Billy through injury. To make matters worse, our centre-back Ger Connors was sent-off early in the second-half after he collided with Kevin Martin. Tullamore were eight points ahead. It didn't look good.

I was switched to centre-back… my first time to play in defence for the club.

We were trailing in the closing stages and managed to rescue it from the jaws of defeat. Michael Mulrooney scored a goal and Johnny put over a couple of points. A young player Kevin Abbott, who has since passed away, scored the crucial winning point that evening. It was the only senior game he hurled for Clareen, but what an impact!

After that, we didn't lose a knock-out championship match for three years.

A COUPLE OF weeks after losing the All-Ireland final to Clare, we got back on the horse with Clareen. We beat Kilcormac/Killoughey and Belmont to send us into the semi-final against reigning All-Ireland champions Birr. It was fixed for the day after Michael and Edel Duignan's wedding, which wasn't ideal preparation for a county semi-final. It turned out to be one of our greatest ever wins.

After a slow start, Mick Mulrooney grabbed two goals and Eugene Coughlan added another before half-time. Birr put us under pressure. Brian Whelahan was moved up front in the closing stages. We hung on to win by a point, 3-8 to 1-13.

The final against St Rynagh's was a tight affair. I had a tough afternoon in the company of Michael Conneely. We led by five points at the interval and looked on the verge of victory when we were three points ahead with time almost up. The thought crossed my mind, *Am I actually about to lift the Sean Robbins Cup?*

Damien Coleman had other ideas. He latched onto a rebound from a 20-metre free and drilled it home to level the game. Our hearts sank at the final whistle. It felt like a defeat. It was a job to lift ourselves for the replay. St Rynagh's had never been beaten in a replay, so the view was we'd left our chance behind us.

★★★

JOHNNY

WE WERE COMING off the back of a campaign with Offaly where Éamonn Cregan would stand up on the Thursday night of an All-Ireland and talk for 15 minutes. 'Lads this is what's going to happen, this is how we're going to play.' The selectors and captain would contribute a few words. All over in no time. Out the door... happy days.

Then we'd get to a county final with Clareen and after training, the whole team would head up to the hall, have a cup of tea and a few sandwiches. Gerry Kirwan would sit down at the top of the table flanked by two selectors and he'd talk for 45 minutes. He'd go through 'The will, the want and the heart'... everything.

The team meeting used to go on for close to 90 minutes. Everyone had to speak. After Gerry, the selectors and captain spoke. Then, they'd start in the corner and every player in the room had to say a few words. Right around, nobody was skipped... down to the very last sub.

I came out of one of those meetings and travelled home with Joe in the car. I was exhausted. It was close to 11pm and I had been on the go from 6am.

'Jesus Joe, I'm wrecked! I'm talked to death.'

In one way it made me appreciate that when I was heading to Birr that Sunday this was what our little club was trying to achieve. Maybe that's what we needed. At the time, I felt I didn't need it.

It came down to another dogfight. When you're trying to win a game like that, you really have to run yourself into the ground. The replay was another hard, competitive game. Rynagh's had a really tough backline with some serious operators in there. Their defence was close to county level and they had David Hughes in goals.

Since I was a teenager, I was occasionally picked up by Martin Hanamy. It was never an easy afternoon in his company. When I saw him jogging towards me before the throw-in, I knew I was in for a dog of a day.

He was a class defender. Martin would be whispering in my ear, 'Shocking aul' day, this is awful weather.'

We were good friends, we'd been on plenty of county holidays and different trips together. One day we played against them and the game was 10 minutes old when this ball hops between us.

It was a real cold day, with rain pelting down and hailstones. Martin leathers me along the back of my leg as hard as he could but close enough to the ball that a free wasn't awarded.

He'd be clever enough to know where the line was. And then he'd come back with a word, 'Jays, sorry about that John!' This sort of thing. It was all part and parcel of the game.

Our lads at the far end were similarly ruthless. A fair bit of peeling went on in that replay but it was all honest, hard-hitting stuff.

It was usually the fella that put his neck on the line that was awarded a free. Placed balls were hugely valuable because the scorelines were so low. We beat them 0-10 to 0-9. All eight of my scores came from frees. Eugene Coughlan and Joe chipped in with the other points.

We were a point up late on when Michael Connelly struck a bullet at the goals. Paddy Connors was on the line beside our 'keeper Liam Coughlan. The ball was travelling too fast for him to react in time with his hurl. He stuck out his head and it hit him smack on the forehead. It rebounded about 20 yards back into play. It showed the character of Paddy and what he was willing to sacrifice for us to win.

★★★

BILLY

OF THE FOUR county finals I won, 1995 was my most enjoyable. I was too young to appreciate it in 1988. I didn't even score in the final but it wasn't a game for any polished stuff. That was a day we had to dog it out. And we did that.

One of the worst belts I ever got on a hurling field arrived in that replay. To rub salt in the wounds it was a case of friendly fire.

I was being marked by Michael Rigney and his brother Hubert was picking up Mick Coughlan. Midway through the second-half, a high ball comes in our direction down the wing.

I told Mick to keep out of the way, but he wouldn't understand that concept!

When the ball dropped I had Michael Rigney behind me, and Mick drifted in front of us. As I put my hand up to catch it, Mick turned and pulled his dead living best with his hurl in one hand. He connected with me clean on the forehead, absolutely pasting me. I was lying on the ground and Mick Murphy came over to throw some water on me.

'COME ON, COME ON... GET UP!! There's 20 minutes to go!'

We were due out in Leinster the following Sunday against Naomh Eoin, the Carlow champions.

It was Tuesday by the time I got myself checked out. Myself and Seamus were building a house at the back of the hospital in Tullamore. Because we were so close and I was in a fair bit of pain, I went around to A&E to see what was wrong with me. Only for that I mightn't even have gone in there.

All around my eyes were black and the bruises went down to my cheekbones. The nurse looked at me.

'When did this happen?'

I couldn't bring myself to say it was Saturday.

'It happened on Sunday. I couldn't make it in yesterday.'

'Jesus that's in an awful state!' It turned out my nose was broken in two places. Fortunately, it had set fairly well. She looked at the X-ray.

'I don't think we'll have to go near it. We'll leave it for the time being and see what happens.' Every time I moved my head I'd get a dart of pain. I still managed to tog out the following week for our Leinster club opener. That's the way hurling was back then.

JOE

I'D PUT THAT county final win down as the best day of my hurling career. That it came only six weeks after the crushing blow of losing the All-Ireland final to Clare certainly helped shake off some of the disappointment from that day.

To captain our club to the county title, it was the stuff of dreams. Shane was mascot for the day so it gave him a taste of what county final day might be like. To put the icing on the cake, I was later named Offaly Hurler of the Year. I played at midfield with the club during those years and loved it. I mainly operated in a defensive role, dropping deep to get on the ball and spraying it quickly into the forwards. I'd break forward for a score a couple of times in each half, usually when my marker was least expecting it.

We got back on the horse again in 1996. We had serious momentum that year. We returned to the final after seeing off Kilcormac/Killoughey in the semi-final replay. We had a great rivalry with them during the 90s. We seemed to meet them more than any other team. In a few close encounters, we always managed to beat them… we were the itch they just couldn't scratch.

The final pitted us against Rynagh's once again. It turned out to be another battle. We were leading throughout and even though they pressed hard near the end and scored a goal, we held on to win by two points.

It gave us back-to-back championships for the first time in the club's history. All of a sudden, we had three county medals. It was a proud day for our family because it was the only county final where all five brothers started on the team. Kieran played on the half-back line and Seamus was at corner-forward.

★★★

JOHNNY

THERE WAS A bit more satisfaction in putting titles back-to-back. You sort of felt like… *We're here now… we're establishing ourselves. We're not just one of these teams that bottle it when the game is there to be won.*

Even though 1995 was so enjoyable, I felt '96 put us on the map as an established, successful team. We were no longer serial underachievers. We had an honest, committed group of players, all different types of characters. The one thing I always respected about them is that when myself, Billy, Joe and Kevin Kinahan came back from the county, we'd be at a fairly high fitness level.

The club would be after having a bit of a sabbatical. They'd be taking it handy through the summer and maybe playing the odd challenge match.

Gerry Kirwan was big into his 10-minute runs around the field. The four of us would take off and we'd try to show up the club lads a bit… to show them what our fitness levels were like. The boys would be panting, you could hear all the groaning and grunting going on behind us. The only other lad who was up with us was our brother-in-law Nicky Dunne. He loved running… the harder the better for him.

But if you gave it three weeks or a month, the lads would be gaining on us all the time. And they would work their socks off… no one would throw in the towel. There were no lads pulling up with hamstrings or twinges… they were unheard of.

If we got to the county final, those guys would be right up with the four of us in the runs. I'd give them huge credit for that. It was a testament to their character. And it wasn't that we were falling back to make it easy or allow them to feel good about themselves.

★★★

JOE

BY 1997 A TRIP to the county final was becoming an annual pilgrimage. Our three in-a-row bid brought us up against Birr, who were coming again with a strong team. Brian Whelahan's younger brothers Barry and Simon were emerging, in addition to Gary and Darren Hanniffy.

Around that time, I was battling a serious injury that I thought was going to end my career.

During the semi-final defeat of Tullamore, the ball was in a ruck when Mick Coughlan pulled on it. He mowed me across the back of my foot, damaging the sacroiliac joint in the heel. It's a serious injury if not treated right.

It wasn't too bad at first. I was working in Cork the following week and went for a run instead of travelling back up for training. I shouldn't have done anything. I only made it worse. I needed a painkilling injection before the final and another one at half-time because the first one wasn't strong enough to kill the pain.

We lost by four points and I had no impact on the game. I was playing centrefield before they stuck me in full-forward. I just couldn't run. One ball broke in the second-half and Barry Whelahan easily beat me to it. I came off before the game was over.

I wasn't able to walk properly for two months afterwards. My hurling days looked in jeopardy. By playing I did fierce damage. Trying to get by with an injection meant it could have been a career threatening injury.

Suddenly, in December, it cleared up. I was genuinely starting to think that I'd have to retire. It was that bad.

★★★

BILLY

EUGENE COUGHLAN RETIRED after the 1997 final. He was 41 at that stage and had been hurling senior for Clareen since 1973. He gave some service to the club. He had 15 years of senior hurling put down before even he won a championship.

He was the father of the group in his later years and a real gentleman as well. He was the first real star in Clareen. He was winning All Stars and All-Irelands when no one else from Clareen had achieved anything of note in hurling. He was Hurler of the Year in 1985.

Even to this day, when people talk about great full-backs of the game, Eugene is always mentioned. His skill levels were incredible. He played everywhere for us. Full-back, centre-back, centre-forward and full-forward. He wasn't a dirty hurler by any means but if you wanted to mix it with him, that was fine too. He enjoyed the physical stuff.

People often ask me what it was like to hurl with him? We sort of took it for granted because every time we went to the field to train, he was there. He just blended in with us and we weren't in awe of him like others were. That's how he wanted it.

GERRY KIRWAN DEPARTED after 1997 and Michael Connolly took over. He was known as the Chip.

Once more we ended up taking St Rynagh's to a replay in the final. Not for the first time, they did us a favour by ending Birr's interests in the semi-final. We dug ourselves into a five-point hole during the second-half the first day. We scored the last five points to draw the game. Johnny converted them all from placed balls, four frees and a '65'.

As he was striking the '65' to level the game, the referee spotted something and blew his whistle just as it was sailing between the posts. So Johnny had to retake it. He held his nerve and put it over at the second time of asking to send us to a replay.

We were so relieved to get another chance at it because it looked like it was gone from us. We took full advantage the next time and beat them by six points. To be reigning All-Ireland and county champions in the same year was a special achievement.

I've pictures in my house of the four county title-winning teams. It's only myself, Johnny, Joe, Mick Coughlan, Ger Connors,and Liam Coughlan that started the four of them.

The perception was that Clareen had reached the end of the road heading into that season.

★★★

JOE

1999 WAS THE first time since '93 we failed to reach the county final.

We lost heavily to Birr in the semi-final. The bulk of our team was well into their thirties.

We were coming near the end of our tether.

Birr were building their next great team and getting stronger all the time. We were heading in the other direction.

We played them in the 2000 final. It turned out to be our last appearance in a senior decider.

It had been a very wet winter. Due to a few disputed dates, unplayable pitches and then the Foot and Mouth outbreak, the final ended up being delayed until the following March.

In hindsight, if it had gone ahead in December, it would have suited us better than the dry ground in March.

They hammered us 3-21 to 1-9.

That was our last stand as a team.

BILLY

EVERY FINAL YOU play in you should appreciate it. We've lads in our club now that would be delighted to even get to a senior final, but if I was involved with them I'd be telling them there's no point in getting there unless you win it.

I reached the county final 10 times in my career. Joe always says if you win half of them it's not too bad, but we didn't do that. We won four... lost six. Joe was involved in the 1985 defeat as well before we came along.

But if you asked me to go back and play them all again, I'd take what I got. Because we won some against Banagher that were extremely tight. We lost some against Birr that were very narrow as well.

So when Mick Coughlan asks us, 'Play 10, I'll give you four there now would you take it?' I'd take it. If you were a gambling man you'd have to.

★★★

JOHNNY

I NEVER GOT too beat up over not winning a Leinster with the club. We were such a small, little rural parish that we were so consumed by trying to get out of the county and beat the likes of Birr. Whereas Birr freewheeled a bit and then once they got out of Offaly, they kicked on and expressed themselves better. They possibly had a more balanced team overall. They had a lot of lads who played county and maybe didn't get fazed by playing in other pitches outside the county.

We definitely could have got to two Leinster finals. In 1995, Kilkenny's Glenmore beat us and went on to lift the club All-Ireland. In 1996, we lost to Dublin champions O'Tooles in a semi-final replay in Portlaoise. Kevin Kinahan was playing great stuff. He was unbeatable in the county final. He got a punctured rib up against Trim in the first round of Leinster and we drew with O'Tooles the first day.

If we had him that day I'd safely say we could have gotten over the line. We were being beaten by good teams to be fair. In 1988, we lost to Tony Doran's Buffer's Alley and they went on to win the club All-Ireland.

Overall, I think 1996 was our big chance. To be honest. I never lost too much sleep over it. Prevailing in Offaly was always the big prize for us.

XI

Davy

Three seasons...blink of an eye

Enter Babs!

The name's Bond...

Missing minutes

Thurles, it is!

WHELAHAN UP FRONT

★★★

JOHNNY

IN 2009, I HEADED off to Spain with friends on a golf trip. There were a few former Offaly hurlers among the crew. Before we boarded our flight from Dublin, I was in a mischievous mood.

In a bookshop in the airport I spotted Davy Fitzgerald's autobiography, which came out a few years earlier. I bought it for the laugh… to see if I'd get a reaction out of one of the lads when they saw me sitting by the pool reading it at some stage during the holiday.

During the flight, curiosity got the better of me. I pulled it out of my bag and had a flick through. The chapter on the eventful 1998 season caught my attention.

'I have nothing against Offaly, but we were the better team that year by a long shot,' Davy wrote. 'I acknowledge that the 1995 All-Ireland final could have gone either way, we got the breaks and we won it, but we were a far superior team three years later.

'Offaly won the All-Ireland, but as far as I was concerned, those players have OUR medals and it was OUR All-Ireland.'

That passage annoyed me when I read it… it didn't sit well with me. I closed the book and never read another word. For him to say that we had their medals was really unfair. We played in four All-Irelands. We felt we were entitled to win two. We proved ourselves over the three days against Clare.

Okay, the ball hopped in our favour when we were granted that third game, but then again we played far better than Clare the first day and they got a soft free to level it. It would have been an injustice if our summer ended like that. I felt it was very unsportsmanlike to be saying we had their medals in our pockets. He'd get up my nose a bit anyway. In fairness, he did give us bits of credit other than that. But that jibe was always something that stuck with me.

AS YOU GET older, each year that passes raises in its importance. The last thing you want to do is let one slip by. After the heights of 1994, three seasons passed in the blink of an eye without much success.

At the start of 1998 Michael 'Babs' Keating succeeded John McIntyre as manager. I was looking forward to working with him. He was an exciting appointment... he had pedigree. He'd won All-Irelands as a player and manager with Tipperary. He also had a big personality and came with a great reputation for fundraising. What I liked about him was that he had big ideas.

That much was clear when he introduced himself to us in a meeting at the County Arms Hotel. County board chairman Brendan Ward was there too.

'We're going to win the Leinster, then we're going to win the All-Ireland... and then we're going on a three-week world cruise!'

Brendan's jaw dropped. It was clearly the first he'd heard of it.

Babs had us winning the All-Ireland and we wouldn't be going on any Mickey Mouse holidays, *we were going on a world cruise.* We were obviously thrilled with this. We were thinking, *That's something to aim at now.* It was a nice carrot to dangle in front of us as we prepared to go back into the winter slog.

Then as the year went on I couldn't help thinking, *Is his heart really in it?*

I had an inkling it wasn't going to plan from the early stages. Even though he talked about winning the All-Ireland, I'm not sure if he really believed in us. A month or two in, there were a few guys on the panel whose names he still wasn't able to pronounce correctly. By that stage you should know your players inside out.

We didn't connect with his philosophy on hurling either.

The modern game is all about keeping possession and playing it short. That's exactly how he was trying to get us to play. One Sunday morning in training, we all stood around while he gave a demonstration for a drill. Babs was in the middle, with his arse out holding off a player.

He started roll rising the ball and backing into the player. 'This is how you do it. You win the ball and take him on.'

We looked at each other thinking, *Is this lad for real? Does he actually want us to play like this?* It was the complete opposite to everything we were ever told. Under Éamonn Cregan, the philosophy was never to get over the ball. Let it fly, move it fast and follow it in.

★★★

BILLY

ONE OF THE first things Babs did was put us on the Nutron diet. It was a new fad at the time. Tommy Lyons had the Offaly footballers on it in 1997 and they won the Leinster championship.

Before Christmas, we all headed down to Athlone to get blood tests that uncovered food intolerances. The results were analysed and we were told what we could and couldn't eat.

Potatoes, butter and gravy were on my red list. A lot of sweet things were ruled out. I was eating an awful lot of fruit, rice, chicken, fish… all that stuff. Some of the lighter lads could have potatoes or some steak or beef. Everyone bought into it. We followed this plan for a couple of months. After that, you gained a certain amount of weight back, but the idea was you didn't go back to what you originally were.

The weight flew off me. I lost a stone and three quarters.

I was up in our home house one evening. It was someone's birthday and the kitchen was full of cakes, buns and creams. My mother kept offering me a bun.

'No, I'm alright!'

My father looked at me.

'Are you alright? Will ya eat a bun.'

While the Nutron diet lost us weight, we weren't eating substantially. I was drinking three or four litres of water a day. I was probably after losing too much weight.

If you take away potatoes from your dinner every day for eight weeks, that's going to make a big difference on its own.

JOE

BABS WAS A player I looked up to as a young fella. When he came in as manager, I wasn't overly pally with him. In fact, I felt he was looking to push me out of the starting team. While I was 34, I made a big effort to keep myself in good shape.

I got the sense he was trying to get more young fellas into the team. When I was left on the bench for a couple of league games that spring, I could see I wasn't in his initial plans. That didn't bother me… I kept my head down and stayed training hard.

Babs had his favourites. He'd talk to some players and wouldn't talk to others. I fell into the latter category. That's just the way he was. His fitness trainer was Johnny Murray, an ex-army man. The training was torturous, up another level on what Derry O'Donovan had us doing. We started off in a gym in Shinrone doing circuit training. It was all bodyweight exercises, stuff he learned in the army. Then we moved onto the field in Banagher. Every night, we'd start and finish the sessions with these 3km runs. They were against the clock and we had to finish inside certain time limits as the year went on.

Johnny Murray was a lovely fella and that training certainly stood to us at the end of the season. However, as we came into the summer months the heavy stamina training continued. Traditionally at that time of year, we'd have done very little physical work… we'd usually do shorter, sharper stuff mixed in with plenty of hurling.

Babs let him take most of the training sessions and took things easy himself. Sometimes while we were warming up, he'd be inside on the physio table getting a rub. He had a back problem from playing golf. That sent out the wrong signals. A few minor things like that didn't rest easy with the players or his fellow selectors.

Our league form that year was quite poor. We only had a win over Antrim to show for our efforts. Then we hit a bit of turbulence when Babs resigned in May after only half the squad showed up to a play challenge match against Tipperary.

Like a few years earlier under Éamonn Cregan, the game had been organised the same day as a round the Offaly club championship. The match was fixed for Clonmel. The National League semi-finals took place in Semple Stadium earlier that day and a large crowd of 35,000 showed up.

Our game was on in the evening and I travelled with Johnny and Kevin Martin. The games in Thurles were over and we got caught in the traffic heading home. We just couldn't go south. It was chock-a-block.

After a while making no progress, we were between Thurles and Cashel when we took the decision to turn back. We weren't going to get there until 8.30pm or 9pm anyway. Babs wasn't happy about it.

The game had been arranged to raise money for John Leahy. Offaly had to borrow a couple of players from Tipperary to make a team. Babs took a bit of stick from the crowd for it. He felt let down, particularly because Clonmel was pretty much his hometown.

Babs stepped down that night but was coaxed back later in the week.

WE BEAT MEATH well in the Leinster quarter-final and went on to play Wexford in the semi-final. Considering they'd knocked us out in 1996 and '97, this was a big one for us. We struggled through most of that game. Our hurling wasn't fluent, yet they couldn't put us away. We stayed hanging in there and were two points down in the last minute when Johnny struck a goal. Brian Whelahan lobbed in a long-range free and a heap of players contested it. It dropped to the ground and Johnny pounced. He pulled on it through a forest of legs and it flew into the corner of the net past Damien Fitzhenry.

It was probably a goal that won us the All-Ireland. If he hadn't scored it, we were gone. There was no backdoor unless we got to the Leinster final. We got out of jail and stumbled on to face Kilkenny.

★★★

JOHNNY

LEADING INTO THAT Wexford game, I spent six weeks out injured with a broken thumb. I got a nasty belt in a club game against Kilcormac/Killoughey that left me with two fractures. I was off work for six weeks and couldn't do any of the hurling training with Offaly.

I used to get up every morning and do a 3km run near my house and a few sprints after. I might do the same in the evenings. The plaster on my hand didn't prevent me from running so I had no excuse not to fall behind the rest fitness-wise. I was probably never as fit when I rejoined full training shortly after the Meath game.

I was worried I wouldn't start against Wexford as we'd performed very well in the win over Meath. Paudie Mulhare had played in my position and was in good form. I hadn't much hurling done. Jesus, this looks like I'm going to be sitting on the bench.

Arriving at training on the Sunday before the semi-final, it felt strange... like I was playing for my place on the team. I normally wouldn't get too worked up about a training session because I never felt under any major pressure for a starting place.

We played a full in-house game. I was more spiky than I'd normally be. I was picked on the B team which really got my dander up and confirmed my concerns over a starting place. I went in thinking, *I need to create a bit of an impression here.*

I don't know how true that was, but in my head I needed to.

Myself and Paudie hopped off each other and had to be pulled apart at one stage. I was the instigator. He wasn't one to take a step back either. We ended up having a bit of a tussle although it didn't go as far as us coming to blows. I was trying to show I was ready to start the following week.

Thankfully, I got selected. I let it be known I was serious about getting back on the team.

John Troy was hitting the frees in my absence and he remained in the role after I returned. In fairness, John was hitting them well so management were right to stick with him. It was nearly a release for me, not having the extra pressure of free-taking duties on my shoulders.

I actually hurled better.

In a way, when you're not on the frees, it just allows your mind to really go hell for leather and concentrate on making an impact from general play. Not that you wouldn't anyway, but I think it takes a little bit of weight off your shoulders as regards responsibility.

I played quite well against Wexford.

I scored 1-3 and set-up a couple of scores even though it was my first day back.

JOE

I'LL NEVER FORGET the Sunday before the Leinster final. Normally a week out from a game of that magnitude, we'd play a good 60-minute training match in O'Connor Park and then ease off the following week to keep fresh for the game.

This time, Johnny Murray had us doing what resembled something you'd reserve for pre-season. Before the stadium was redeveloped, there was a hilly grass bank on the hospital side of the pitch. Deciding we needed a blow-out, Johnny had us sprinting up the hill about 20 times, one after another.

It was nearly something you'd do to prevent a lad from playing well the following week. It was completely contrary to what we were used to.

★★★

BILLY

DURING THE SAME session, Babs left early as he had somewhere to be. That didn't send a good message to the squad. I felt it was bad preparation and other players were the same. We felt he was letting us down a small bit. Then the wheels came off in the Leinster final.

We lost a dour game to Kilkenny 3-10 to 1-11. DJ Carey scored two goals from frees. If you took them out, there wasn't much in it. We were fit but sluggish, lacking that bit of sharpness. Kilkenny were fairly flat too.

The introduction of the backdoor meant we were still in the championship. Still alive. I don't know why Babs was so offended by our performance. Maybe his resentment over the Clonmel episode was still lingering.

To go out and speak about us the way he did after the game with those infamous comments to the media, I felt he was setting himself up to leave. He described the players as 'sheep running around in a heap'.

He said what he was trying to teach us was 'falling on deaf ears' and wondered if he was wasting his time with us. 'I'm not being listened to,' he continued. 'It's a vein running through this Offaly team of individualism, of not thinking of their colleagues. The players just sail along. There's not a lot of disappointment in that dressing-room. They just take every day as it comes.'

How could he expect to come back into an Offaly dressing-room after saying those things about his players? I don't buy the argument that he was trying to rile us up to get a reaction for the next day. In my view, his mind was made up that his race with us was run.

★★★

JOHNNY

NOT LONG AFTER Babs made those remarks to the press it filtered back to the team. We'd gotten to know a few reporters over the years and one of them mentioned to a player that Babs had given us a bit of a roasting. I found his words hurtful.

I don't think we deserved to be spoken of like that. Most managers nowadays will back their players in public even if they say something different inside the sanctity of the group. If Babs had to say what he said in the dressing-room, I don't think any of us would have had an issue with it.

To go out and call us 'sheep in a heap' like that, it didn't sit well with us. As an Offaly team, we were never disrespectful to any manager. We always bought into whoever was in charge of us. We gave every man his fair chance. We might not have agreed with all his methods, but whatever he was trying to get us to do, we did our best to implement.

We felt our underperformance that day was down to the fact we hadn't enough hurling done. The type of ball work we were doing wasn't lending itself to how we played. That was the biggest thing. I'd put it down to a clash of hurling styles and a lack of involvement from the manager on the training field.

As we always did on the Monday after a Leinster final, we went out for a few pints during the day. A crew of us had gathered in Whelahan's pub and were chatting about the fall-out from the game. Then Johnny Pilkington walked in the door.

Things went nuclear.

'Wait till you see tomorrow's paper!'

'What are you after saying now?'

It was quite funny. We had a few drinks on board at that stage and were in that sort of humour, but in the cold light of day you're scratching your head thinking, *was that the right thing for him to do?*

★★★

BILLY

FOR THE FOLLOWING day's *Irish Independent*, Johnny Pilkington did an interview unloading on Babs. He questioned his training methods and the decision to move John Troy out of centre-forward against Kilkenny.

'He's making it look like the Offaly players are idiots and undisciplined. It's stupid and unfair… Babs is washing his hands of all responsibility…You can't blame him for everything but you can't blame the players for everything either… we're all a team, We go down together and we win together. What he said will only cause trouble… we don't need this kind of stuff from Babs. It's very unprofessional of him.'

At the time we were a bit sceptical of the good it was going to do us. On the other hand, it was a case of the players fighting back. It was Johnny Pilkington leading the charge. There was nothing wrong about what he said, he was speaking from the heart and telling the truth.

I wouldn't have come out like that myself, but he did. Things happen for a reason. We probably wouldn't have won the All-Ireland if he didn't give that interview. We knew that night things were heading in a certain direction. Brendan Ward, to be fair to him, stood behind the players. By Tuesday evening, Babs was gone. Nineteen days out from an All-Ireland quarter-final, we were managerless and in disarray.

Although it made plenty of headlines, we didn't have much time to think about it. We were back in the firing line straightaway and had a big game coming up fast. By Babs leaving, it put more pressure on us as players. The whole country was watching this thing play out. *Here's Offaly with another manager gone. Three managers in the space of 18 months and these guys think they can win an All-Ireland?*

It was a black mark against us, but we felt Babs wasn't giving his all and looked for an excuse to go. It certainly wasn't a case of player power.

Paudge Mulhare took training on Tuesday and it was quite a good session. What that whole saga did was, it galvanised the troops.

We had a cause again. A siege mentality.

★★★

JOE

THE THURSDAY EVENING after the Leinster final, Michael Bond strolled into the Offaly dressing room for the first time.

I was living in Tullamore and was normally one of the first to arrive at training. Killian Farrell was in early too. Michael said nothing, just took off his coat and hung it up. He proceeded to take off his shoes and tog into a tracksuit.

Killian and I looked at one another. *Who is this fella? Where is he after coming out of?*

'Excuse me, is it any harm to ask you who you are?' I asked.

'I'm your new trainer.'

'Well, if you are, you may introduce yourself.'

'I'm Michael Bond… from Loughrea.'

That was my first meeting with him. We got no forewarning before we attended training that we had a new manager or that he was going to be there. He had experience coaching some club sides in Galway but hadn't managed at county level since he led the Galway under-21s to the All-Ireland in 1983. We knew none of this at the time.

He was principal of Loughrea Vocational School. He had an air of authority about him. He strived to make everyone feel valued in the set-up. He always made time to chat to wives and girlfriends, which showed his class. Behind his angelic face though he had a hard side. He was a good communicator and wouldn't be slow in telling you to pull your hurl when you had to. He had a cutting edge.

Not once did he mention the stuff that had gone on with Babs. He was extremely positive. Before one training session, I was pucking the ball back and forth with Brian Whelahan. I'd kill the ball dead as it arrived. As Bond walked by, he passed a comment to me… 'You have a brilliant first touch!'

Nobody ever gave me a compliment like that in all my years hurling. I kind of knew it myself, but he reinforced that. There's a great saying that, 'players will forget what a coach says, but they'll never forget how a coach makes them feel'. That was certainly the case with Bond.

Most importantly, Bond wanted to play the style of hurling that suited us. His approach to training was a breath of fresh air. We went back to ground hurling. For the first few weeks, my tongue was hanging out at training.

Earlier in the summer, the only ball that could come inside to me in the corner was when someone out the field mishit it. Everybody was shooting for their own score... we weren't playing like a team. You'd want a tracksuit on you playing corner-forward. Bond changed all that.

Now the ball was coming in... fast. Everything was done at speed. During training games, the ball would hardly be gone dead and another one would be fired in. The benefit of all the heavy training we did under Johnny Murray meant that when we focused more on speed work and hurling skills, we improved immensely.

Because he only had a fortnight to prepare us for Antrim, he scheduled a load of consecutive nights of training. We met up 11 times over his first two weeks. Now, we didn't go flat out every night... it was all short, sharp stuff. Some sessions might be purely focused on ball striking or we might go for a swim to recover.

One new drill he introduced for the forwards was executing a drop puck in front of goals. It's almost impossible for a goalkeeper to read. It could be executed in tight spaces. Although it seemed like a futile drill at the time, it paid off in spades when Joe Errity scored a goal from a drop puck in the All-Ireland final. Then after his second effort was saved, it was tapped home by Brian Whelahan.

★★★

JOHNNY

THINGS WERE HUMMING nicely in training. You could feel the whole atmosphere change within a couple of sessions... *We're actually at something here now.* We started to kick into gear. Then Michael Bond organised a challenge match with Kilkenny in Nowlan Park.

We shipped a heavy beating and they didn't even have a full team out. Shortly after half-time, I controlled a ball on the end of my hurl. Out of the corner of my eye, I could see a Kilkenny player coming in from my right side. As he attempted to cut out the ball, he followed through with the nose of his hurl, catching me clean across my cheekbone.

It was a country mile from the ball.

That was the last thing I remember. I was knocked unconscious. He badly broke my cheekbone. I vaguely remember being dragged off the field. I was rushed to hospital… I needed 18 stitches from just under my eye down to the lip.

I was drifting in and out of consciousness while the doctor was stitching up my face. He had his knee up on the trolley. I woke up in a panic. I probably had a concussion too, although it wasn't diagnosed at the time.

It was a scary moment. I walked in the door at home and my face was in pretty bad condition. It was all swollen… black and blue, with a load of stitches laced up along. Sinéad was that shocked when she saw me, that she started to cry. Joe had her pre-warned.

I still have a scar on my face from it. I didn't know who did it. I just knew it was an under-21 player that had been brought into the squad on trial. It was a careless stroke from a guy trying to make a name for himself.

A few years later in 2001, I was among a few Offaly lads brought out to hurl for the weekend in New York. We were representing the Offaly club and after the game we were having a few drinks in Gaelic Park.

I was sitting at the bar when this guy comes over and shakes my hand.

'I'm the guy that did that to you!' he said, pointing at my scar. That's how he introduced himself. I was shocked because I'd never met the guy before. Never knew his name… never even knew who he was.

I just replied, 'Oh right!' I didn't fall out with him but I didn't engage him in conversation either. I was a bit taken aback to be honest.

So I was sidelined again for a couple of weeks. I missed the Antrim game, which we won by nine points. It wasn't a vintage performance. Joe clipped four points, while Billy and John Troy scored 1-2 apiece.

We were starting to get our mojo back as our old friends from Clare appeared on the horizon.

BILLY

AT THE TIME we were in turmoil, a volcano had erupted in Clare.

Colin Lynch was sent-off at the start of a fiery Munster final replay. He was slapped with a three-month suspension. Brian Lohan received his marching orders in the same game and was also banned for the All-Ireland semi-final. After a bad-tempered bid to fight their case that became a big media frenzy, Ger Loughnane was banished from the sideline too.

If we thought we had problems, the stuff going on down there was crazy.

★★★

JOHNNY

A LOT OF it was self-inflicted. They were bringing a lot of scrutiny on themselves… it was self-destructive. They didn't need to be doing any of it because they had a serious team. They were reigning All-Ireland champions after a brilliant season in 1997 and going for a third All-Ireland in four years.

Loughnane was the one driving it and I felt it was a distraction to them. It wasn't good management in my book. Okay, you fight your players' case but there were better ways of handling it. All that stuff didn't do Clare any favours in the long run either.

★★★

BILLY

LOCALLY, THERE WASN'T much optimism about our chances. We were coming off a poor Leinster final and a single digit win over Antrim. The Tullamore Show was taking place the same weekend and quite a small Offaly crowd travelled to Croke Park.

The organisers of the Tullamore Show actually asked Joe if he could get the

All-Ireland semi-final changed to the following weekend. That's how much interest there was in our game.

We were completely written off coming in. The bookies had us as 10/1 outsiders. Pete Finnerty had written a newspaper column that ran with the headline, **Offaly should ring in sick.**

Bond stuck it up in the warm-up area, along with some other similarly themed clippings from other media coverage of us. Proper dressing-room wall material! Hand on heart, it was the most determined team I ever saw in a dressing-room. Here we were, four years after winning the All-Ireland and three years after falling to Clare by a point in the final, being completely overlooked.

That all fuelled our fire.

We threw caution to the wind on the first day and hit them with everything. We should have beaten Clare there and then. In hindsight, it was just as well we didn't. The two extra games really prepared us for the final and got the crowd invested too.

Johnny Pilkington scored 1-1 late in the game to overturn a losing position and edge us one clear. Jimmy Cooney awarded a very soft free against Kevin Kinahan and Jamesie O'Connor dispatched it. We headed for a replay not knowing the drama that was about to unfold.

Even though we could have sneaked it, our performance restored a bit of pride in the jersey.

Our preparation for the replay was far from ideal. That morning, we learned of the passing of Ted Mulhare, father of Paudie and a relative of Paudge. Paudie's unavailability meant we were without a starting forward.

Then the team bus was held up by the Tall Ships event in Dublin and only got to Croke Park about half an hour before throw-in. Normally you'd need close to an hour for fellas to get themselves warmed up and ready... factoring in rubs, strappings, tactics talks and all that.

Everything was rushed. We hardly had time to tog out.

To make matters worse, Brian Whelahan was left behind in the Lucan Spa Hotel, where we had gathered earlier in the day. There was a mix-up and we ended up going without him.

He was in an awful rush to get across to Croke Park, requiring a Garda escort there.

JOE

IT FELT LIKE it was going to be one of those days. I missed a penalty in the first-half and four minutes into the second period we were 10 down. At the interval, management made a few switches that eventually bore fruit.

Johnny was brought out from corner-forward to midfield. Michael Duignan went back to the half-back line and Brian Whelahan pushed into the attack. Billy was introduced off the bench. Johnny, in particular, had a brilliant second-half, probably as good a half hour of hurling as he ever put down. He drove us on, getting on a mountain of ball in midfield.

Billy sniped 1-1, and then Joe Errity won a penalty and drilled it into the net himself. We kept plugging away, although we were lucky not to lose Michael Duignan to a red card. He probably should have gone for a loose stroke on David Forde, but he managed to talk Jimmy Cooney around.

We were back within three points when Jimmy sounded the final whistle. I wasn't aware it had been blown up short. When you're in the heat of battle, you don't tend to be following the clock. Devastated our comeback had fallen short, I trudged straight into the dressing-rooms and thought no more of it. We were out of the All-Ireland.

BILLY

THERE WAS A bit of a raucous going on with the referee, and a few players had gathered around him. Duignan was in his face straightaway. Yet at the same time when we left the field and went into the dressing-rooms, as far as we were concerned the match was done and dusted.

What stood to us was the fact Ger Loughnane admitted in a TV interview on the field straight afterwards that the game was blown up early. For Jimmy Cooney it was a genuine mistake but for us, I think he saved our bacon. Clare were fairly confident at the time and there were still three points in it.

★★★

JOHNNY

WE WERE REALLY after coming back into the game. There were two minutes of normal time and three minutes of injury time left. *Would we have levelled it? Who knows?* Maybe we would have…if you were a betting man you'd probably say it was doubtful.

Five minutes is a long time in any game and considering what we had done in 1994, we deserved a chance. For Ger Loughnane to come out and call it as it was in that interview, that certainly helped our case. And our supporters were the biggest thing.

I MOVED OFF the pitch fairly quickly and into the dressing-rooms. It was there where I first heard of a possible timekeeping issue. I did feel there was an injustice done, but expected it was just going to be one of those things. *You're going to have to suck it up and get on with it.*

After losing a big game, I didn't like hanging around. I showered, togged in and headed straight up to the bar. Within 10 minutes of that final whistle going, I was sitting up in the players' lounge with a pint of Heineken in my hand.

A couple of the Offaly lads were standing at the big glass facade that faced out onto the pitch. I walked over and looked down. I couldn't believe my eyes. Our supporters had staged a protest, taking to the field and sitting down in the sunshine.

I hadn't realised any of this was going on. I was shocked. As I watched the Offaly people execute a coup, I started to think, *Is this possible? Could we get another crack at it?*

★★★

BILLY

KERRY WERE DUE to play Kildare in an All-Ireland under-21 'B' hurling final afterwards and that was put on ice. Brendan Ward came out and asked supporters to move off the pitch. He showed a great level of authority, both in how he promised the crowd we would 'fight tooth and nail' for our cause, and the way he dealt with the media afterwards.

If the fans hadn't invaded the pitch, I think the whole thing would have been brushed under the carpet. They were brilliant the way they made a big deal out of the injustice.

★★★

JOE

MY OWN VIEW at the time was there had to be a replay…without a doubt. The GAA had no other choice. How could you have 10,000 people sitting on a pitch and not give a replay, particularly when Jimmy Cooney blew up early and admitted to blowing up early?

We were having a few pints after the game and were all getting steamed up and dehydrated. The only rehydration in those days was a pint of Smithwick's or Heineken.

Drinking water after games was alien to us.

By the time we got back to the hotel, the Lucan Spa, we decided we'd have a team meeting. It was starting to look like there might be a replay, but we'd heard nothing official.

We couldn't get a private room. So once we finished our grub in the big function room we were in, we had it out. All our partners were there as well, off to one side. Michael Bond chaired it. He believed a replay would be called and wanted to train the following evening at 4pm.

Johnny Pilkington said he wouldn't train as there was no point, we weren't going to be in the championship. Michael Duignan agreed with him.

Billy stood up anyway and said, 'If training is tomorrow evening at 4pm, Michael… I'll be there. I'm not listening to any more of this' and he walked out the door. I spoke as well, echoing Billy's sentiments.

The thought of saying I wouldn't be going training wouldn't have entered my head.

BILLY

ONE MORE TRAINING session wasn't going to kill us, regardless of whether we got the replay or not. We landed back in Birr that night around 10.30pm and instead of continuing on with the night as we normally would, everyone just packed up and went home.

When the news came through the following morning, it was like winning the lotto.

We were handed a lifeline.

I was dropped for the first game against Clare and only came off the bench in the 62nd minute. I was disappointed to have been left off again the second day. The fact I scored a goal after coming on, I felt I had put myself back in the frame to start. I arrived at training determined to make an impression. That's the way I was thinking.

I had a spring in my step walking into O'Connor Park that evening. And the crowd that showed up! It felt like something different was happening. There was a different vibe again, a new energy there.

And we knew that this was going to be a cracker of a game. Our confidence was growing all the time. Even though we were losing that game by three, we'd come back from 10 points down. And we were starting to say, *We have the measure of these lads now. If we play the way we can, we can take them out.*

All roads led to Thurles the following Saturday.

That was one of the best weeks of training we ever put down. There was just an energy about the place… everyone was looking for tickets. Playing an All-Ireland semi-final in Thurles was a new experience for us as well.

The media narrative was that Semple Stadium was like a home pitch for Clare and they don't lose there. We went down and did a training session there on Wednesday evening.

It just felt brilliant… the pitch was perfect.

JOE

THURLES WAS A bit of fresh scenery for us. It's only 30 miles down the road from Birr, so it almost felt like playing at home.

Spirits were high the night we trained in Semple. We drove down in cars. I travelled down with Kevin Martin. We did a light session to get a feel of the place... mainly some ground hurling and shooting practice.

We had a puck around on the field and did some shooting drills at both ends. There was no place on the field that I couldn't put the ball over from. No matter where I got it, I could split the posts. There are times in your life when everything feels right. There were often other occasions when I couldn't see the ball going over. I was just in that vein of form.

The second replay came around quickly. We landed in Thurles on the bus and there was a carnival atmosphere about the place... the buzz was electrifying. There were people everywhere. When we crawled through the square in the town, the Offaly crowd gathered on either side of the bus.

Marie was on the team bus and what she remembers was the eerie silence as we passed through.

There was no shouting from the fans. They started banging on the side of the bus, almost like an Indian war chant.

When we walked into the grounds, every second steward in Semple wished us luck, which was most unusual given we were playing a Munster side. We felt everyone outside of Clare was on our side that day, as opposed to 1995 when the whole country wanted them to beat us.

Marie's mother lived across the road from the Poor Clare nuns enclosed order on College Road in Cork. The family were very friendly with Sister Paul Warner, who was a nun with a big interest in Offaly hurling. The week before the game, she sent us an envelope with a bunch of blessed miraculous holy medals. I handed them out to the players in the dressing-room.

All the lads pinned them to the inside of their shorts.

★★★

JOHNNY

BOND HAD THE perfect habit of just saying enough at the right time. He was all about showing heart and grit… letting fly and winning your position.

He was the first manager we saw that dragged the wing-forwards back out the field. He wanted them 70 or 80 yards from goal to clog up Clare's attacking end of the field. It was more of a defensive role and it left space in front of our corner-forwards. That tactic bottled Clare up and they didn't get as much space as they were used to. It worked a treat. We held them to 0-13, their lowest total of the championship.

I was enjoying a new role at midfield alongside Johnny Pilkington. I'd played there regularly with the club and felt I was a good reader of the game. I tried to make myself available for a pass out of defence and just kept moving all the time. I remained in that role for the last five years of my career. Even though I was moving further away from goal, I was able to pick my moments to get forward five or six times in a game to get a shot off.

As an atmosphere, I'd put that clash up there with an All-Ireland final. The contest was 100 miles an hour. You only had split seconds on the ball. That was the way we liked to play anyway… let it fly, follow it in and see where that takes you.

We led by three at half-time. My concern was could we keep that level of intensity up for 70 minutes? I had no need to be worried. All our big players came up trumps. Joe scored five points in a Man of the Match display.

★★★

BILLY

CLARE THOUGHT THEY'D bully us that day, but we didn't allow it. We were so well-prepared mentally for anything that was thrown at us. Stephen Byrne made a few great saves in goals that kept us in front.

We won by three points. After everything we'd overcome that summer, it was an incredible feeling when the final whistle went. It was an unforgettable victory.

Ger Loughnane came into our dressing-room and was full of praise for us.

'What a difference a week makes!' he said. 'I was in here last week commiserating with you. Here I am to congratulate you on behalf of every hurling person in Clare. For your tremendous display today and your deserved win today.'

Even though we came out on top against the reigning All-Ireland champions in an epic trilogy, we didn't feel complete unless we lifted the Liam MacCarthy. Kilkenny waited five weeks to play us in the final. We only had a two-week wait from the All-Ireland semi-final, which suited us perfectly.

The final coming around so quickly was perfect for us.

EVEN THOUGH MANAGEMENT never said anything to us, I knew before the match something was up with Brian Whelahan. He had a 'flu on him and wasn't feeling well. They gave him some tablets and let him at it.

You could see he wasn't himself. Brian McEvoy got off to a fast start on him. Michael Bond jigged things around. Michael Duignan went back to wing-back and Brian Whelahan was moved up to full-forward. That move revitalised him and he started coming into the game… it worked a treat.

I was playing in the corner and being marked by Willie O'Connor. He was an exceptionally clever hurler, a ball-playing corner-back. Against Waterford he swept up a load of dirty ball that Pat O'Neill broke down to him. Bond's tactic was to get Willie far enough from goal so he couldn't do that against us.

So I drifted way out from my usual position. Willie couldn't leave me on my own 40 yards from goal because I was within shooting range. He had to come after me. Joe was playing at corner-forward that day. The move left loads of room inside for himself and Brian to make hay.

★★★

JOHNNY

LIKE IN ANY game, if you're feeling unwell sometimes you can play your way through it. Once Brian got on a few balls, things started to roll for us. The whole team fed off the back of that.

Myself and Johnny Pilkington knew we'd have to put in a huge shift defensively and work our socks off to link the play from defence to attack. Even though we were a new midfield partnership, we had a good understanding of each other's games. We agreed in the dressing-room before we went out that he would sit a bit deeper and I'd try and get forward to support our attack.

I just tried to keep the ball moving as much as possible. Like the third Clare game, it was a real battle at midfield… we were up against Peter Barry and Philip Larkin. One of them clattered into me about five minutes into the second-half. I got a knee straight into my thigh, giving me a dead leg. It was fairly painful.

The physio came in. I told him, 'I'm gonna keep going!' Even though it was throbbing with pain, I started to run it off. The key with a dead leg is to keep it moving because if you stop at all, you can feel it tightening up.

As the half progressed, I couldn't sustain it. I was pulling my left leg behind with a few minutes left. I signalled to the bench to take me off. Billy had gone off a few minutes earlier after getting a bang on the knee. The two of us were side by side on the bench, praying we'd see it out.

It was only in the end that we pulled away. We were leading by two points when I came off and it was still hanging in the balance. DJ stood over a 20-metre free and drilled it over the bar. Then Brian got his goal near the end.

★★★

BILLY

WHILE THE FINAL score of 2-16 to 1-13 looked reasonably comfortable, it was only in the last three or four minutes that we made it safe.

It was a nice place to be knowing we had the game won a few minutes out. It's a lovely feeling. It was nowhere near as chaotic as 1994. They had better control over the crowd that year, even though a good few still made it out onto the field when it ended.

The fact we defeated one of hurling's big three in the final made it even sweeter. That's not to make light of Galway or Limerick, but there's a level of satisfaction in beating a traditional power in the All-Ireland.

To win a second one was huge for us. From the time we won the first one we were saying to ourselves, did we want to be known as the team that just won the one All-Ireland. In 1994 they said we stole it. Until you get back there and win the second one… that was always going to be thrown at us.

JOE

PERSONALLY, 1998 WAS the most memorable All-Ireland win I was involved in.

I was 35 and played consistently well over the year. I scored 1-20 from play over the course of the championship and showed I was still able to keep up with the younger lads. I worked harder than any other year to keep myself in shape.

Michael Bond gave me the licence to make switches on the field if I felt they'd benefit the team. I scored my first point off Tom Hickey in the corner and my second off Pat O'Neill after moving into full-forward. It was a day where every score counted.

Given all that happened with the Babs saga, Bond coming in and the three epic games with Clare, it was an unreal year. We played eight championship games, the most we had ever done. In 1994 it only took us four games to lift the Liam MacCarthy Cup. In 1981, we needed just three.

I had the honour of being the first Offaly hurler to win three All-Ireland medals on the field of play, equalling Martin Furlong's record in football. It was a good return from five appearances in the final.

★★★

BILLY

LONG BEFORE I ever won one, I was fascinated by the pictures of the All Star teams in pubs. In Percy's in Kinnitty, they had a wall adorned with photos of teams from the 70s and 80s. I nearly knew all the names off by heart at one stage.

To actually make it onto one of them was a huge honour. While it's a team game, when you're called onto the stage and handed one of those awards, it makes it very personal. I won the first of my two All Stars in 1994. It was the same year there was a mix-up with Brian Whelahan. He was chosen as Hurler of the Year, yet missed out on an All Star. He was nominated in both wing-back positions. The people voting on it presumed he was going to get it on the other wing. So Davy Clarke from Limerick got one and Kevin Martin took the other slot.

I didn't know I was going to win that year. The football was announced beforehand… The hurlers had to wait until the ceremony itself. Myself, Johnny and Kevin Kinahan were all winners that night. It was a fair haul for Clareen to have three players named on the same All Star team. It meant a lot to our club.

When I was interviewed, I spoke about my pride in the club for producing us. There were a lot of people that helped us all through the years that allowed us reach the heights we did.

Our father was always very proud when any of us won an All Star. He wasn't a man that would be clapping you on the back or anything like that. But he would say privately, 'Well done!'

★★★

JOE

TO SEE BILLY, Johnny and Kevin Kinahan bring home All Stars in 1994 was brilliant for Clareen. I'd be lying if I said I wasn't disappointed that I didn't join them. On the night they were announced, RTE teed it up by remarking that it looked like us three brothers were going to win one each. Ultimately, the two lads got chosen and I didn't. It was a very public thing, we were all interviewed on the night before the awards were announced.

I had a very good season. I scored 1-2 from play in the final. I felt that if I wasn't replaced against Limerick, I'd have finished it with an All Star. John Leahy was selected ahead of me on the basis of his league performances, which was unusual. He was the only player to win an All Star without playing in a championship game.

The bottom line is that it's an All-Ireland medal that really matters. That being said, All Stars are nice to win. It would have been lovely for the three of us to win one together, but it didn't happen.

I was 36-years-old when I was finally selected on the All Star team in 1998. That was huge.

All Stars are hard won. I was nominated for the first time aged 20. I had a number of nominations over my career, so to win it near the end was even sweeter.

★★★

JOHNNY

I GOT EIGHT consecutive All Star nominations between 1994 and 2001. I was fortunate enough to make the team three times in my career. It's a brilliant honour, but only in hindsight do you really appreciate what it means.

They're a bonus at the end of the year. You do feel for the others that don't get one. When you're part of a team, you're only as good as the lads you have around you. They're such small margins. You could have three lads vying for one position who had super years and two of them would lose out. You need a few things to run your way and that's not to underestimate getting one or anything like that. But you do need to be a little bit fortunate.

Billy and I missed out on the chance to head off on All Star tours in 1994 and '95. The trips that were there in the 80s were discontinued in the early 90s. They were eventually revived in 1999 after eight years.

★★★

JOE

MUCH LATER IN my career, hurling provided the opportunity for memorable trips to Inverness in Scotland. A less exotic location than All Star tours, but it was a privilege to manage the Irish Shinty team for three years. I had Jim McKernan of Antrim and Waterford's Kevin Ryan assisting me. My good friend Ciaran 'Sod' Daly also helped out on those trips. It was a different challenge. You were picking players from the weaker counties and allowed four marquee players from the Liam MacCarthy Cup teams.

The lads from the top counties were always delighted to be asked along. It was an honour for them to wear the Ireland jersey. We always went out to win and managed to do that for three consecutive years. The two associations kept tinkering with the rules to try and sway things in Scotland's favour. We were hell bent on not letting them beat us.

The Scots were well supported in Bught Park. Hearing them passionately singing the *Flower of Scotland* before games was an experience. The Shinty Association in Scotland are great people. Very tough on the field but when the game is over they're very hospitable.

One year the Scots were pulling timber. Jackie Tyrrell was in the middle of it and things were getting heated. He pulled a stroke at a ball and pushed in his marker's front teeth. The Scotland player had to be replaced... he had to go off and get them straightened back out but landed down to the function that evening. It was all left on the field. Himself and Jackie had a great night together.

I REPRESENTED LEINSTER a few times during my playing career but was never fortunate enough to win a Railway Cup medal. So, it was a privilege to get the opportunity to also manage Leinster between 2012-14. I was appointed by Leinster Council chairman Martin Skelly. John Conran, Derek Lyng and Humphrey Kelleher were my selectors.

When we had a few training sessions, the first players to show up were always the Kilkenny lads. They were very easy to work with... they all rowed in. As soon as they hit the field, they trained as if it was a championship game.

In 2012, when we won the competition, our side from number two to nine was all black and amber... Paul Murphy, Noel Hickey, Jackie Tyrrell, Tommy Walsh, Brian Hogan, JJ Delaney, Michael Fennelly and Michael Rice. It was a formidable side. Our front six included Eoin Larkin, TJ Reid, Richie Power and Richie Hogan. Shane and Ryan O'Dwyer made up the attack Joe Bergin, Rory Hannify and David Kenny were the other Offaly lads selected, so it was great to have them involved. We beat Munster in the semi-final and Connacht in the final. We won the competition again in 2014, beating Connacht in the final in Croke Park before an International Rules game.

When I was young, the Railway Cup was a huge thing. It's a pity they can't find somewhere for it in the calendar. Every player I rang to be involved, not one of them said no... it was always yes.

XII

A father's advice

1999

First retirement?

THE GREAT LOSS

The cats are back

Cork

Billy goes

The last hurrah?

JOHNNY

THE MORNING AFTER Cork beat us in the 1999 All-Ireland semi-final, myself and Joe visited our father in Tullamore Hospital.

We were due to meet the Offaly lads in town that afternoon for a few end of season pints. The Monday session was always a good day, even though disappointment naturally lingered. It was nice to chill out with your teammates and unwind at the end of a long campaign. But first on the agenda that day was saying hello to our dad and getting his views on the game. He'd always have it well analysed by that stage. Where it went right or wrong, or some incident that took place.

Even though he could hardly talk at this stage, he remained very forthright. Just as we were wrapping up our visit, he turned to Joe.

'Sure, you may retire now!'

He took Joe by surprise. I could see he was taken aback.

***

JOE

I JUST REPLIED, 'Ah sure we'll see!'

His comment always stuck with me because he'd rarely have said something like that. He probably knew he wasn't going to be around for much longer and could see the toll it was taking on me to hang in there with Offaly. He saw first-hand the effort I had to put in to keep playing at that level. A couple of years earlier after we lost to Wexford in 1997, I was captain and down in the dumps. He called to my house in Tullamore and we went for a few pints.

He knew I'd be disappointed and perhaps thought it was my last game with the county. It was most unusual for him to take the time out from farming. So after 1999, I could see why he thought I should pack it in. This time he was more direct.

His heart was always in the right place. But still I didn't listen to him.

DESPITE TURNING 36 before the start of the 1999 season, the thought of retirement didn't cross my mind. We had an All-Ireland title to defend and I wasn't going to walk away from that challenge.

Michael Bond stayed on as manager and he gave me some time away from the team. I didn't return to collective training until early April and only featured in one National League game.

Bond gave me plenty of space and didn't hound me to come back. He knew, along with the dogs on the street, that I was doing my training in the Tullamore Harriers Athletic Club, a running track right on my doorstep.

Having the trust of the manager to delay my return certainly helped the longevity of my county career. I always came back in good shape, just requiring some match sharpness to get up to speed. I used to start my training on my own on St Stephen's Day every year. After that, I trained every second day without fail. I always tried to have a little bit more work done than everyone else, especially as I got older.

Marie and I flew out to Boston in March to support a fundraiser for a local Offaly man. I still maintained my training regime over there. I was there for five days and got my running done on three of them.

Being able to do my own training reduced the risk of getting injured and meant I was fresh when the summer came around. My breakfast during the championship consisted of two raw eggs mixed in orange juice. Another thing that aided me in my later years was working closer to home. Between 1991 and early '98, I commuted to the ESB's head office in Dublin. I worked in the accounts department. It involved getting the train up every morning from Tullamore. I'd cycle from Heuston Station over to Fitzwilliam Street and return again in the evenings. It was an 11-hour day.

That was a busy time, so moving back to the midlands after seven years made a huge difference to the body. I got a position as HR manager alongside former Offaly footballer Sean Lowry. It was a tough few years in the ESB around the midlands. The peat stations in Rhode, Ferbane and Shannonbridge in Offaly, plus Lanesboro in Longford, were being closed. I got on great with Sean and we often reminisce about those days. Our job was to manage the de-manning of the closure stations. We had to manage the voluntary redundancy process for those wishing to leave the company. The ones that stayed were reassigned, retrained and reskilled to work in other parts of the company.

Following that process, I went to work as HR manager for the two new peat-power stations built in Shannonbridge and Lanesboro. They were state of the art stations with new work practices from the old ones.

In 2010, I moved to ESB Networks Business as property manager. It's a wide-ranging, national role that takes me all over the country. I've been with the ESB all my working life. They're a great company to work for. The camaraderie there is a huge thing. I met some fantastic people there over the years. I worked in so many different areas, there's loads of opportunities for anyone who wants to better themselves. It's encouraged all the time.

I completed an MBA over two years from Coventry University after retiring from Offaly. More recently I completed a diploma in personal and executive coaching.

WHEN OUR FATHER got sick in April 1999, it was a huge blow to all of us. It came out of the blue. He was a healthy man who'd been farming all his life. He was very active and on the go the whole time. I'll never forget the day I got the news. It started out with a toothache that didn't go away. He got it checked out and was referred to the ENT surgeon in Tullamore, Dr Kieran O'Driscoll.

They took a biopsy and sent it away for testing. I was sitting at work in the ESB offices in Ferbane when Dr O'Driscoll called me.

'Can you bring your father down to see me? The results of his biopsy are back and I need to talk with him.'

I rang my mother straightaway. 'Daddy has to go down to Tullamore to see the surgeon. I'll collect ye in half an hour!' I didn't fully know how bad the news was at the time, but because of the urgency I knew it wasn't good.

When I arrived my father was sitting at the kitchen table. He was dressed in his good clothes and ready to go. When I walked in the door, I could tell he was searching my facial expression for signs if I knew anything. I found it very hard to hold it together. Inside, I was choking up.

Like any man of that generation, he was never one to show much emotion. Deep down, he probably knew something wasn't right. That's why it caught me off guard when, as we walked out the front door towards the car, he stopped and started to sob. He used a handkerchief to wipe away his tears. Mam was still inside the house.

I wrapped my arms around him to console him.

His only words were, 'I hope I don't suffer much!'

Those words will stay with me for the rest of my life. In the hospital the bad news was delivered to him. Throat cancer.

He always had a particular dread of throat cancer. A man he knew from Clareen died of it years before that and my father often spoke about how much everyone said he suffered. Dr O'Driscoll performed a huge operation on him soon after. It was followed by chemotherapy and radium treatment.

But the reality is he suffered a lot in his last year. We all witnessed that and felt for him. It was a tough year for the family. Especially my mother, who looked after him in every way she could.

★★★

BILLY

HE BROUGHT ME into the cow shed one day and told me the news.

'I've to go for an operation. It's not good. We have to try and get some of our affairs in order.'

I knew then it was going to be the end. He was very brave about it. You could see he had a big battle ahead of him… He was a full year in and out of hospital before he passed away.

He had his operation at the end of May. At the time it was a 30-70 success rate.

If he didn't have it, he wouldn't have had much time. We hoped for the best, that it would remove all of the cancer. At the time we thought it had, but it came back.

He lost part of his tongue due to the surgery and found it hard to communicate. The farm was busy at the time. Even though he found it hard to talk after the surgery, he could write notes. His head was still in the farming space for the first few months. He'd write a note asking has a cow calved yet?

★★★

JOHNNY

MY MOTHER RANG me to see if we were around, as they were on the way back from the hospital.

'Can we meet ye somewhere quiet, we have something to tell ye.'

I didn't ask too many questions but I thought it was strange they wouldn't call down to the house. In hindsight, Jack was 21 months old and Emma was only born six weeks earlier, so they'd be a handful. I suggested the back bar in Spollens which I knew would be quiet.

The minute they walked in I knew something was seriously wrong. My father welled up and gave both myself and Sinéad a big hug. I had never seen him show emotion like that before.

'The news is not good,' he said. 'I have the boyo and I have a huge battle on my hands.' He explained what he'd just been told and gave a brief outline of what was to follow. He was determined to fight this thing to the bitter end. The four of us just sat there drinking a few pints and glasses of Guinness, chatting about anything and everything. We were trying not to think about what lay ahead.

★★★

JOE

ONE DAY. I brought him home from St Luke's Hospital in Dublin where he was getting treatment. We passed through a number of small villages as we approached home. As we were coming into Kinnitty, the final village on the route, he asked, 'Are we not going to stop for a drink?'

It was the tradition of the old people that if you went somewhere as far as Dublin, you never came home without stopping in to have a drink. Life was too short not to have time for a chat and a drink.

Even though at the time, he could hardly drink because he never fully regained his swallow after the operation. We pulled into Giltraps and he managed to drink a glass of Guinness. I thought he'd want to get home as quickly as possible. But he was that sort of man.

★★★

JOHNNY

FOLLOWING HIS OPERATION, I'd go in early in the mornings before work and visit him. I'd head to work and go training afterwards.

He had such an interest in hurling that we were trying to do anything we could to give him a lift. He couldn't go to the matches anymore and was watching them on TV. We were conscious that seeing Offaly win might raise his spirits a bit.

Trying to keep performing on the hurling field while all this was going on, it was a lot to deal with. That's the part of sport people on the outside don't realise. They don't know what's going on in a player's personal life. They see you in a match on a Sunday and wonder why you're not performing as well as you should be. You might be after spending the whole week in and out of the hospital… Hurling could be the last thing on your mind. You just don't know what's going on inside a player's head.

★★★

JOE

HURLING WHILE ALL this was going on was tough, there's no denying it. But what else would we do? We weren't going to stay at home and sit looking at one another. He wouldn't want that.

It was much harder on our mother than anyone. At least we had our own families. And we could go out and play hurling to take our mind off things for an hour or two. Having that outlet was a release for us. We saw off Wexford in the Leinster semi-final, scoring 1-13 between the three of us.

I played corner-forward and posted 1-5… it was only my second game since the previous September's All-Ireland final.

★★★

BILLY

KILKENNY BEAT US pretty well in the Leinster final for the second year running, banishing some demons for the 1998 All-Ireland in the process. Brian Cody was in his first year as manager and it was plain to see they had an abundance of talent coming through. Henry Shefflin and John Power emerged to join a forward line that was already capable of racking up big scores. The 5-14 they put past us was no fluke… defensively they were solid too.

Our team was starting to slip somewhat. A little bit of staleness was creeping in. While we were always capable of producing a performance, we couldn't do it consistently anymore. Although we were still the second best team in Leinster, Kilkenny seemed to be streaking away from us all the time. We picked up a lot of injuries during the league so Michael Bond focused more on hurling than the hard work we probably needed early in the year. He didn't have a fitness trainer with him. He was doing it all himself, which wasn't ideal.

JOE SAT OUT the All-Ireland quarter-final with Antrim with a dead leg. It was the first championship game he missed for Offaly in six years.

The Kilkenny defeat didn't bother us too much. We had another shot through the backdoor. We were always at our best when our backs were against the ball. Having been fortunate in previous years with injury, we seemed to pick up a lot of them that season. We defeated Antrim easily enough and faced Cork in the semi-final. They beat us by two points in a brilliant game of hurling. We were really fired up for it. We started well and led by a point at the interval, although it should have been three or four.

We needed every score we could get because Cork were always going to come back at us. They were younger and fitter. We were 0-16 to 0-14 up with 62 minutes gone. They outscored us 0-5 to 0-2 in the last 10 minutes, which was a killer. We left it behind us. I always say that we just didn't train hard enough in 1999. We were a better hurling team than Cork but didn't have the legs to stay with them over 75 minutes.

★★★

JOHNNY

I HURLED OKAY on the day. I was marking Mickey O'Connell, who was an up and coming midfielder. He scored five points in the Munster final. I looked forward to the challenge and measuring myself off him.

I felt that was our last chance to win an All-Ireland. We still had the nucleus of a serious outfit. It turned out to be Billy's last game in an Offaly jersey. Martin Hanamy followed him into retirement too. John Troy and Hubert Rigney were on and off the panel the next year for various reasons.

That's four players from your starting 15. If we'd gotten through to the final that year, I felt we would have had a better chance of winning it than we did in 2000. For most of the Cork game, we were in control. We played really well despite the talk that the Offaly team were on the slide. John Troy snatched a ball off Brian Corcoran and put it over. Johnny Pilkington went to a new role at wing-forward and scored a brace.

Dickie Murphy's performance was criticised afterwards. We always had a little issue with him. He would smile and laugh, but at the same time we always felt he was hard on us. That goes for the 1995 final and especially the '99 semi-final.

★★★

BILLY

THERE WAS A vital moment in that game where John Troy did his trademark move where he chopped the ball into his hand and split the posts. Dickie Murphy blew him for picking it off the ground. John Gardiner drove the free over the bar.

That's a two-point swing and it cost us on the day.

That's not to say Cork didn't deserve to win. They were a young, coming team but we were well in with them. We were after taking plenty of stick after losing the Leinster final by 10 points. The win seemed to fill Cork with confidence. They went on and beat Kilkenny in the final, 0-13 to 0-12.

The Cork game was the last time the three of us hurled together for Offaly.

★★★

JOHNNY

OUR FATHER PASSED away on April 7, 2000. We knew he was near the end. Thankfully, the whole family was at his bedside in the hospital when he peacefully passed away.

They're tough times to think back on. You adjust to the idea that he's going to die, but it doesn't make it any easier when the time comes. He was 64 then, still a young man. He was coming to the end of his working career on the farm. He was getting ready to hand it over to Billy. He loved a pint, chatting about hurling and heading to matches. He could have had a great 15 or 20 years of retirement if he didn't get sick.

He spent his whole life working hard to get all of us up, reared and out the door. This was his time to live and enjoy his later years, but he missed all that. He was great with the grandkids.

He got a raw deal in the overall scheme of things.

It would have been great for Mam to have that company as she got older as well.

BILLY

IT LEFT A big void in our mother's life. She was only 58 when he died.

She was a very young woman with nine children that were all nearly grown up. And next thing your husband dies on you.

It took her a long time to recover from it. She was after putting in a very hard 12 months before that as well. We were in and out of the hospital, but mammy was there all the time.

She took the brunt of it.

★★★

JOE

OUR NATIONAL LEAGUE game against Dublin that Sunday was called off as a mark of respect.

A huge crowd showed up to his funeral. Micháel Ó Muircheartaigh was one man who turned up at the house and stood by his coffin. He'd have been very happy with that. And lots of other big names in the GAA from far and wide. I suppose we were fairly prominent on the county scene for over a decade.

He got a great send-off.

I was asked to do a eulogy at the funeral Mass. While it was tough to do, it was easy to speak about the man and the life he lived.

I still miss him to this day. He was a man you could turn to when you'd be in need of something, even a bit of advice.

Any time Shane was taking an important free, I'd always ask my father to help steer it over.

And in fairness, he'd come up trumps most of the time.

He would have taken a fair bit of joy out of Shane's hurling career and all his grandchildren. I suppose Shane was the one that played the most for Offaly. Even his successes with Tullamore footballers and hurlers… to captain Tullamore to win a county championship, he'd have been very proud of that.

More recently, he would have been very proud of Shinrone's win in the senior county final with Mary's four sons, Sean, Michael, Adrian and Ciaran, playing their part.

JOHNNY

HE WAS NEVER one to be in the limelight. He'd come to the dressing-room after matches whether we won or lost... he'd always have a word for you. Sometimes he'd just have an auld wry smile and didn't need to say anything.

For every match I ever left the house to play, he only ever said one thing as I was going out the door.

'Pull your hucking hurl today now.'

That was it. He wasn't a man for cursing, so he'd say 'hucking'. He said it with such determination, you could nearly hear him grinding his teeth as he spoke.

And what more did he need to say? I suppose it just meant that I was to do whatever I could to help the team win the match. Stand up to your man, be man enough not to back off. You could take it 100 different ways, but that's what I took from it.

He got huge satisfaction and pride out of our careers. I'm sure he had great memories from the days watching us. And he was a great man to have a quiet word when you were down.

The Tuesday after we lost to Clare in 1995, we were in the house moping around. Everyone was feeling low.

'You'll have a lot worse days!' he said to me. 'It's only a match at the end of the day. There will be worse things in life than this.'

And he was completely right. When you lose a family member, hurling pales in significance. In that moment you think it's the be-all and end-all... but it's not life and death.

It's sport... it's a game.

XIII

Captaincy
2000
Pat Fleury
17 hours on the drink
Kilkenny... again!
Young rebels quietened
Cody gets his first

★★★

JOHNNY

EVERYONE HAS THEIR own style of leadership. Martin Hanamy was the best captain I played under. He was well liked among the whole squad.

He led by example. He was as tough as nails. So calm and consistent. What you saw from him in training was what you'd get in a match. He was as tough on a dirty night in January as he would be in Croke Park in the middle of the championship.

He wasn't one for shouting and roaring in the dressing-room, but what he did was, he left everything on the pitch. He had natural leadership qualities that really came to the fore in 1994.

Michael Bond stepped down at the end of the 1999 season and Pat Fleury replaced him. One of his first acts was to appoint me captain. It was a big deal for me.

When I took it on, I thought back to Martin's time as captain. I just tried to go out and lead by example in every training session. Be the first man there and do everything right… every match, be there and try to lead professionally. Try to show the way for the younger players. Teach them what was required. Like him, I wasn't a huge guy for speaking in a dressing-room. Now, I had no problem doing it when I felt something needed to be said.

So much went on in 2000, I could nearly write a book on that season alone. Between retirements, fall-outs between the team and management, players leaving the panel and other rumblings, it was hectic stuff. There was a lot of fire-fighting going on all year long and as captain, I was stuck right in the middle of it.

After we only beat Derry by six points in the All-Ireland quarter-final, we looked in danger of self-combusting. The first night we came back to training, I could detect self-pity in the camp. So many voices, unhappy about one thing or another.

I pulled the players into a circle before the warm-up.

'Look. There's too much talking going on, too many lads feeling sorry for themselves.

'If people don't like it, they should go.

'We're heading for an All-Ireland semi-final now. The Derry game is behind us. We have to get back on track here and we have to try and get our issues sorted out. We all need to pull together.' In the midst of it all, my father passing away knocked the stuffing out of me for a while. I was only going through the motions, asking myself what I was doing there at all.

As the evenings lengthened, my hunger came back. The captaincy galvanised me.

If we could win the All-Ireland this year, I'll lift the Liam MacCarthy Cup as captain in his honour.

That was in my head all season. It helped me put in an extra effort.

I was probably hiding my grief with hurling, instead focusing on the next game. I didn't deal with it. Being a competitor, my instinct was to use his death to drive me on the hurling field. I worked well with Pat Fleury and really enjoyed my hurling that year.

I'd put it down as my most consistent season with Offaly. I didn't miss any games. I was almost contributing as much to the scoreboard from play as I had been at wing-forward. You get a little bit more space to operate in midfield. Even though I was only 29, I knew in my heart and soul that I was nearing the end of my career. With the way my knees were, I was running out of time.

So I put everything into that season.

When it was all over, it was like a bubble burst inside me.

I took it pretty bad.

BILLY

I RETIRED THAT spring. It would have been lovely to play on when Johnny was captain. He phoned me when I was mulling over my decision… we talked about it. He understood my reasons for going.

When our father got sick, I had to run the farm as well as my day job. I had started with Offaly County Council as a tradesman a few years earlier.

Fiona gave birth to our eldest son Sean on November 17, 1999, so we had a lot of balls to juggle. I was stretched to the limit. I had to find time to visit my father in hospital as well.

It wasn't really viable to keep hurling with Offaly. Under different circumstances, I would have loved to play on. It was easier for Johnny and Joe… they were based in Tullamore where we trained and weren't working in the evenings as well.

Fiona and I built our house next door to my home place. It was nice to be able to ramble up to my mother any evening and keep her company.

So I packed it in at 31. It wasn't a decision I took lightly. I massively enjoyed my time with Offaly. You can't have your time back, so you have to make the best of it when you're there. I certainly did that. I never regretted my decision to walk away.

When Offaly reached the All-Ireland that September, the whole family went up to it. It didn't upset me too much not being out there. I just really wanted the lads to win.

IT ALWAYS LOOKED like I'd be taking over the farm at some stage. Back in the early 90s my father made the decision that between myself and Johnny, one of us would take it over. Joe had gone to Tullamore, Seamus had some land and was a building contractor. Kieran also had a bit of land and was working with Banagher Concrete.

Then Johnny got the job in the Office of Public Works and Sinéad was working in the civil service, so they moved to Tullamore. That's how it came around that I was the one to inherit the farm. After he died, my father left it to me. So, I kept it going as he'd have wanted.

I spent 12 years as a tradesman with the County Council before I was promoted to a General Service Supervisor in Birr in 2010. It's a historical town… it's a busy job. I work alongside my former Offaly teammate Brendan Kelly. I have 15 people working with me at the moment.

★★★

JOHNNY

MY SEVEN YEARS with the Office of Public Works was probably my most enjoyable time professionally. We worked on the banks of the Royal and Grand Canals, making, fitting and repairing lock gates and jetties.

I made great friends there. A lot of them were solid GAA people. Every day we'd chat about sport and there would be all sorts of slagging going on or lies being told. I wasn't worked to the bone either, so I had plenty of recovery time for training.

I struck up a great rapport with Michael Brophy, from Killeigh. He was like a second father to me. He had the good sense to protect me from any hurling talk coming up to big games. He was nearly more nervous than I would be the week of an All-Ireland. He always looked forward to retirement. Unfortunately, he passed away just six months after he retired. He was a lovely man and a very good friend of mine.

Working on both canals, we had a huge area to cover. Depending on where in the country we were based, I could be leaving home at 6am and not returning until 7.30pm. So that led to me leaving in 2000.

I joined the HSE. Initially I worked as a foreman in Mountmellick over a community nursing unit. Then I moved on as building inspector in Birr where they were building a new £20 million elderly care unit. It was a great learning experience. It was mayhem at times. Things moved at such pace.

I got transferred back to Tullamore as clerk of works on the new €100 million hospital project. I've been based there ever since. In my current role I work on all construction projects large and small in Laois and Offaly. There's great satisfaction in seeing a building being completed to a high standard. In Offaly we sometimes forget how lucky we are to have the state of the art Tullamore General Hospital on our doorstep. Nobody wants to be in a hospital, so it helps if the surroundings are modern and clean. It's the least the patients deserve.

★★★

BILLY

IN MY EARLY days on the Offaly panel, when I was working on the building site and then farming in the evenings, it was very physically taxing. The manual work stood to me in some ways… it built up a lot of strength in my arms and core. This was before the era of strength and conditioning.

In other ways, I used to arrive at training after working hard all day wondering why I was feeling so tired. But in hindsight there was no comparison to the work I was doing and a fella that was sitting in an office all day. By God, I used to be tired at the end of the week.

During the 1994 season, Seamus and I were plastering houses in Tullamore. We'd been on the site from 7.30am and didn't finish until 6pm. I had Offaly training at 7pm. There wasn't much point in me turning the car for Clareen, only to turn around and drive back to Tullamore.

So I used to pull up outside O'Connor Park and sleep in the car for 45 minutes. It was a long day before I arrived home that evening. You'd be fit for nothing, only the bed. Then on the evenings we weren't training, I worked on the farm.

That's one of the biggest changes I see in the county game nowadays. You don't see anywhere near as many tradesmen or farmers anymore. You take any top hurling side at the minute, 12 of the starting team could be either in college or teaching.

Now I'm not saying teaching isn't hard work, it is more so taxing on the mind than anything. But they can finish up early and unwind for a couple of hours. Go home and do some stretching. It suits them to have the summer free to dedicate themselves full-time to the game.

JOE

I PLAYED WITH Pat Fleury during my first four years on the panel. We always got on well. He was a brilliant motivator in his days as captain. I think he found the step up to the hot seat a little bit more difficult, as most people do. 2000 was such an up and down year. He possibly found us difficult to manage.

One incident in particular summed that up.

We had a decent league and felt we were tipping along nicely. As part of fine-tuning our preparations for the championship, we travelled down to Ennis to play Clare in a challenge match. It was a Saturday evening… three weeks out from our Leinster semi-final date with Wexford.

We had an overnight stay in the Auburn Lodge Hotel. For whatever reason, Clare seemed way more up for the game than us.

★★★

JOHNNY

THEY WERE HOPPING off the ground. Absolutely flying it. They beat us by 18 points. They ran rings around us and did a training session afterwards.

We were feeling sorry for ourselves and headed for the hotel bar. We were due to have an early morning training session on Sunday, but the game went so pear shaped that we needed a blow-out. We had a great night out in Ennis that night.

When we landed back at the hotel, we had a sing song that went on into the early hours of the morning. When I came down for breakfast around 10.30am the following morning, I could hear a few familiar voices in full flow again. Round two was kicking off again at the bar.

Management took one look at us and made the wise decision to cancel training. The feeling among the players was that we had performed so poorly against Clare, there was no benefit to training that morning.

We decided we'd try and get it out of our system in a different way. We'd talk it out. So we went and had another good day of it.

JOE

TIPPERARY WERE PLAYING Galway in Ennis that day. A crowd of supporters from both counties started to filter into the hotel for their lunch, and Johnny Pilkington stood up on a table and got a sing song going.

He had the whole hotel rocking with *Sweet Caroline* before lunchtime on a Sunday.

The team bus brought us to Portumna where the session continued. Some lads were sitting outside in the May sunshine with large bottles of Bulmers. Others sat inside and watched the league final on TV.

Everyone was getting into better form.

We made it back to Molloy's Pub in Birr, which is a great GAA bar. When Michael Duignan and I got back to Tullamore, of course we didn't go straight home either. We ended up in the Bridge House bar.

It was a long day

★★★

JOHNNY

THREE WEEKS OUT from the championship, we spent about 17 hours drinking. Clare were on a drinking ban.

We went out in Leinster and hammered Wexford by 3-15 to 1-8. Clare fell at the first hurdle in Munster against Tipperary, losing by eight points. Their season was over. We went on to contest the All-Ireland final. I wouldn't advocate it all the same. It's just funny the way it worked out. It was good for team morale.

I certainly don't think management anticipated things to transpire like that. By allowing us to have a few pints on the Saturday night, they didn't know what they were letting themselves in for. Pat Fleury had Pat Cleary, Ger Coughlan and Tom Donoghue in with him. They liked a pint but would have been reasonably straight-laced. They weren't huge socialisers.

They gave us an inch and we took a mile.

BILLY

KILKENNY DISMISSED OFFALY in the Leinster final for the third year running. They were just phenomenal that year.

You could see Cody was starting to get his teeth into them. He transformed Kilkenny. They were a little bit like us in the late 90s... they had a few guys that weren't living like elite athletes. It was his way or the highway.

He moved on so many quality players. From the team that beat Offaly in 2000, about six All Stars had moved off the panel by 2003. Any guy that didn't commit, he didn't want.

★★★

JOE

FEELING HE NEEDED to freshen up the team, Pat Fleury made a raft of changes for the All-Ireland quarter-final with Derry. I was one of the players dropped and I wasn't pleased about it. Once I started back training with Offaly, I felt I needed every minute on the pitch to sharpen my game.

In all likelihood we were going to beat Derry and had Cork coming down the line. I knew I'd be back in for the semi-final, so it wasn't doing me much good sitting on the bench when I could have been getting tuned up. I came onto the field about 10 minutes into the second-half. Things weren't going to plan... Derry were giving us loads of it.

John Troy was taken off 14 minutes from the end. He was replaced by Joe Errity when the game was still on the line. He ended up leaving the panel after that and missed the Cork game.

It was one of a number of curious decisions management made that day. Michael Duignan was the only defender not to have conceded a score off his man. He got moved up to the forwards when Brian Whelahan was introduced, and was subsequently taken off.

He wasn't too pleased either.

Luckily for us, we weathered the storm.

Johnny was on fire. He scored 12 points and carried us to a six-point win.

★★★

JOHNNY

I WENT INTO the dressing-room at half-time with a worst-case scenario lashing through my mind. *This could be worse than Antrim in 1989.*

Leaving off a couple of regulars backfired on Pat Fleury that day. They tried out some young lads, maybe assuming we were going to win easily. When it was still in the balance with 15 minutes to go, Joe, Brian Whelahan and Joe Errity were brought in to try and rescue us.

Established players don't like being left off the team if they feel they deserve to be starting. They don't like being taken off either when the game is there to be won. We had a lot of disquiet in the panel around that time and the Derry result fed into it. We were lucky to get out alive. Despite all that, we managed to refocus on Cork and enjoyed a good run-in to that game. We were given no chance beforehand. They were reigning All-Ireland champions and after cruising through Munster a second time.

John Troy, an All Star in 1999, left the panel. Hubert Rigney was coming back from illness. Factoring in the retirements of Billy and Martin Hanamy, we were down four key men.

While we were slipping, we had young blood like John Ryan, Brendan Murphy, Gary Hanniffy, Simon Whelahan and Ger Oakley competing for places. But nobody saw the performance against Cork coming.

Where did it come from? It was just in our psyche. Tell us we don't have a chance and you'll get our dander up. When Cork beat us the year before, there was only the puck of a ball between the teams. Twelve months later... and we're supposedly rubbish.

I looked around the dressing-room at Sid, Kevin Kinahan, Johnny Pilkington... there was a lot of pride there. We wouldn't fear anybody. We certainly weren't quaking in our boots playing Cork. We felt like they were still a young team and we had the upper hand in experience.

JOE

WHEN WE WALKED around the parade before the game, I was the last man on the Offaly side. I looked across at the Cork players' physiques and thought to myself, *How are we going to contain these lads today?*

Cork started quickly, reeling off the first couple of points. We hung in there, even though they were well on top. Myself and Johnny P sneaked a couple of points to keep us in touch.

Joe Deane was doing a lot of damage and had eight points to his name by half-time. Pat Fleury gave his marker Kevin Kinahan a telling off in the dressing-room. Kevin gave his answer back in the second-half, showing tremendous guts to completely shut down Deane.

Trailing by three after 42 minutes, we roared back into the contest. Cork wouldn't score again for 18 minutes.

Our forwards worked hard to prevent Cork from spraying nice ball into their attack, forcing them to launch it long into Deane, which suited Kinahan. Our defenders were tenacious, led by Man of the Match Simon Whelahan.

We started to win other key battles all over the field… Gary Hanniffy on Brian Corcoran, Joe Errity on Fergal McCormack, Johnny Pilkington on Sean Óg Ó hAiplín, John Ryan on Diarmuid O'Sullivan.

Brendan Murphy was switched to midfield and Johnny went to wing-forward, which allowed both play their way into the game.

I won a ball off O'Sullivan and passed to Murphy for the go-ahead score. I clipped my second of the day shortly after. When it went over, I raced back out to my position in front of the Cork dug-out to show them, *We're still full of running, even the older lads.*

Johnny hit three vital scores in the last 10 minutes and finished with 0-7. Brian Whelahan, Michael Duignan, Kevin Martin and I were all back to our 1998 levels. All of a sudden, we had all the momentum and the Offaly crowd roaring us on.

Despite the talk about Cork's superior fitness, we didn't even use a sub until stoppage-time, while they had two players introduced by the 60th minute.

Everybody played well. It was just one of those days. The dying kick of our team.

We had four points to spare at the finish. Without a doubt it ranked as one of the sweetest victories of my career. After the disappointment of losing to Cork in 1984 and '99, it was great to be part of the first Offaly side to beat them in the championship.

We broke new ground and were back in another All-Ireland final. For a county that had opposed the backdoor system, we availed of it to reach the final for the second time in three years.

THE FOUR-WEEK run-in to the final meant there was plenty of time to get the minds right. John Troy returned to the squad after going back to his club. The bodies on the other hand were breaking down... a few players carried niggles, including Brian Whelahan who was injured a lot that summer.

Even though we lost that final, Kilkenny were there for the taking. We missed a couple of early goal chances and one after half-time. If we'd stayed close to them we might have had a chance of beating them.

If Brian Cody had been beaten in his second successive final, I don't think he'd have lasted. The whole course of hurling history could have changed. DJ Carey and Henry Shefflin ran in a couple of early goals which killed us.

They came against the run of play. Our tactic was to frustrate them and hold them for as long as we could until such a time as the pressure would come on in the closing stages. If the pressure built with 15 minutes to go, we'd be in a good position to pounce.

They came into that game under savage pressure. But the early goals settled them and gave them a bit of confidence... they led by eight points inside nine minutes. We were back within five shortly before the break, when Charlie Carter struck the game's crucial goal.

We went in 10 behind at half-time. Cutting the deficit to eight on two occasions in the second period was as close as we could get to them. We had a lot of mileage on the clock and even moving Brian Whelahan up to the forward line, where he caused wreck in 1998, couldn't unhinge the Kilkenny defence.

★★★

JOHNNY

IT HIT ME like a double whammy in the days that followed. It sort of dawned on me the year I was after having. You lose your father, you lose the All-Ireland as captain… it's a lot to deal with.

Sinéad would say it too, I was down for so long after that. After my father died I put all my eggs into the one basket… winning the All-Ireland in his honour.

I was completely deflated in the days that followed. There's photos of us going home after the game and we looked so gutted. It felt worse than 1995 because we knew it was our last chance. We had a feeling there might not be any more opportunities with that team.

I wasn't disappointed with the game itself because I knew Kilkenny were the better team. When you're beaten by a superior side on the day, I'd be man enough to admit it.

XIV

Playing with pain

Joe's 19 years

Back with Clareen

Billy's long goodbye

JOHNNY ALONE

JOE Vs SHANE

TIME TO MANAGE

★★★

JOHNNY

I DON'T KNOW why my knees were so bad. Sometimes it can be hereditary. Strangely enough, Billy and Joe never had knee injuries. It may have been down to the way I played. I wasn't a straight-line runner. I liked to jink and sidestep, often jumping from one knee to the other.

The first time I injured my knee was the week before the All-Ireland under-21 final in 1992. We were playing an in-house game and I landed awkwardly after catching a ball. I knew straightaway I did some damage. The next morning, it had swollen so badly I couldn't see the kneecap. I was sure I was gone for the final.

I'm not sure if management had a word with them, but the team doctors insisted they could get me back in time to play the game. I received a cortisone injection into the knee joint… the swelling and pain went away. By Wednesday, it felt great. Being young and innocent, I was delighted. I was eager to play the game. Being honest, I'd probably still do the same thing again.

In hindsight, I'm not so sure it was a good decision to get those injections. I was now playing on a damaged knee joint. I played on for a couple of months after that until the cortisone wore off. It numbs the pain, but it doesn't mean the damage is repaired.

By 1993, both my knees were giving me trouble. It was a wear and tear issue. I had arthritis and cartilage damage… they would constantly swell up, especially in summer time on the hard ground. Every morning when I'd wake up after training or a game, my knees would be swollen and sore. I was constantly taking painkillers and anti-inflammatories before games.

I went up to Blackrock Clinic for an X-ray and consultation with Dr Colville, who really put the frighteners on me.

'Your knees are in really bad shape. They're that bad, you'll have two new knee replacements by the time you're 30!'

I was 22 at this stage. I came home that evening thinking, *That's it. It's all over.*

He was giving me the worst case scenario. He did keyhole surgery on the left knee to clean it out, sand down and smoothen off the bones, and tidy up the cartilage. I had three more of those procedures done over the next six years... one more on the left and two on the right. They were minor procedures to tidy up the cartilage. I'd get them done in the winter, whenever we finished up with the club.

I'd normally miss six or eight weeks at the start of the season. I did the rehab, starting back in the swimming pool, then onto the bike to build up the muscles around the joint. It was a constant process. As the 90s went on, my knees got worse and worse. I could feel moving parts in them, bits of grit and cartilage as I ran.

By the time 2001 came around, I was in constant pain and starting to get frustrated. I wasn't enjoying the training as much because of the discomfort.

JOE

INITIALLY, I INTENDED on continuing with Offaly in 2001. Michael Bond was back as manager. I was fit, as we'd been training away with Clareen over the winter in preparation for the delayed county final against Birr.

Towards the end of March, Marie's mother got sick, very suddenly. It was bad news. She had cancer and passed away shortly afterwards. She was very close to Marie and all of us. She was a kind hearted person... she came up from Cork to Tullamore at the drop of a hat to look after our kids when we went away on team holidays.

Her passing was a big blow. She had become close to my mother after daddy passed away. I decided I had enough then. I was needed at home and no longer had the heart to continue. After 19 years, my time with Offaly was up.

I could see the team of the 90s was breaking up. I always said I'd like to get out at the top… coming off the back of an All-Ireland final wasn't a bad way to go. I was glad I could do it on my own terms, without having a falling out with managers. I didn't want to wait to be pushed. Michael Duignan retired around the same time even though it wasn't planned that way.

A couple of days later, I received a handwritten letter from Bro Denis with the Presentation Brothers letterhead:

Dear Joe,

So the end has come at last! Well you really can have no complaints. You had a good innings. I just want to add my sincere congratulations to you on a wonderful career.

I think it was 1975 that you arrived in Birr. Bro Cronan had you in his team the following yea,r 1976. You shared all the school successes of 1978, '79 & '80. Bro Cronan's address is Presentation Brothers Maiville, Turner's Cross, Cork. He'd be delighted to hear from you.

When you are next in Birr, call in because I have a framed photograph of the 1979 team which you may like to have.

I hope the Dooley effect rubs off in Tullamore. It would be great to see a juvenile team from Tullamore winning a championship.

Again, thanks for all the great days over twenty five years.

From now on you can relax and enjoy the game from other angles – even perhaps as a coach!

With every good wish for the future.

God bless,

Bro Denis

★★★

BILLY

THE BENEFIT OF retiring from county hurling at 31 was that it prolonged my club career. I was able to give Clareen some of my good years. I hurled on until 2008… when I was 39. That brought me to 22 years at adult level with the club.

It was tough on Johnny having to pack in the hurling in 2003. I often felt for him. Even his last couple of years with Offaly were a struggle. He tried to stay on for as long as he could. Some people in the club might have wondered why he couldn't give us a few years hurling, but he just wasn't able. His body gave up on him.

As frustrating as it might have been for people in the club thinking we could have done with him, it was far worse on him not being able to even train. He had a very good career. He played loads of hurling and was hugely successful.

But I had a grand few years hurling with the club before I finished. A long goodbye. I was able to wind down gradually. I was glad to get out when it was over. The difference was I could choose when I packed it in. It came to a sudden stop for Johnny. To this day he still struggles with his knees.

Losing him was a big blow for us. We started slipping in later years. It was frustrating to go from competing for county titles to battling for survival. I played in two relegation finals… thankfully, we won both.

A bit like Offaly, a special group of players came together in the late 80s and 90s. The year I finished up, our under-21s won the county title. There was a new batch of youngsters emerging, fellas like Joe Bergin and Dermot Mooney. Almost every one of the 16 players on that squad went on to represent the club at senior level. Because our pick was so small, we couldn't afford to let anyone slip through the net. That was always the way in Clareen. Since the days we were young, if you were a hurler aged between 16 and 40 you were up training with the seniors.

I was a wide-eyed 16-year-old when I first joined the set-up. In a training game one evening I was marking Sean Coughlan, a brother of Eugene and Mick. He was a grizzled veteran, 19 years my senior. I got out in front to win a ball, went around him and pucked it over the bar. Sean never liked anyone getting the better of him, especially a young fella.

Sure enough the next ball that arrived in, I picked it up and went to turn… Sean ploughed straight into me and put me out over the sideline.

'Welcome to senior hurling!' he says.

He wasn't going to let me do it twice. It was all part of the learning curve.

Johnny Abbott was another senior player not to be messed with. He was a fine hurler in his day. He played with Offaly in his day and won a Leinster title. We were marking one another in training when a high ball was pucked out between us.

I gave him a slight nudge with the hurl and caught the ball behind him. I split the posts. The game went on for another 15 minutes. Another ball dropped between us near the wing. I stood with my hand up in the air waiting for it to arrive.

Johnny was still stung from my earlier score. I hadn't thought a whole lot about it. He let in the handle of his hurl to push me away, but caught me in the corner of my eye. The lining of my eye was cut and I spent three days in the Eye and Ear Hospital in Dublin over it.

My mother rang me the next day to see how I was. 'I'm grand, but I'll be in here for a couple of more days.' And that was it.

I never held anything against him because he didn't mean to hurt me. It just happened. They were the sort of hits that went on in training.

The worst belt I ever got came in a junior game against Shinrone. It was a miserable day. I was moving towards goal when I went down to rise the ball and the full-back came out and drew on it. His hurl followed through up along my stick and connected with me straight in the eye.

The pain was unmerciful. I had a big cut along the side of my eye. It almost finished me… I ended up with another visit to the Eye and Ear Hospital.

★★★

JOHNNY

I WAS STILL hurling reasonably well in 2001. I was on a bounce from the previous season which was probably my most consistent for Offaly. I was enjoying playing in a more defensive role at midfield.

We were pleased to see Michael Bond return as manager that season. We had great time for him. His personality and theory on how hurling should be played fit in well with us. He resonated with the players and Offaly people in general.

Yet again, he had no fitness coach and took that side of training himself. I felt we weren't as well-prepared fitness wise as we should have been. We were showing signs of fatigue. The retirements of Joe and Mike Duignan were blows. The guys in my age group and a couple of years older were declining physically. Standards were starting to slip.

Kilkenny had moved onto a different level under Brian Cody. They looked capable of giving any team a good beating… which they did when they had 14 points to spare over us in the Leinster semi-final.

Only beaten provincial finalists went through the backdoor, meaning our season was over in early June. I managed my knees through that campaign. I was on prescriptions for Difene, which is a strong painkiller, and Voltarol, an anti-inflammatory. It was heavy stuff and hard on the tummy, so I had to take other tablets to counteract an upset stomach.

It was at its worst in the summertime. When the ground got hard it had the most impact on the knees. When 2002 came around, things really got bad.

They were giving me trouble from early in the year. After I had a routine procedure, my left one just didn't feel right. It actually felt worse than it did going in. Every time I bent it or went to run, I could feel something bulging out of the side.

I went back in for another scope. It transpired there was a piece of cut off cartilage that had grown into a 25mm ball of gristle that had lodged in the joint. They removed that and I played on. I had a bandage on but I was still pulling the leg behind me. I shouldn't have been allowed to train. The start of the championship was looming, where we had a date in Thurles with Kilkenny in the Leinster semi-final.

I was in no fit state to play. Concerned with matters, I went to the famous physio Alan Kelly in Tallaght. I told him I wanted to be fit to hurl in a couple of weeks. He got me to take off my tracksuit bottoms and walk over and back across the floor a number of times.

He looked at me.

'Are you for real? You're mad. You're in no condition to be training.'

He knew by the level of muscle wastage around my left knee.

'Go back and tell the manager you're pulling off the panel. With the condition of that knee, you're in no fit state to be playing. If you were with a provincial rugby team, you'd be put into a factory reset for six to eight weeks to build the muscles around the joint. You wouldn't even be allowed on a pitch.'

I went back and explained this to Fr Tom Fogarty, who had taken over as manager that year. I was fairly sure he wasn't listening to me.

'Sure you'll be alright to train on Thursday night.'

Maybe I was happy to hear it. I knew my time with Offaly was coming to an end and we had Kilkenny coming up. I continued to train. Looking back now, it was a stupid thing to do. I was only codding myself by continuing after getting advice like that from such a well-renowned physio.

On Thursday night, we did some running in O'Connor Park. I was falling further and further behind the group. I was running with a limp and still no one told me to stop. I partly blame myself for that. *What did I think I was at?*

They took some mercy on me and I wasn't selected for the Kilkenny game. Instead, Fr Tom asked me to sit beside him in the dugout so he could bounce things off me during the game. It was a strange request. I felt a little awkward sitting on the bench alongside the three selectors.

As it turned out, my input wasn't really required. Kilkenny beat us well. We lost by 2-20 to 1-14. Henry Shefflin had an unbelievable game… he scored 0-11, six from play.

We entered the expanded qualifiers and faced Meath, managed by Michael Duignan, in the first round. It was my final time to make an impact in an Offaly jersey. My knee felt really uncomfortable in the warm-up… I took my place among the substitutes. With 20 minutes to go we managed to get ourselves in a sticky situation.

They scored a goal and were just a point behind when I was introduced. Even though I was only 31, the state of my knee meant I couldn't cover much ground. I tried to read the play and use my experience to take up good positions on the wing. I scored three points from play over near the sideline from quite a distance out. We got out of Navan with our pride intact.

A 2-19 to 1-9 loss against Tipperary in round 2 was my last ever appearance for the Faithful.

I travelled to Portlaoise with Kevin Martin. All the way over, all he talked about was fishing and shooting. He had plenty of other interests outside of hurling and was a great man to stay relaxed before a match. At one stage I said, 'Kevin, do you realise we're going over to play Tipperary in the championship?'

In fairness, that's what worked for him. He was always a man to perform on the big day.

Tipp were reigning All-Ireland champions. Again, I started on the bench. I came on when we were nine points down. I went in on Philip Maher, a 6'3" All Star defender, big and strong. I had no business being on the field.

On the way back to Tullamore, lo and behold Kevin was still talking about fishing and shooting. I thought it was funny how he could switch off and on. My mind drifted to my knee. *I can't keep going like this.* I had a feeling that might be it.

★★★

JOE

IN JULY, MARIE, my good friend Paul Bell and RTE's Marty Morrissey organised a surprise 'This is Your Life' event to mark my retirement. I had no idea it was happening.

I was out golfing with Johnny and Johnny Flaherty earlier in the day and nothing was mentioned. The plan was to keep me occupied to allow Marie to do some last minute organising for the evening.

I went out to the Bridge House Hotel for what I thought was a family meal with Marie, Shane, Aideen and Niamh. But I was lured there under false pretences. Marty came strolling up to our table in the restaurant and announced... 'Joe Dooley, This is Your Life.' An eruption of applause went up in the main ballroom. We were brought through onto a stage in the ballroom where almost a thousand people and a camera crew had gathered.

How they all kept it from me, I'll never know. We sat up on stage as family, friends, former teammates, managers and opponents all came up to say kind words. Those who couldn't make it, such as Nicky English and Ger Cunningham, recorded video messages that were played on the night.

A host of players from the Offaly teams of the 80s and 90s turned out. Diarmuid Healy, Michael Bond, Éamonn Cregan and Derry O'Donovan were there too. Huge names from the GAA world were among the guests... Brian Cody, Cyril Farrell, Ger Loughnane, Jimmy Barry Murphy, Martin Storey, DJ Carey, Joe Quaid, Conal Bonnar, Brian McEvoy, Tomás Mulcahy, Pete Finnerty, Sean Lowry, Dickie Murphy, Micheál Ó Muircheartaigh and John Dowling showed up.

Brian Cowen, a great friend of mine, also spoke on the night. He said that the 'best tribute I can pay to Joe, is that he is the equivalent in hurling of Martin Furlong in football - a man who spanned three decades, and the only other

Offaly man to win three All-Ireland medals (on the field of play)'. It wasn't just a celebration of my career, but also a tribute to what Offaly hurling had achieved in the previous two decades.

I GOT SO much enjoyment out of hurling... my goal was always to play it as long as possible. I was 48 when I eventually packed it in for good. Once I was fit and avoiding injuries, what else would I be doing?

I hurled on with the club at senior level for another couple of years after retiring from Offaly. During my final campaign in 2004, I played championship hurling against Shane. He made his senior debut for Tullamore the year before and spent the summer lining out with the Offaly minors.

When we were drawn in the same group as Tullamore, we knew it was on the cards. Not much was said between us that morning. We left the house and drove to Rath separately. I played wing-forward and Billy was centre-back... Shane started at corner-forward for Tullamore.

During the first-half he picked up a ball along the end line and ran towards goal. Kevin Kinahan picked him up and dropped him out over the line. *Thou shalt not pass.* He didn't get any privileges against Clareen just because he was a Dooley! It was a nice welcome to senior club hurling.

It was a fairly unique occasion to play against your son. There was a picture of the two of us in the *Tullamore Tribune* the following week. It's a nice one to have.

I DROPPED DOWN to junior in 2005. The commitment obviously wasn't the same. While I didn't have to go to the team training every week, I kept in shape by doing the work on my own. Going out to play games without being in shape for them just didn't make sense to me. I made sure to get the miles into the legs.

We went on to reach the county final where Drumcullen beat us. We gave it another crack in 2006 and scraped past Birr in the quarter-final. They had a right good team... Johnny Pilkington, Joe Errity and Brian Hennessy were on it. Billy and Kevin Kinahan were involved with us for that victory but ended up playing senior before the summer was out. We made it back to the final where we faced St Rynagh's.

Marking me that afternoon was Martin Hanamy. There was huge interest in the game as people knew we'd be sparring partners.

'Do you know we're the monkeys in the circus here today?' Martin grinned before throw-in.

I grabbed an early goal and we prevailed by a narrow margin. My father won a junior medal with Clareen in 1956 so it was lovely to emulate him.

We had great celebrations afterwards.

Our team was filled with players I hurled senior with for most of my career.

I was at full-forward, Seamus played corner-forward, our cousin TJ Dooley was in the other corner... Mick Mulrooney was in goals and Mick Coughlan lined out at centre-forward. We had a good few younger lads in the side too, including my brother-in-law Kevin Carey and nephew Brian Dunne.

I played on for another couple of years at junior B before hanging up the hurl for good in 2009... a full 30 years after my first game at adult level. I loved every minute of wearing the black and amber, equally as much as I loved wearing the green, white and gold county jersey.

★★★

JOHNNY

I WASN'T WILLING to close the book on Offaly just yet. I had another operation on my left knee in the winter of 2002, in the hope it might give me another lease of life.

I know I'm in the twilight of my career. If I can just take a break over the winter and get the knee right.

I wasn't saying, *This is it.* I felt I was young enough to play on for another few years. I did the rehab diligently. I got back in the gym and built up the muscles around the knee. I worked on my conditioning, building towards a return to the field. *Maybe, just maybe.*

I didn't go back in with Offaly. *I'll start off with the club and see how it goes.*

I came on as a sub for Clareen in a league game against Kinnitty. I only played about 20 minutes, but I didn't feel right. I had that familiar grinding sensation in the knee when I ran. Every step I took was a struggle.

It turned out to be my last ever game of hurling.

When I woke up the next morning, I couldn't see my knee. My whole leg had swelled up like a balloon. I went into my GP, Dr Brendan Lee.

'I can't stick this anymore. I'm after having three procedures on this knee now and it's not improving.'

Dr Lee called it straight. 'Make up your mind if you want to hurl now… or walk later. If you give up sport, you'll stop agitating the joint. You have to consider what's going to happen in the next 10, 15, 20 years.'

The stark reality of those words hit me hard. I was gone. It was over.

He was on the ball. When I stopped, things did settle down. I was able to go off the tablets. I had a good 10 to 15 years reasonably pain free. It's only in the last five years my knees have started to act up again. But it was definitely the right call to pack in hurling, even though it wasn't very popular with Clareen, more so than Offaly. The county team probably knew at that stage I was done.

I'd have loved to have given a few years to Clareen. It just wasn't possible. I used to feel like people in the club were looking at me thinking, *Why aren't you still playing?*

I felt they thought I was overreacting or copping out. It was nothing like that. I'd have loved nothing more than to play on with them. My four brothers were still hurling long after I finished and I was the youngest.

Someone in the club would ring me up at the start of every year and ask if I was coming up to train.

'I can't come up to train. If I do that I'm back to square one.'

'Ah you'll come up… you'll come up!' This went on for about five years after I retired. Then after that, they wanted me to play a bit of junior hurling. I used to find it very uncomfortable to even go to club matches because, even though I explained my situation. I felt people were looking at me going, *What's wrong with him?*

In fairness, the club just wanted to see me playing. It wasn't for any bad reason. They wanted me there and involved. Outside of that, I didn't find retirement terribly bad. I find I can move on pretty quickly. I immersed myself in playing a bit of golf to fill the gaps and replace the social interaction.

I tried to keep myself occupied but it's a serious drop off when you stop everything. I first wore the Offaly jersey as a minor in 1987 and played the whole way through until 2002. That's 16 full seasons. We had long campaigns with the club as well. So even though retiring at 31 meant I had a short career, we got through an awful lot.

We were fortunate. Including replays I played in 21 major finals... 11 senior county finals and 10 All-Ireland finals between senior, under-21 and minor. So nearly every year we were playing in a final... two some years. Mentally, I felt like I'd gone through the mill. There was a lot of pressure riding on those games. When you factor in the responsibility of taking frees and managing my knees in later years, there was a release when I retired.

I HAD THE knee that ended my career replaced a couple of years ago. It's still giving me a bit of trouble. It felt like there was a reaction to it and it didn't bed in properly. I had to go back to the consultant. I'm just unlucky, only about three percent of operations don't go to plan and I'm in that category.

A review panel of professors are going to try and figure out why it didn't go right. Unfortunately, that's where I'm at. I have to get the right knee done as well... but I'll be holding off until we get this one sorted first.

★★★

BILLY

GETTING ROUGH TREATMENT from defenders was part of the game.

As a county player playing club hurling, we were always in for extra treatment. In fairness there was no double marking back then, you had your marker and that was it. But our Offaly teammates didn't spare us.

They'd leather you as much as anyone. It was never anything malicious. If you stood over the ball or put your hand out for it, it was open country... they were going to pull. And rightly so. That's the way it should be.

John Troy's brother Mick from Lusmagh took no prisoners. Kilcormac/ Killoughey's Seamus Kiely was a tough customer too. Then again you'd win a couple of frees and get the odd score off them.

Birr were a different proposition. I could be on Brian Hennessy or Joe Erritty who wouldn't give the same physical attention. They'd be out a yard in front, so it was nearly harder to play on them.

I always had respect for a lad that was hard-hitting and played it fair. I'd respect him over a fella that draws a mean stroke. Once the games were over, it would all be forgotten about.

I always felt that as a corner-forward it was important not to let yourself be blackguarded by a back. There were loads of times under a dropping ball when I was given a belt on the back of my hand or hit in the side of the neck with the handle of a hurl.

That riled me up and I'd be sure to bide my time to exact revenge. I could be watching my marker for 10 or 15 minutes, knowing I'd get him sooner or later.

I was never a dirty player. I'd never pull at a lad's head or anything like that, but you have to protect yourself. You have to fight your corner.

★★★

JOE

HAVING MANAGED CLAREEN to the county title in 1988, management was always something I was going to give a proper go at some stage.

When I finished with Offaly, I did a season as player-manager with Clareen. In 2003, Tipperary side Toomevara approached me about taking over as manager. I agreed and combined it with my own club hurling. They had bags of talent... George Frend, Tony Delaney, Benny, Terry, Ken and Tommy Dunne, Mikey Bevans, John and Paddy O'Brien. Although they were unsuccessful the year before I took over, Toomevara had claimed seven senior county titles in the previous decade and were well-established at the top of Tipperary hurling.

I felt things were going well. We won the Tipperary All County League and reached the semi-finals of the North Senior Championship. In the early days on my drives from Tullamore to Toomevara, I'd pass through Birr. At the time they were reigning All-Ireland club champions and on the way to retaining the Tommy Moore Cup.

I envisaged Toomevara playing Birr in an All-Ireland club final. I thought they were good enough to get that far and maybe even win it. I always felt it was an All-Ireland we were working towards, not just a Tipperary title. They had the players to go all the way to St Patrick's Day, but failed to deliver on that.

Training was geared towards cranking it up as the year progressed. I didn't want us to peak too early. After going unbeaten for five months, I walked away in June. It was a week before the North Tipp final against Newport. Some club officers and one or two influential players weren't happy with how things were progressing. I was told they felt a change was needed. They didn't say what the issue was and I didn't ask. When I heard about concerns over my management, I just walked away. I didn't feel I needed to stand around and fight my corner.

If some people don't want me, that's fine. I don't need it.

They had asked me to go down and take over. I didn't go looking for the job. There was some speculation in the media afterwards that some players weren't happy with my training methods. About two thirds of the squad rang me afterwards and that's not the impression I got from them. It was more to do with some of the people I was working with in the club rather than the players themselves.

The club was very divided after I left. A lot of people weren't happy with how the whole thing was handled. I received a letter of apology from the club sometime later. It was a good lesson to learn early in my managerial career.

MIDWAY THROUGH THE 2005 championship, the Tullamore manager stepped down. They were mired in a relegation battle and chairman Jim Buckley phoned me to see if I would take over. It made sense.

I was finished playing senior for Clareen at that stage. We'd been living in Tullamore a long time and Shane was a regular on the senior team. The main motivation was, there was a great crowd of young lads coming through in the club.

We avoided relegation and I stayed in charge for the following year. 2006 was a thoroughly enjoyable campaign. We won the league and although we weren't successful in the championship, the big thing was all those young guys bought into playing senior hurling for Tullamore.

While he was still very young, Shane was hitting frees for Tullamore in both those seasons. He had two brilliant campaigns and was called into the Offaly senior hurling panel on the back of those performances.

I stepped away at the end of that season. I felt it was going to take Tullamore two or three years to win a county title and there were loads of people around the town that could take them the next step. I had enough done. Besides, the Offaly job was on my radar.

Traditionally more of a football town, Tullamore went on to win the Offaly senior hurling championship in 2009. That team, managed by Kevin Martin, was backboned by the 2006 league-winning side. Shane captained Tullamore to that county final win in 2009. It was a brilliant occasion.

I met Páidí Ó Sé once through Brian Cowen and we became friendly. He said once that he found it fierce difficult to watch his young lad play, and I'd agree. It's human nature that you're watching your son more than any other player. More often than not he played well, but you'd be on tender hooks throughout the game, particularly when he's on frees.

Shane has had a great career with Offaly and Tullamore. He put a lot of time into his skills and free-taking. As he got older he worked hard on his fitness and physical strength. He was mad into hurling from day one. On weekend mornings when he was very young, he'd be up early watching video tapes of old Offaly hurling games. I brought him along to all the Offaly games and training sessions in Clareen. I used to bring him down to the local pitch in Ballinagar and put him in goals. I'd take shots and he wouldn't flinch. He was always keen to be the one taking the shots.

Offaly were well into the lean years by the time he broke onto the scene. They didn't enjoy anything like the sort of success we had during the glory days of the 80s and 90s. He arrived off the bench in all four championship games during his debut season under John McIntyre. I was in Páirc Uí Chaoimh when Cork knocked Offaly out. It wasn't pretty. The home side dished out a 2-17 to 0-11 hammering. Driving home that evening I said to Marie, 'That was hard to look at. I can offer something here.'

John McIntyre stepped aside in the wake of that defeat. The county board put together a selection committee to find his replacement.

I put my backroom team in place. I got some good people on board… Brendan Kelly and the late Pat McLoughney as my selectors. Brian Murray came on as my physical trainer and Micheál Spain agreed to join as kitman if I got the job. He's a good character, a real solid, dependable guy. He's still there to this day… 16 years later.

Tony Murphy agreed to return as team secretary, having been away from it for a few years. Deirdre Dooley was the physio and our team doctor was Shane Carroll. We worked very well as a management team. Everything we discussed remained in-house.

I went for an interview and some time later was offered the position. Seven years after my retirement, I was the new Offaly manager.

XV

Facing Cody
Father and son
Davy Fitz... no fists!
Billy on the sideline
Johnny and the minors
Seeing red
A game to love

★★★

JOE

MANAGING A COUNTY team completely consumes you for nine months of the year. From October up until July, it dominated my thoughts nearly every waking minute of the day.

I had four very enjoyable years with Offaly. We had a good solid panel. Over my tenure, no player left the squad. Anyone that came in could see we were making progress and things were being done right. My only regret is that we didn't get the rub of the green on a few occasions, especially in the championship.

As manager, my main aim was to create an atmosphere where everybody felt valued and could contribute. We achieved that. Secondly, it was important to know how to pick the side, select players in their best positions and get them playing as a team. They have to be motivated too. A lot of it is self-motivation, but it still comes from the top.

Pat McLoughney was a great help to me. He hurled with Offaly during the 70s and was a very shrewd hurling man. When my father passed away, he was almost like a second father to me. I could ring him at any time of the day or night and he'd answer. He'd also ring me for a chat most days. Brendan Kelly was also a great selector, who always did what was best for the team and was very loyal.

IN 2008, WE beat Laois well in the first round of the championship and went on to play Kilkenny in the semi-final. They were in their pomp at that stage...

the best Kilkenny team of all-time and in the middle of their four in-a-row run.

I had huge respect for Brian Cody, but he didn't frighten me. He was just another manager. He had five All-Irelands already won at that stage and became an even bigger name in the few years after that. We gave them a good game until half-time. They overran us in the second-half and had 18 points to spare by the finish.

I WAS TOUGH on Shane at times. It was for his own good, but maybe I went over the top on occasion. If he wasn't my son I wouldn't have been as hard on him. When you know a fella has the ability, sometimes you do it for their own sake... to get them to perform at their best.

I remember one occasion in O'Connor Park where I particularly tore into him at half-time. After I did it I could sense the rest of the team thinking, *You went over the top there.* He was only 21 when I took over. Being so young, I was conscious of people saying he was only there because of his father. He had to prove himself that little bit extra than others. If there was a 50-50 call in that first year, it went against him. But once he got into the team against Limerick in the qualifiers, he was a starter from there on out.

While I was bitterly disappointed with the Kilkenny result, we had four weeks to regroup for Limerick. They were big guns at the time, fresh from a run to the All-Ireland final in 2007. They had beaten us well in the league in the spring. Our preparations and fitness levels were always geared towards being right for the summer.

We played them in the Gaelic Grounds and I can't recall a pitch looking so good. It was like a carpet. We freshened the team up by introducing a number of young lads from the start... Shane, Joe Bergin and Dan Currams. It was a really youthful starting team... they joined fellow under-21s Conor Mahon, Diarmuid Horan and Derek Molloy.

In his first championship start, Shane turned in 0-5 from play. Joe Bergin had a brilliant game at full-forward, registering a hat-trick of goals. Limerick couldn't deal with the long ball into him. Brian Carroll chipped in with a few points. At the back, David Kenny and Diarmuid Horan were immense.

We led by 2-11 to 0-6 at half-time and never let up in the second-half. A large crowd travelled from Offaly and roared us on. It was a brilliant win, one of my most enjoyable days as Offaly manager.

Davy Fitzgerald's Waterford were next up in Thurles. It was a game we never settled into. They enjoyed a blistering start and hit us for two goals inside the first 20 minutes. Eoin Kelly scored both of them. He was at the top of his game and finished with 2-13. After giving them a seven-point head start, we managed to claw ourselves back to within two points on a couple of occasions. That was as close as we could get and they ran out six-point winners.

Near the end of the game, things were getting tense. I jogged down the sideline to follow the action. There was an argument over a sideline ball… I felt a jostle in my back and turned around only to see it was Davy.

I clenched my fists. I didn't swing out, luckily. It could easily have turned into something nasty. It got a good bit of media attention afterwards. I rang Davy the following day to clear the air… I didn't want it lingering on. He was grand about it. It was a heat of the moment thing. There was no issue between us.

★★★

BILLY

I GOT A huge buzz from coaching. You often hear people say it doesn't come close to playing. I'd disagree. I got a fair kick out of it. It's not something I'd knock.

When you're playing, you can concentrate on your own game. When you have 30 lads under you and you're trying to get them to perform the way you want them to, that's a massive challenge.

Granted it's at a lower level, but the feeling after winning championship games as Clareen manager was immense. It wasn't something we were doing too often in the years before I took charge. We didn't win a county title in my two years over them, but every evening I came home after winning a championship game I felt a sense of pride.

I filled the time after my Offaly retirement by doing a couple of years with the Seir Kieran and Kinnitty amalgamation at under-21 level. When my young lads started hurling, I went back to basics. I took them from under-8 up to under-12. It's good fun at those grades. When you have a load of young lads looking up into your eyes asking you, 'Where do I go?' You'd have to laugh at them sometimes with the attitude they have. If I told them to run around the field three times, they'd do that. No questions asked.

I did five years of the most relaxed coaching you could do. The same year I finished up hurling with Clareen, I took over the under-21s again alongside Eugene Coughlan and Barry Bergin. We knew we had a good crop of youngsters emerging and we convinced the club to break the amalgamation with Kinnitty. Rather than having six or seven starting and the rest on the bench, we felt we were good enough to fill our own team.

That side was good enough to win a number of county titles. Sometimes when two clubs join forces it doesn't really click and that's what was happening. The following season we won the championship. We only had a 16-man panel and a lot of them were only 17 or 18… we beat a Kilcormac/Killoughey and Drumcullen amalgamation in the final. It sealed the first ever under-21 'A' title in the club's history. We only lost two players off that team for the next season. Coolderry narrowly beat us in the next two finals. They were gut wrenching to lose.

★

JOHNNY

A COUPLE OF years after I retired, we had a scare shortly after our youngest daughter Hannah was born.

Hannah was around nine months old at the time and as the child minder was off that day, I took the day off work to mind her at home. I was changing her nappy and had her on a baby changing unit on the breakfast counter. I bent down to pick up some baby wipes and as she was getting stronger and more active, she managed to propel herself off the unit, dropping onto the tiles. She landed on her head. I could hear the thud. I knew it was serious. I picked her up and I ran my hand along the side of her head… I could feel it had been crushed in. The side of her head was completely hollow. Baby's skulls are soft. It takes a good number of years before they fully develop. But her skull had completely caved in.

I started to panic. I rang Sinéad to let her know what had happened. She left work straightaway. I strapped Hannah into the child seat and sped up towards the hospital in Tullamore. She was in so much shock she couldn't even cry. Halfway along the journey as we were going up through Arden View, she started to get sick all over the place. Then she went into convulsions.

I had to pull in the car and try and make sure she wouldn't smother herself. I managed that and continued on up to the hospital.

Sinéad arrived around the same time as us and we brought her in. I'll never forget the A&E. There was a flurry of activity around us and the nursing staff's faces told us it was serious. An ambulance backed up to the door and the surgeon explained that Hannah's brain was swelling and she needed to be moved to Beaumont Hospital immediately.

We were terrified. He said an anaesthetist and registrar were travelling in the ambulance as well, because they may need to perform surgery if the brain continued to swell. Sinéad had to give the commitment that she would step aside if that happened.

They strapped Hannah onto Sinéad on the stretcher and whisked them off. The main concern was that the skull had pushed in her brain… there was a high risk of brain damage. We were told there was only a 50 percent chance of a good outcome.

I followed behind in the car. The things that would be going through your head. I can't say I remember one part of that drive. To this day, Sinéad is convinced nothing short of a miracle happened on that journey. She held a medal of Our Lady that Joe's wife Marie gave her as they were leaving in the ambulance. As she held it to Hannah's head, she felt the skull move. At that point she knew Hannah would be okay. Sinéad isn't religious by any means, but she is certain of divine intervention that day. Hannah was kept in for a few days and her consultant's words backed Sinéad's experienced.

'Mom and Dad, I should be here explaining by these X-rays why your daughter suffered serious brain damage, but I have no answers. There's no medical reason as to why she is perfect. Take her home, be grateful and enjoy her.'

Sometimes Hannah laughs at it now. Anything that ever goes wrong, it's always my fault. 'Sure you dropped me on my head!' She always throws that at me in a funny way. It was by no means funny at the time.

EARLIER THAT YEAR, I dipped my toes in coaching for the first time. I was friendly with Morgan Lawlor from Ballyskenagh. He was over Kildare and asked me to go in and help out a bit. It was handy enough. I went up one night a week to do some ball work with them.

My first proper gig in management was with the Offaly minors in 2005. I spent two enjoyable years over them... I was young, energetic and fresh out of playing. I had all the modern training methods. I picked bits and pieces from the best managers I played under.

Tony Murphy came on board as team secretary. He was a Clareen man and operated for over 35 years in the same role with the senior team. He worked with north of 15 managers during that time. Before the modern era of massive backroom teams, Tony performed the work of 10... Between booking pitches, meals, organising challenge matches, buses, ordering hurls and balls, he did it all.

We had a good team. About 10 lads went on to play for the county at senior level. I put in a huge effort both years. Back then, the manager did everything... the warm-ups, stretching, fitness, ball work... contacting the players. We were a little unfortunate. In both seasons, we were knocked out by a team we'd beaten earlier in the championship.

After defeating Laois and Dublin in April, we lost to Wexford. That set-up a rematch with Dublin, who improved hugely from our first meeting. They exacted revenge on us in Birr, 0-14 to 1-5. They were a strong outfit, with future Leinster senior medalists Johnny McCaffrey, Joey Boland and Shane Durkin in their ranks. They went on to defeat Kilkenny and Wexford to take the Leinster title. 2006 ended on a more disappointing note. We saw off Carlow, Laois and Westmeath to top our round-robin group, before losing to Carlow in the Leinster semi-final.

★★★

JOE

TWO WEEKS BEFORE the 2009 Division 2 league final against Wexford, we went on a warm weather training camp to Benalmadena in Spain.

The players all raised money individually and a few sponsors came on board. We had a great five days over there. They got to live like professional athletes for a few days. We trained every day, mainly focusing on speed and ball work.

At home, we didn't have great training facilities, mainly operating out of the barracks field Crinkle, which served its purpose but was fairly basic. The training camp was an ideal way to fit in a bank of work ahead of the league final. The fact we went away put pressure on us ahead of the Wexford game, which would decide who was promoted to the top division.

A Dan Currams goal helped us to a 1-13 to 0-13 victory in Thurles. The game was played before the Division 1 final between Tipperary and Kilkenny. The work we did in Spain paid off.

However, it counted for little when we met in the Leinster quarter-final three weeks later. Colm Bonnar's team turned that result on its head, beating us by seven points. We were flat on the day and couldn't raise a gallop. We were like the walking wounded going to play Cork in a first round qualifier, down six or seven first choice players through injury. They just hit us at the wrong time. Ger Oakley and Rory Hanniffy were huge losses.

The hardest thing after that defeat was returning to training to play Antrim in a relegation play-off semi-final. The players showed huge commitment by how they prepared for that game. We won 1-28 to 0-13 and secured our place in the Liam MacCarthy Cup for 2010.

I NEVER WENT looking for altercations with other managers on the sideline. Sometimes they seemed to come my way.

We took on Antrim in our 2010 championship opener minus Conor Mahon, who went to America for the summer. He was a key player for us, bringing physicality to the middle third. We did everything in our power to persuade him to stay, but the attempts were unsuccessful.

The Saffrons looked on the verge of sealing a first championship win over Offaly since 1989, when we were awarded a late free to level the game. It was over on the 20-metre line near the sideline. As Shane was lining up to hit the free, Antrim manager Dinny Cahill started shouting onto the field. He made it seem as if he was giving instructions to some of his defenders. It was a thinly-veiled attempt to put Shane off. When I saw his antics, I saw red. I legged it down the sideline and dropped the shoulder into Dinny, spinning him around. We had words. The free went over and the game went to extra-time.

We went into the Parnell Park dressing-rooms annoyed and heated up. We managed to channel that anger and won the extra period 2-26 to 3-16.

The week before we played Galway in the Leinster semi-final, we went down to play Cork in a challenge game. It was played as a curtain-raiser before a Cork-Kerry Munster football championship match. A good crowd showed up to watch Cork hockey us. We overnighted in Cork. It probably helped boost team morale after such a poor showing. Coming back up on the bus, the management team huddled together. The mood was one of concern. *Jeepers, how are we going to manage against Galway?*

But deep down I was happy enough. I knew we had the work done. Sometimes a defeat like that before a big game is a good thing. It keeps everyone grounded and focused.

We went out in Croke Park and surprised a lot of people. It was a victory we left behind us, even though we needed two late scores to rescue a draw. It was a riveting game. We tore into them and made light of our underdogs tag by rifling in three first-half goals. John McIntyre was in charge of Galway and his team fought back. They struck two goals. Midway through the second period we lost Dan Currams to a very soft red card.

In the days before Hawk-Eye, they had a point awarded that was later shown to be wide on TV replays. It was looking like Galway were going to scrape through before Shane's pressure free with the last puck from way out on the sideline earned us a replay.

Galway rejigged their team for the rematch in Portlaoise and hit us hard from the off. After falling nine points behind at the interval, we battled back bravely. When Damien Hayes scored his second goal, it looked like our goose was cooked. We saw a chink of light when David Burke was sent-off for retaliating after being fouled. Joe Bergin bagged a goal as part of a run of 1-2 without reply. With six minutes left, we took the lead for the first time.

O'Moore Park was heaving. Galway equalised and the game looked destined for extra-time. In stoppage-time, Joe Canning and Ger Farragher popped up with scores to send them through. After two enormous efforts, it was a heartbreaking way to lose. The same Galway team got to the All-Ireland final two years later. They were big and powerful, yet we more than held our own against them.

We bounced back and beat Limerick in the backdoor. They were in disarray at the time. In solidarity with 12 players dropped by Justin McCarthy from the panel, a further 11 walked in January.

Unusually, we held the favourites tag. We dealt with it admirably and were good value for our 1-19 to 1-13 win. That pitted us against Tipperary. After a shock Munster quarter-final exit, Liam Sheedy's team found their groove in the qualifiers. They beat us by six points and went on to stop Kilkenny's 'Drive for Five' in September.

Considering the quality they had, we gave a very respectable showing. We didn't concede a goal against them. After playing us, they went on to put three past Galway, three against Waterford and they buried four in the final defeat of Kilkenny.

We weren't good enough to beat Tipp but they didn't annihilate us either. Shane had a fine season. He finished as the championship top-scorer and was given an All Star nomination.

I felt 2010 was our best year, without a doubt. We had size and hurlers. Everyone was playing to their potential and morale was high.

★★★

JOHNNY

I WAS AT a loose end after the minors. Westmeath county board contacted me about joining Seamus Qualter's management team as coach. I met Seamus and decided to come on board. It was a good experience in Westmeath. They've loads of quality hurlers.

The majority come from north of the county and they're similar personalities to ourselves in Offaly. Lots of great characters with a droll sense of humour.

While Westmeath were a step below where Offaly were at, they were very competitive. The year before I joined, they beat Dublin in the championship. Even though the campaign ended in relegation to the Christy Ring, a 10,000-strong crowd packed into Cusack Park for the Leinster semi-final with Kilkenny. You can't buy that sort of experience.

In 2007, we won the expanded Christy Ring Cup to gain promotion back to hurling's top tier.

We had no shortage of talent – really naturally gifted hurlers – but what shocked me was the attendances at some training sessions. The players lacked application at times. They just wouldn't commit themselves fully.

Seamus stepped down at the end of the season and I took over. At the same time, Joe was appointed Offaly manager. We were denied a unique sideline meeting when the draw for the Leinster Championship pitted us on opposite sides.

Things started off well. We won the Division 2 league, beating Carlow in the final down in Limerick. We had a great night. We brought the cup back to the Brewery Tap in Tullamore and had a few drinks. We were eight weeks out from facing Dublin in the first round of Leinster.

I gave the squad two weeks off to let them recharge the batteries. The intention was to reset and go gung-ho for the championship. This was the bit that got to me.

I fixed our first training session back for Killucan on Sunday morning at 10am. It was a fresh, brisk morning and I woke up feeling really good. I drove over nice and early to get everything set up. The sun was shining. *This is the start of a six-week run-in to Dublin.*

We had 26 on the panel. With training about to start, we had 12 or 13 out on the pitch. No sign of the rest. It reminded me of Cregan back in 1993.

What's going on here, where is everyone?

I could see a few lads sauntering in, walking along the side of the field to watch the session. None of them were togged out. I couldn't figure out what the problem was. I was getting thick looking over at them. *Should I just pack it in and head home?*

If I went over, that was giving them an out. They would have poured out their story, explained what was wrong with them and headed out the gate. So I made them wait.

'Don't go anywhere!' I shouted over at them.

I ran the full 90-minute training session with the dozen lads that bothered to tog out. I left the rest standing on the line, watching on. Once it finished, I asked them one by one, 'What's the story?'

I got all sorts of excuses. Migraine, twinges, hamstrings… you name it. A few were genuine, to be fair. My take on it was they switched off. They didn't see the merit of revving up training six weeks out from championship. Now, it did improve dramatically. Strangely enough, as we got closer to the Dublin game the injuries cleared up, all of them.

I tried every trick in the book I had learned over my playing career to improve the situation. In fairness to the players, eventually they did commit. Every session we had a lad back. Then when we were two weeks out we had 24 at training. On the week of the game, every lad was chomping at the bit. To me, that's counterproductive. The heavy training has to be done in the four weeks beforehand.

We didn't have one player unavailable on the day we played Dublin, but our chickens came home to roost. They got an early run on us and beat us well.

We recovered and reached the Christy Ring final. We lost to Carlow after extra-time in a brilliant game of hurling in Tullamore... 3-22 to 4-16. The lads put in a huge shift that day.

A lot of them were going for their third Christy Ring title in four years. It would have been a great finish to the year if we'd manage to win the league and Christy Ring.

I stood down after the game. I had my mind made up from earlier in the year, maybe even from that Sunday morning. I wasn't enjoying it as much as I might have liked.

THE MAIN REASON was my son Jack was starting out at underage level in Tullamore and I wanted to get involved with his group. I spent the next five or six years coaching young lads in Tullamore. I have to say I enjoyed it. We had some great times.

When you have someone belonging to you involved, you get in there and try to do your bit. As was done for us when we were underage in Clareen 30 years earlier.

When Jack started playing senior for Tullamore, I'd give him the odd pointer here and there, but the main thing is just to go out and enjoy it. GAA is all about making friends and if you can be successful as well, then all the better. Jack has huge interest in it and he loves being involved with Tullamore.

I did the same with our daughters Emma and Hannah. I trained them at underage level and took the Tullamore senior camogie team for a couple of years. One thing I noticed about training girls was how determined they are... They have no fear.

They'll take on everything you say.

★★★

BILLY

THE MOST IMPORTANT quality I look for in a hurler is instinct. You might work with a fella who has the skill, but his reactions are slow or he just doesn't think quick enough. I could see that in a player a mile off.

If you can get a player that thinks quick, it's much better than him being quick on his feet as you can move the ball to a teammate a lot quicker than you'll move yourself. I can see it with my son Gearóid. He's not the fastest player, but he has the instinct. That counts for a lot.

I took on the seniors in 2014 and '15. After the success we had with the under-21s, I was going to have to do it at some point. Our team was filled with young lads from those teams.

I brought Hughie Hannon and Joey Mooney in as my coaches/selectors. It was a good learning experience. We went in with the best of intentions. All my lifetime, I was around the club, be it as a player, underage coach or supporter. There's a line you have to draw when you become the senior manager. You can't get too friendly with the players, even when you're living locally.

I could meet a fella on a Saturday around the village and I'd chat away. When we got back to the field on a Tuesday night, it was a different story. I was back on my side of the line. Whether you hurled with a guy in the past goes out the window. You have to forget about the personalities in a club.

I never had any issue dropping a player. Lads know themselves when they're not going well. Sometimes you hit a bad run of form and there's nothing you can do about it. Oftentimes, leaving a player off for a match or two might see his attitude towards training change. I might get a bit more aggression out of him. They'd be fairly quick in letting you know they weren't happy sitting on the line.

Without blackguarding him, you're doing it for his sake. You play the long game. That's all part of management. If they don't react well to it, that's their problem.

I was disappointed we couldn't reach a county final. We had a good group of players but they never really pushed on. We were reasonably successful. We reached a league final and got to a county semi-final in 2014, which we hadn't done in years. We had a great 3-17 to 0-15 over Birr in the quarter-final. It was our first championship victory over them since the 1995 county final. St Rynagh's were too strong for us in the semi-final.

JOE

MY INITIAL THREE-YEAR term ended at the end of that season. The county board made it clear they wanted me to stay on. I weighed things up and decided to commit for an extra season.

I had freshened up the backroom team the previous year with the addition of Galway native Franny Forde. He helped out as coach on the training ground, which freed me up to focus on other aspects of managing the team. He was a brilliant addition. He could run a coaching session for 90 minutes without repeating a drill.

Franny went on to coach Galway to All-Ireland success in 2017. Sod Daly came on board to help out with the kit. I brought in Clara man Joe Quinn as our S&C coach.

During the winter, we lost long-serving players Brian Mullins and Ger Oakley to retirement. With Ger went the last playing link to the 1998 All-Ireland winning side... but coming off the county's best season in some time, we returned to the grindstone in high spirits.

The championship was always our main priority each year. We always aimed to win a game or two in the National League, doing just enough to stay up. With one team getting relegated from Division 1, I drew a circle around the round 5 clash with Wexford in my diary. Win that game and we felt it would keep us in the top flight.

Sure enough we beat them by 2-15 to 1-16 in Tullamore. But there was another twist in the tale... we lost our final two games to Waterford and Kilkenny. Wexford finished on three points, benefiting from Cork and Tipperary putting out weakened teams against them in the last two games.

So we dropped down to Division 2, which was a fair sting in the tail heading into the championship. To make matters worse, against my wishes the county board played a round of club championship before we opened our championship against Dublin. Rory Hanniffy, Michael Verney and James Rigney picked up knocks that ruled them out of the Dublin game.

Dublin were flying it under Anthony Daly. Winning the National League for the first time in 72 years gave them real momentum. Despite losing Derek Molloy to a second yellow, we fought back from an eight-point deficit only for a late goal from substitute Peadar Carton to send them through. Even though we lost, Shane was awarded Man of the Match after registering 2-13.

We were down a few bodies for the qualifier clash with Cork. When I reflect on my time in charge of Offaly, that was certainly a game we left behind us... we lost by a point on a day where we shot 16 wides. After trailing by 2-13 to 1-9 on 50 minutes, we showed great heart and desire to bring it down to the wire. We moved Currams out from full-forward to midfield for that game and played a blinder. Shane put over a lovely sideline cut and then had a touch of fortune when his 65 dropped into the net.

That brought us within a single point. Just when we had the momentum to push for an equalising score, Johnny Ryan sounded the full-time whistle. We felt aggrieved that he played just one minute of injury-time, considering six substitutions were made in a second-half where there were also a number of injury stoppages.

In the last game Offaly played before I took over, they lost to Cork by 18 points. To go from that to a one-point defeat was a decent turnaround, even if it was little consolation that day.

I batted away questions about my future by the media afterwards.

Deep down, however, I knew my time was up.

That being said, I could easily have done another year. We were getting close to where we wanted to go and improving all the time. Managing at that level takes a huge toll and I was balancing it with a busy job in the ESB.

Above all else, my relationship with the county board pushed me towards the exit door. Things deteriorated as my reign went on. I'd put it down to an accumulation of small things. The main gripe was that we were finding it very difficult to get access to O'Connor Park, our newly renovated county grounds.

In the lead-up to the Cork game, we looked to train there. I sent a request into the county board that we'd like to train there on Tuesday, Thursday and Saturday nights. For some reason, none of those were available. So I said we'd go Monday, Wednesday and Friday. Again, there were issues with those dates.

On one of the evenings, the Tullamore under-14s hurlers were training on the field. The county board said they couldn't have two teams training there on the same night. Johnny was over that Tullamore team and it was put to me that if I asked him to change, we could train there.

That annoyed me.

'I'm not doing that!'

On another occasion, we showed up to train at O'Connor Park only to find the gates accessing the field all locked. When we eventually made it inside through one entry point, players and coaches were asked to leave the field as training wasn't to commence until a later time.

There was also an issue with players' cars parked outside the grounds.

In my 19 years hurling for Offaly, we trained in O'Connor Park for almost every training session during the championship. It went from that to a situation where you had to look for permission to have access to it. Some nights we did train there, the goals were cordoned off for resurfacing. It was not easy.

Finances were tight. A lot of players and medical staff were struggling to get paid travelling and medical expenses.

Thankfully, that has all changed now.

Two weeks before we played Cork, we wrote a letter to the county board secretary Martin Boland outlining our grievances and highlighting the commitments the squad were making. We concluded by saying no further requests would be made to use O'Connor Park, that more games should be played in Birr and that the board should ask clubs to make their facilities available for our training sessions.

Everybody in our group endorsed it. It was signed by the players' GPA representative, the team captain and vice-captain, myself, the two selectors and the team secretary. We all felt the same, that we weren't wanted in O'Connor Park. I've no idea why.

It wasn't directly a factor in my decision to step down, though it certainly didn't help. Sometimes players benefit from a fresh voice. If things were running smoother and I felt more support from the board, I could possibly have been encouraged to stay on for another year. Rory Hanniffy was one of the senior players who said to me at the time, 'I don't know how you manage to handle dealing with the board and not let the hassles filter through to the team'.

★★★

JOHNNY

IN LATE 2016, I received a call from the newly appointed Offaly manager Kevin Ryan. We met in the Tullamore Court Hotel to discuss me coming on board as selector and coach. I liked what I heard. He'd managed Antrim and Carlow. He'd been around the club scene quite a bit. I decided to give it a go.

It was a year I learned a huge amount about the modern way of doing things. He was very analytical. GPS trackers came in. Training was all about small-sided games. Diet sheets were posted up on the WhatsApp group. I didn't agree with everything that went on, however. I feel there's an awful lot of balderdash going on in county set-ups. At the end of the day, you have to go out and play the game.

There's no denying it was a tough season. Offaly hurling was at a low ebb. We had a tough group in the league... Galway annihilated us 6-23 to 1-12 in our opening game. It's difficult to keep morale up when your team is losing games by that margin.

That defeat against Galway heavily influenced Kevin's tactics for the rest of the year. We lost the next three games, but had to travel to Tralee to play Kerry in the final game. If we lost, we were relegated, and if we won we'd seal a quarter-final place against Tipperary in Tullamore.

We won a dogfight by a few points. It was a big victory where the players really put the shoulders to the wheel. Kevin decided to have a team meeting in Banagher before training on the Thursday night before the Tipperary game.

'It's like this lads,' he began. 'The bookies have us at -18 in the betting. If we can keep the margin below 10 points we will have done a massive job. We are going to try to win in five minute segments. When the first segment is up... we'll move onto the next.' And so on.

I'd never heard anything like this before. He continued on in that vein. When the players went out onto the field to start training, I could see they were slightly deflated. If the manager doesn't believe in you, what chance have you got?

I couldn't believe what I was after hearing. I never thought I'd see the day where we were going out to lose by less than 10 points. As it turned out, they beat us by 4-28 to 3-13.

For the championship he decided to play with eight defenders. A lot of teams were dropping one man back, but withdrawing two forwards as sweepers was total defensive negativity. We were struggling to score at the best of times. Playing with just four forwards made things even harder. The idea was the wing-backs had licence to break forward. We were to contain teams, cut out the concession of goals and build from the back. It was a case of damage limitation. In the majority of games we played, we were around -15 in the handicap. He believed in what he was doing and stuck to his guns. Myself and Gary Cahill voiced our concerns.

'Look, I don't think this will go down well.'

He thought I was a dinosaur and living in the past, and told me so! I've thought about it many times since. Maybe he was right. Maybe it was me that just couldn't get my head around how far back we'd fallen.

I'd always respect the manager... but I wasn't going to be a 'Yes' man either.

'This is not going down well on the ground. I can get the vibe. You're not hearing it. You're living down in Waterford, but the vibe locally is that it's way too negative and we're showing no ambition whatsoever.'

He didn't care how it washed with the public.

We beat Westmeath in the first round of Leinster. Galway were next. They were a serious outfit... reigning All-Ireland champions. We went ultra-defensive.

You might frustrate a team for 30, 40 minutes. The plan then was to push up and go for it if we were close enough. We kept the goals out, but they popped over the points from midfield all day long. It finished 0-33 to 1-11.

Waterford put 1-35 past us in the qualifiers to end our summer. Kevin's reign finished after that. The upside following his reign was that we were still in the Division 1 league and the Leinster championship.

Maybe Kevin should have been given a second year. The county board was very quick to move him on. Little did we know just how much worse things were about to get.

BILLY

I TOOK A few years out, and in 2022 I was appointed manager of our intermediates. Barry Whelahan is over the senior team and they all train together.

My sons Conor and Seán are involved with us. They stuck at the hurling even when they went away to college, which was a great sign. Conor made his senior debut this year, and Sean is strong enough to do the same over the next year or two. I'd be nervous enough watching them as a supporter, but managing them is fine. There's so many other things going on as manager, I can just treat them the same as the other players. It is nice having to have Dooleys still representing the club. Our history with the club dates back 80 years, so hopefully Conor, Seán and Gearóid can continue that tradition.

IT WAS TOUGH to watch Offaly hurling fall so far from the heights we enjoyed during our playing days. We have lads in with Offaly at the moment training four and five times a week. You have to hand it to them, they're really putting the shoulder to the wheel. They do all that training but I feel when it comes to the match, they need to do more.

You can say their skill levels aren't as good as the top teams, but I feel their determination isn't as good either. They're not committing themselves to the cause enough. They need a little bit more grit between their teeth… especially when they're hosting a team in Tullamore or Birr. You go out and get stuck in. I think that's partly the reason. When a Kilkenny lad pulls on the jersey, he'll kill for the cause. Offaly need to get more of that into their play.

JOE

WE REACHED A low ebb two or three years ago. There are a number of reasons for it. The clubs took their eye off the ball as regards underage coaching. The schools haven't been producing the teams either. The third factor was the county board neglecting that side of things. Ultimately, it's their job to oversee all of that and ensure the proper coaching structures are in place.

While it's up to clubs to coach their own players, it's really the county board's role to make sure it's happening correctly. And that didn't happen. A lot of that has been corrected and there's huge work being done at underage level now.

We were too easy on ourselves. We shouldn't be accepting defeat from some of the teams that beat us. That shouldn't be happening, irrespective of everything else. We just didn't perform.

In my time as manager, we trained in Crinkle. It was a barracks and a poorly lit stoney field. Whereas now, the new Faithful Fields training facility is a brilliant asset. All the teams train there in both codes, they have a gym and plenty more. It has been paid for in full without any loans, unlike O'Connor Park where the county board has a big debt to pay off for developing the grounds. I think the burden of repaying that debt consumed a lot of the board's time, energy and funds. That was probably a contributing factor in our decline as well.

Now we have that facility in place, loads more funding and manpower is going into coaching in schools and clubs, plus the appointment of several games development officers. Hopefully that will all bear fruition at some stage in the future.

Michael Duignan went in as county board chairman. Along with his officers, they have put a lot of the right structures in place. There's no guarantee we'll see Offaly competing for senior All-Irelands again in my lifetime. We're a small county and we don't have a huge pick.

If we could be lucky enough to get a bunch of talented players to come through together, we have everything in place to make it a success.

The Dooley Brothers in the famous Green, White and Gold

Joe Dooley beats Ollie Kilkenny to the ball in Offaly's All-Ireland final victory over Galway in 1985 (top) and in the final in 1994 he evades Limerick's Dave Clarke and Ciaran Carey.

Joe on the sideline managing Offaly in the Leinster Senior Championship in 2010.

Billy Dooley finds a way against Limerick in the 1994 All-Ireland final (top) and celebrates his late goal in the same game. Billy in full stride (below) in Croke Park.

Johnny Dooley breaks clear against Limerick in the 1994 All-Ireland final (top) and experiences the pain as a losing captain after the 2000 All-Ireland final.

The Offaly team which defeated Galway in the 1985 All-Ireland final (top), and the teams which defeated Limerick (middle) and Kilkenny in 1994 and '98 to lift the Liam MacCarthy Cup on the double with the Dooley brothers.

The Liam MacCarthy Cup is lifted high by captain Pat Fleury after the 1985 All-Ireland final win over Galway (top), and Martin Hanamy (centre) and Hubert Rigney also honour their Faithful supporters in 1994 and '98.

The triumphant Offaly squad which lifted the Liam MacCarthy Cup in 1994 reunite as the GAA's Jubilee team before the 2019 All-Ireland final in Croke Park.

EPILOGUE

★★★

BETTY

THE LADS ALWAYS had a love for hurling.

When they were young, anytime they went out the door the hurl would be swinging after them. No matter what they went to do, the hurl and ball were brought along. If they went farming up in the field, they'd be pucking to each other as they went along.

When Joe didn't have a ball, he'd puck around with stones. One time Seán was having a snooze in his chair in the kitchen. Joe pucked a stone and missed the wall. It flew through the kitchen window, passed by Seán's ear and out the back window. Seán woke up and let out a roar when he realised what was after happening.

The girls were big into it too… Clareen had a camogie team going for a while. One year I played on it with Sandra, Mary, Patricia and Eilish. They didn't want the rest of the team knowing I was their mother. We were playing one evening in Birr in the field at the back of the County Arms Hotel. This ball came in towards me and Mary came flying after it. She started to call for the ball. She shouted, 'MAMMY, MAMMY… MAMMY… pass it here'

They all knew after that!

★★★

SEAMUS

THERE WAS NO brotherly love when we were hurling in the yard. You could be killed in the middle of it… we all hated losing. We'd make little teams up between the lads and girls. There would be war.

We fell out many times. Sometimes the aul' chap would have to come out of the house and give out to us. We'd scatter for the night. There wouldn't be a word about it then the next evening. We'd go back hurling… getting stuck into each other again.

We had an ass that we used as transport up to the top of the lane.

When we went to hurl with the neighbours in Connors' on Sunday evenings, there could be three or four of us on his back. We'd get off, tie it up and hurl until nightfall. You'd have to nearly kick him to get up the lane, but there was no bother getting him back down to the house once we were finished.

The very minute we hopped up on him, he'd be gone like a shot. And a load of us on his back, in the pitch dark, hanging on for dear life.

★★★

SANDRA

ALL WE EVER talked about at home was hurling, hurling… *hurling*. It was a religion in our house. We discussed it before and after the match, what they did right or wrong…who played well or didn't .

The girls were huge into it too. We all played club camogie for a long time. We played with the lads up until under-14. I played with Johnny and Billy in national school… we won a Bord na Scoil title together. They were exceptional at that age.

As they got older, we never missed one of their Offaly matches if we could get to it. It was a huge thing for us to watch them play. At the time, we didn't realise how remarkable it was to have the three of them in the one forward line.

Coming from such a big family, we were never let get too far ahead of ourselves. If someone had a bad game or missed a free, you'd know about it. If you played really well, there mightn't be anything said to you. You were never going to be praised too much.

One thing that was always drilled into us was that one person is never going to win a game, you have to play as a team. You always pass to the person in the best position. That stood to the lads when it came to playing with the county.

★★★

PATRICIA

I WAS CLOSEST to Johnny in age. I was the little tomboy of the family and from the time I could hold a hurl, he would drag me along everywhere. I drew the short straw. I was the one that had to try and get the ball off him.

He used to practise his solo running over and back across my head every day. Eventually I'd get cross and I might hit the ball away. He'd pick it up and do it with his left hand to really annoy me.

We used to have a high ceiling in the kitchen. He'd throw the ball up in the air. 'Try and catch it now Tricia!' I could never get it off him. Then he'd say, 'Right, I'll do it with my right arm behind my back and I'll try catch it with my bad arm.' That's how he used to practise his fielding.

As soon as he'd come home from school, he'd go out and puck the ball against the gable end of the house. It was the same before school. It was nearly like a drug… he had to hit the ball off the end of the wall so many times in the mornings and evenings.

Half the parish used to have these little Honda 50 motorbikes. We had a couple of them in the yard. Anyone could drive them. Once you pushed them, they got going. As soon as I was old enough to puck a ball past the '45', Johnny used to throw me up on the back of the motorbike with a bag of balls. He'd spin down to the hurling field to work on his frees.

I was his sidekick.

He'd take so many off his left and right. He'd take them down the middle and on the wings. Sometimes when he was standing over one I'd shout in, 'Offaly are a point down and there's a minute left in the All-Ireland!' He always liked to practise as if it counted.

And just when I thought we were finished, he'd put me in goals and take a few penalties.

It helped me too. When the camogie team in Clareen disbanded I played with Kinnitty. Eilish played with Birr and we actually came up against each other in a county final one time.

I played with Offaly for a good number of years. Eilish and I were part of the squad that won the county's first ever Leinster under-14 title. We got to a camogie junior All-Ireland final one year in Croke Park. Unfortunately, I got injured before it so I missed out on the chance to play there.

★★★

KIERAN

I WAS FIRST brought onto the Offaly senior panel in 1985. I hurled with them the whole way up until 1990. I played in all the league campaigns, but never got to hurl in the championship.

In those days they rarely brought on subs. They might only use one if someone was injured or if things were going badly wrong. The closest I came to coming on was in the 1987 Leinster final. Padraig Horan was full-forward and he got a belt. Georgie Leahy shouted over at me, 'Get ready, you're coming on!'

I warmed up on the sideline. Then they wrapped a bandage around Padraig's head and he stayed on. That was my big chance to play in Croke Park.

The only time myself, Joe, Billy and Johnny hurled for Offaly on the one day came in 1990 in Ennis. Billy and I both ended up in Ennis Hospital after the game. Both of us got split open. I was cut over the eye and he was bleeding on his head.

We weren't wearing helmets. Paudge Mulhare brought us to the A&E. The three of us sitting in the waiting room is my abiding memory from that day.

★★★

BETTY

SEÁN WAS NEVER one to give out too much praise to the lads, but in his own way he was delighted for them. They achieved great things. There was so much excitement when they played in All-Ireland finals. It's all people would talk about. You could see the joy it brought to them. It lifted their hearts.

On the day of an All-Ireland, myself and Seán would wake up early. Seán would go herding cattle and I'd do the milking or feed the calves. Then we'd come in and make a whole lot of sandwiches. We'd fill up a couple of flasks of boiling water… we'd put them all into a basket along with tea bags and milk.

Mary and her husband Michael would collect us and we'd all head off to Croke Park. When we parked up in Dublin, we'd have our sandwiches and tea. We'd head down to the Hogan Stand pub for a few drinks… then onto Croke Park.

I'd be nervous watching them. So would Seán. He'd be delighted when they all hurled well. If they didn't, there might be complaints going on around us. I didn't like listening to them.

I missed Johnny's goal against Limerick in 1994. When he was about to take the free, I had my head down between my hands. I couldn't watch it. I didn't know what he was going to do with it. I suppose he had to go for goal. Then I heard the roars and looked up. Pat Connors got the other goal and Billy scored a few points. All of a sudden Offaly were six points up. It was great.

Shane was only about eight and he was down in front of us with Marie. The second the full-time whistle went, he bolted out onto the field. He went straight across to Joe. And Joe lifted him up. That was a nice memory.

★★★

SANDRA

THE 1994 ALL-IRELAND was just exceptional. I was in Hill 16 right behind the goal Johnny scored into… it was outrageous. I can remember the sensation when we saw the ball hit the net… the best feeling ever.

When the match was over we tried to get out from the Hill onto the field. There were so many people streaming down, we were finding it hard to get on. Then somebody just grabbed my hand and pulled me up over the wall.

★★★

EILISH

I'M THE YOUNGEST of the family. I was only a teenager when the lads were hurling. 1994 was great because I was still living at home... I did my Leaving Cert that summer.

I was able to enjoy the build-up with mam and dad. RTÉ came to the house and interviewed them. For two people that were never used to the limelight, they spoke so well... they came across brilliantly in all the interviews they did.

It was really special to see just how proud they were of the lads.

For the 1998 All-Ireland I was in New York on a J1. I was playing a camogie blitz the first day they played Clare. The news came from the pub across the road that we'd lost.

Next thing, someone shouted over that the Offaly supporters were sitting on the pitch... we didn't know what was going on.

It was a mad summer for Offaly. We were up, we were down, we were in... we were out. The whole Babs thing, the backdoor... it was surreal. All the Offaly natives over there were completely engrossed in everything that was happening. When people found out I had three brothers on the team, I was like a mini celebrity in the Irish community.

I went over with a girl from Kilkenny. So on the morning of the final, we went our separate ways. We headed to different pubs to watch it. Finbarr Furey was in the same pub that night.

When he found out I was a Dooley, he bought me a drink. It was a nice thing to happen.

Not long after the All-Ireland, my parents and three sisters all went on *The Late Late Show*. I was like, *Thank God I'm in America and I don't have to go on TV.*

God forbid, to go on television would have been my worst nightmare!

★★★

MARY

MY HUSBAND MICHAEL and I have great memories of going to the games. When our sons Seán and Michael were young they used to come with us. We'd bring my mother and father as well.

We were all together for the 1994 All-Ireland. We were sitting in the Hogan Stand, down in the dumps. We weren't going to leave early because we wanted to meet the boys after the match. It was important to be there for them in good and bad times.

Then the whole thing changed. It was like coming from a nightmare into a dream... I can recall it as if it was yesterday. We went out onto the field to meet them after the final whistle. The euphoria of the whole thing... it was just fantastic.

The 1995 All-Ireland was particularly tough. It was the opposite of the Limerick game. We thought we had it. They were devastated.

★★★

KIERAN

WE HAD GREAT times with the club. The best day we ever had was when Joe trained us to win our first county final in 1988. I was 21 and got Man of the Match in that final. It was even more special because we were after losing finals in 1985 and '87.

I spent the summer of 1987 in New York. I hurled with the Tipperary club over there and lived with three Irish lads on Gun Hill Road in the Bronx. I intended on staying long-term.

Seamus was working over in England. When we reached the county final, the club flew the two of us home. We didn't start... both of us came on as subs. I broke my ankle in the game It meant I couldn't fly back Stateside as planned on Monday. I decided to stay at home. So I wrote a letter to the boys in the apartment. In those days you didn't keep money in the bank. I had about $1,500 of savings stashed under a floorboard in the back of the hot press.

I instructed them to pack up my clothes and take whatever money was needed to send them in a parcel. And stick in the rest of the money with it. But these boys were borderline alcoholics. They were drinking five or six days a week. I'd say when they opened the letter, it was like they were after winning the lotto. No money arrived, no clothes… *nothing.*

I never heard from them again. I'd say they drank for a week straight. My name was probably sung out a few times in the pub! Anyway, it was a good thing I stayed at home because we won the county title the following year.

★★★

SEAMUS

I'M IN THE building trade and had Billy working with me in 1994. The morning after they beat Galway in the All-Ireland semi-final, we were working on plastering a house below in Borrisokane. There was a lad from Clonaslee with us as well.

We all went on a bit of a session after the match and were feeling a bit under the weather.

We decided to take a break from the plastering. We went down to this pub in Borrisokane for the cure. So we sat down the back of this pub and had three large bottles of cider. There were a couple of locals, elderly guys, sitting at the bar. They had the paper out and were reading about Offaly and Galway the day before.

During that match, Billy got a ball and scored a goal after coming in along the end line. The Galway 'keeper poleaxed him just as he hit it. Billy collided off the post and the way he was lying there, you'd have thought he was out for the count.

Yer man was looking at a picture of Billy laid out on the ground in the paper.

I was at the bar getting a round.

'Jaysus,' he said. 'Billy Dooley took some wrap there yesterday!'

'Oh yeah,' I replied. 'Doesn't yer man down there sitting at the table look fierce like him.'

He looked over at Billy. He glanced down at the paper and back up again.

'It's fecking him, is it?' he said.

'That's him!' I replied.

A couple of minutes later, three large bottles arrived down to the table courtesy of our friend. We were elected. We got another couple of hours out of it. We didn't go back to work that day.

★★★

EILISH

I CAN RECALL the boys being sent-off a few times in club games. If you hit one of them, it was like you hit them all.

If you thought you were only going to have a row with one of them… forget about it.

One big row down in Kilcormac stood out. I was standing in front of it and I thought they were going to be killed. And it only seemed to be my five brothers involved against the entire Birr team.

Playing with Offaly for so long, I think the toughest thing for the lads was the physicality. There's a picture of the three of them in O'Connor Park a few days before one of the All-Ireland finals. They look happy in it, but you can see the physical toll it was taking.

The management had them on a diet and they were just skin and bone.

Billy was working a very physical job as well as training so much. He was on a building site all week and farming. Johnny was helping out on the farm at home. Joe had three small kids at the time and working in Dublin. There was huge pressure on them and it was hard to balance it all. But they did.

There was never a complaint out of them… ever. Which is amazing when you look back considering they hurled for so long.

★★★

MARY

WE WERE PART of the protest after the second game with Clare in 1998. The Omagh bombing happened the week before… I can still remember the sadness of the minute's silence before throw-in. You could have heard a pin drop.

After the ref blew it up early, we had the twins with us and we all sat out on the field in Croke Park. It was brilliant. We went down to Thurles the following Saturday for the third instalment.

The atmosphere was unreal. We went into Hayes' Hotel for the usual pre-match drink. Kieran and his wife Catherine were there too. We were all sitting down at the back of the pub.

Bertie Ahern was Taoiseach at the time. He was in town to watch the match. He was up the front of the pub when he heard our parents were there. So he made his way all the way down through the crowd to have a chat with us in the corner. Daddy loved that.

Joe got Man of the Match that day… he scored five points. It was one of the best games he ever played. We went down the town afterwards and had another couple of drinks with the team. Our car was parked out the Roscrea Road.

The Offaly team bus was going to be passing by that way so one of the lads said, 'Sure hop on the bus and we'll give ye a lift back to the car.'

We got on the bus. It wouldn't start.

So everyone had to get off and give it a push to get it started. This was on the main street in Thurles. The whole team and management all hopped off. I was pushing beside Paudge Mulhare. When the engine started running, a huge cheer went up.

★★★

SANDRA

WE ALL WENT up to the All Stars in 1998. We had the dinner and a great night afterwards. Then at around 4.30am, I remember daddy leaving the hotel and heading out to the car park.

I said, 'Oh God, what are you at?'

He walked over to the car and pulled out a flask and a couple of sandwiches. He opened the boot and we sat there, having our tea and sandwiches. It was hilarious.

I was thinking, *If anyone saw us now, eating these yokes! Here's the country folk up for the weekend.*

It's funny the things that stay with you.

★★★

EILISH

WE KNEW FROM listening to Joe at home that he'd make a great Offaly manager. He's always been very fair and solid. He had all the qualities to do it.

I'm surprised he hasn't managed other teams in the last couple of years.

We were all so proud to see him manage the county, without a doubt… to see your brother over Offaly was unbelievable.

One thing that always stayed with me was after he got taken off in the 1995 All-Ireland final.

I was in the crowd and watched him as he left the field. I knew he hated being substituted. But he didn't sit on the bench with his head down in disappointment. He was up and down the sideline, like he was one of the selectors. He was roaring and shouting, encouraging the team.

I often say that to my sons when they're hurling, that if they're taken off in a game you don't sulk or go off pucking the ball around on the sideline. You stand there and support your teammates.

I felt that was a moment that really showed Joe's leadership skills.

★★★

BETTY

WHEN THEY WON All-Irelands we'd head over to the team hotel to see the lads. Seán always liked to get back down home and head into Percy's in Kinnitty for a pint.

That's where all the chat about the match went on.

Then we'd be in Birr the Monday night for the homecoming. The crowds were massive. They'd go touring around the county with the cup. When they arrived in Clareen, there was a big bonfire up at the cross.

They got off the bus and all stood on the back of a lorry.

★★★

KIERAN

ON OUR WAY home from the win over Clare in 1998 some of the family went into Breteron's, a small pub in Roscrea. It was packed.

When my mother and father walked in, the whole place stood up and gave them a round of applause. Offaly hadn't even won the All-Ireland, but the entire pub was standing up, clapping them.

There was another pub in Birr called the Dublin Bar. Whenever the boys hurled well in an All-Ireland semi-final or final, the same thing would happen when they'd come in.

They didn't look for that either. They were quiet people. They didn't like attention being thrown their way like that.

Deep down, I'm sure it filled them with pride.